THE COMPLETE GUIDE TO AMERICA'S
NATIONAL PARKS

THE COMPLETE GUIDE TO AMERICA'S
NATIONAL PARKS

NANCY J. HAJESKI

mri

MOSELEY ROAD INC.
GATINEAU QUEBEC CANADA

MOSELEY ROAD INC.

1780 Chemin Queens Park
Gatineau, QC, J9J 1V1, Canada
www.moseleyroad.com

President: Sean Moore
Art and Editorial Director: Lisa Purcell
Cover design by Lisa Purcell

ISBN: 978-1-62669-400-2

Printed in China

26 25 24 23 22   1 2 3 4 5

CONTENTS

INTRODUCTION: *To Preserve and Protect* 6

CHAPTER ONE
PARKS OF THE NORTHEAST AND THE MIDWEST

ACADIA, Maine 12
CUYAHOGA VALLEY, Ohio 18
GATEWAY ARCH, Missouri 20
MORE TO EXPLORE: *National Wildlife Refuges* 22
HOT SPRINGS, Arkansas 26
INDIANA DUNES, Indiana 30
ISLE ROYALE, Michigan 32
VOYAGEURS, Minnesota 36

CHAPTER TWO
PARKS OF THE SOUTH

BISCAYNE, Florida 40
CONGAREE, South Carolina 44
DRY TORTUGAS, Florida 46
EVERGLADES, Florida 48
MORE TO EXPLORE: *National Wild and Scenic Rivers* 54
GREAT SMOKY MOUNTAINS,
Tennessee and North Carolina 58
MAMMOTH CAVE, Kentucky 64
NEW RIVER GORGE, West Virginia 68
SHENANDOAH, Virginia 72

CHAPTER THREE
PARKS OF THE SOUTHWEST

ARCHES, Utah 80

BIG BEND, Texas 84

BLACK CANYON OF THE GUNNISON, Colorado 86

BRYCE CANYON, Utah 90

CANYONLANDS, Utah 96

MORE TO EXPLORE: *National Forests* 102

CAPITOL REEF, Utah 106

CARLSBAD CAVERNS, New Mexico 112

GRAND CANYON, Arizona 116

GREAT BASIN, Nevada 122

GREAT SAND DUNES, Colorado 124

GUADALUPE MOUNTAINS, Texas 126

MESA VERDE, Colorado 128

PETRIFIED FOREST, New Mexico 132

ROCKY MOUNTAIN, Colorado 138

SAGUARO, Arizona 142

WHITE SANDS, New Mexico 146

ZION, Utah 148

CHAPTER FOUR
PARKS OF THE WEST

BADLANDS, South Dakota 156

CHANNEL ISLANDS, California 160

CRATER LAKE, Oregon 164

DEATH VALLEY, California and Nevada 168

DENALI, Alaska 170

GATES OF THE ARCTIC, Alaska 176

GLACIER, Montana 178

MORE TO EXPLORE: *National Preserves* 182

GLACIER BAY, Alaska 186

GRAND TETON, Wyoming 188

JOSHUA TREE, California 192

KATMAI, Alaska 198

KENAI FJORDS, Alaska 202

KINGS CANYON, California 204

KOBUK VALLEY, Alaska 206

LAKE CLARK, Alaska 208

LASSEN VOLCANIC, California 210

MOUNT RAINIER, Washington 212

NORTH CASCADES, Washington 216

OLYMPIC, Washington 218

PINNACLES, California 222

REDWOOD, California 224

SEQUOIA, California 228

THEODORE ROOSEVELT, North Dakota 234

WIND CAVE, South Dakota 236

WRANGELL-ST. ELIAS, Alaska 238

YELLOWSTONE, Wyoming, Montana, and Idaho 240

YOSEMITE, California 246

CHAPTER FIVE
PARKS OF HAWAI'I AND OTHER U.S. ISLANDS

HALEAKALĀ, Maui 254

HAWAI'I VOLCANOES, Big Island 258

MORE TO EXPLORE: *National Seashores and Lakeshores* . . 260

AMERICAN SAMOA, American Samoa 264

VIRGIN ISLANDS, St. John 266

Index 270

Credits 271

INTRODUCTION
TO PRESERVE AND PROTECT

From the vast Wrangell-St. Elias in Alaska, at more than 8 million acres, to the tiny Gateway Arch in Missouri, with fewer than 90, America's national parks allow visitors from around the world to appreciate the diversity of all the wondrous landscapes the nation has to offer.

On March 1, 1872, Congress designated the unique and beautiful Yellowstone region of Wyoming, Montana, and Idaho as America's first national park. Under federal protection, this land would forever be used "as a public park or pleasuring-ground for the benefit and enjoyment of the people." The establishment of Yellowstone National Park went on to generate a worldwide movement; today some 1,200 national parks or preserves exist in more than a hundred countries.

Setting aside land for future generations was a revolutionary concept . . . but one whose time had more than come. With few restrictions to curb them, commercial and industrial concerns seeking timber, game, fish, gold, silver, copper, or water rights showed little restraint when it came to profiting from wilderness resources. Just as no one stepped in when plainsmen and government agents killed off many millions of bison (thus depriving Native Americans of their greatest resource), no one stopped the logging industry from felling 90 percent of California's giant redwoods to build homes for growing cities. Of course, conservationist voices were raised in alarm every time an old-growth forest disappeared or a species became extinct, but America's captains of industry had a voracious appetite for progress, and they turned a deaf ear. As did many in the government, sadly.

THE PEOPLE'S PARKS
Yet with the official declaration of Yellowstone as a precious, significant, and vulnerable site, a new public consciousness began to spread. "These are our wild spaces," people said to themselves, "our heritage. And our children's heritage."

Congress continued to designate national park after national park, and Americans responded by flocking to them in increasing numbers, as did many visitors from other countries. Once tourism replaced commercial exploitation in the parks, literal and figurative guardrails were put in place to prevent damage to delicate ecosystems, pristine waterways, and native animals and plants. New infrastructure—trails, boardwalks, bridges, stairs, and overlooks—was created, while rangers instructed the public on park protocols. In many national parks the only hunting and foraging was done by native people whose subsistence rights allowed them to continue their traditional way of life.

Some national parks contain designated wilderness areas—"undeveloped federal land that retains its primeval character and influence . . ."—which are managed to preserve those natural conditions. A number of national parks are partnered with preserves, where hunting and fishing are allowed.

THE NATIONAL PARK SERVICE
The early national parks were overseen by the Department of the Interior, but a movement arose to create an independent agency to manage them. It was spearheaded by business magnate and conservationist Stephen Mather, city beautification advocate J. Horace McFarland, and journalist Robert Sterling Yard, who wrote a series of articles extolling the inspirational, educational, and recreational possibilities of these parks. In 1916, when President Woodrow Wilson signed the National Park Service Organic Act, the bureau was mandated "to conserve the scenery and the natural and historic objects and wildlife . . . [and] leave them unimpaired for the enjoyment of future generations." Mather himself became the first director of the NPS.

In addition to national parks, the NPS currently manages national monuments, memorials, lakeshores and seashores, recreation areas, wild and scenic waterways, preserves and reserves, parkways, historic sites, historic parks, military parks, battlefield parks, and scenic trails.

~~~~~

This guide offers readers a detailed look at the 63 national parks. Their evolution and culture will come alive, along with the geology that shaped them and their many attractions—landmarks, activities, animal and plant life, native artifacts, museums, visitor centers, lodgings, and tours. The entries also provide stats and state location maps along with vivid photographs that showcase each park's iconic scenery. The "More to Explore" spreads introduce other protected national sites, such as seashores, rivers, forests, reserves, and wildlife refuges.

So travel along from the Eastern seaboard across the Midwest to the Rockies and the Pacific coast, from the Great Lakes to the Southwest deserts, and from the icy northern reaches of Alaska to the balmy shores of Hawai'i, American Samoa, and the Virgin Islands . . . and ultimately discover the history and majesty of America's natural crown jewels—its exceptional national parks.

TEN MOST-VISITED PARKS

According to Park Service stats, these parks receive the most visitors.

1. Great Smoky Mountains National Park
2. Yellowstone National Park
3. Zion National Park
4. Rocky Mountain National Park
5. Grand Teton National Park
6. Grand Canyon National Park
7. Cuyahoga Valley National Park
8. Acadia National Park
9. Olympic National Park
10. Joshua Tree National Park

▲ **The Civilian Conservation Corps** was a voluntary private work relief program that ran from 1933 to 1942 as part of Franklin D. Roosevelt's New Deal. The work of these young men shaped many of the parks we see today, with much of the infrastructure they built still in use. Above President Roosevelt, flanked by members of the Corps, eats lunch at the mess table in Camp Fechner, a Civilian Conservation Corps camp at Shenandoah National Park, in the summer of 1933.

◀ **A CCC boy,** as they were called, helps build a log cabin at Granite Creek, Teton National Forest, Wyoming, in 1937. Among their responsibilities was forest management, flood control, road building, and conservation projects, and the buildings they constructed utilized native materials.

"THERE IS NOTHING SO AMERICAN AS OUR NATIONAL PARKS…. THE FUNDAMENTAL IDEA BEHIND THE PARKS … IS THAT THE COUNTRY BELONGS TO THE PEOPLE, THAT IT IS IN PROCESS OF MAKING FOR THE ENRICHMENT OF THE LIVES OF ALL OF US."

— *Franklin D. Roosevelt*

▲ **John Muir** (right) stands with President Theodore Roosevelt at Glacier Point in Yosemite Valley, California. Muir guided the president on his tour of the park in 1903. In 1864, President Abraham Lincoln had created the Yosemite Grant, which was the first instance of the federal government setting aside parkland specifically for preservation and public use. This precedent set the stage for the 1872 creation of Yellowstone as the first officially designated national park. In 1890, Congress made Yosemite one of three additional national parks, along with Sequoia and General Grant, now part of Kings Canyon.

"THE PARKS DO NOT BELONG TO ONE STATE OR TO ONE SECTION … THE YOSEMITE, THE YELLOWSTONE, THE GRAND CANYON ARE NATIONAL PROPERTIES IN WHICH EVERY CITIZEN HAS A VESTED INTEREST; THEY BELONG AS MUCH TO THE MAN OF MASSACHUSETTS, OF MICHIGAN, OF FLORIDA, AS THEY DO TO THE PEOPLE OF CALIFORNIA, OF WYOMING, AND OF ARIZONA."

— Stephen Mather, first director of the National Park Service

A herd of bison grazes in Hayden Valley at Yellowstone. The first of America's now 63 national parks, it is still one of the most visited.

NATIONAL PARK CHECKLIST
How Many Have You Visited?

PARK NAME	√	PARK NAME	√
ACADIA		INDIANA DUNES	
AMERICAN SAMOA		ISLE ROYALE	
ARCHES		JOSHUA TREE	
BADLANDS		KATMAI	
BIG BEND		KENAI FJORDS	
BISCAYNE		KINGS CANYON	
BLACK CANYON OF THE GUNNISON		KOBUK VALLEY	
BRYCE CANYON		LAKE CLARK	
CANYONLANDS		LASSEN VOLCANIC	
CAPITOL REEF		MAMMOTH CAVE	
CARLSBAD CAVERNS		MESA VERDE	
CHANNEL ISLANDS		MOUNT RAINIER	
CONGAREE		NEW RIVER GORGE	
CRATER LAKE		NORTH CASCADES	
CUYAHOGA VALLEY		OLYMPIC	
DEATH VALLEY		PETRIFIED FOREST	
DENALI		PINNACLES	
DRY TORTUGAS		REDWOOD	
EVERGLADES		ROCKY MOUNTAIN	
GATES OF THE ARCTIC		SAGUARO	
GATEWAY ARCH		SEQUOIA	
GLACIER BAY		SHENANDOAH	
GLACIER		THEODORE ROOSEVELT	
GRAND CANYON		VIRGIN ISLANDS	
GRAND TETON		VOYAGEURS	
GREAT BASIN		WHITE SANDS	
GREAT SAND DUNES		WIND CAVE	
GREAT SMOKY MOUNTAINS		WRANGELL-ST. ELIAS	
GUADALUPE MOUNTAINS		YELLOWSTONE	
HALEAKALĀ		YOSEMITE	
HAWAI'I VOLCANOES		ZION	
HOT SPRINGS			

CHAPTER ONE

PARKS OF THE NORTHEAST AND MIDWEST

The Northeast was home to nine of America's original 13 colonies, and thus was one of the first regions settled, developed, industrialized, and urbanized. National parks are often intended to preserve large areas of wilderness, of which this region had little by the time the system was established. This explains why remote Acadia is the sole Northeastern national park. There are, however, plenty of national monuments and national historic sites in this region for the history-minded traveler to visit.

The Midwest, sometimes called America's "breadbasket," is another area that has been highly developed, in this case converting the vast prairies for agricultural use. Still, some wilderness areas remain, including remnants of the Great Plains grasslands that once sprawled across the center of the nation. There are also a number of protected sites around the Great Lakes, where delicate or vulnerable ecosystems required federal intervention. Other sites, such as Gateway Arch in Missouri and Hot Springs in Arkansas received federal oversight due to their historical significance.

◀ **Hot Springs National Park, Arkansas**

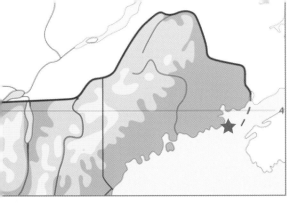

MAINE

ACADIA

Discover an island wilderness where dense woodlands meet the rocky shores of the North Atlantic.

LOCATION Hancock County and Knox County, ME

CLOSEST CITY Bar Harbor, ME

AREA 49,075 acres (198.6 km²)

ESTABLISHED July 8, 1916, as Sieur de Monts National Monument; January 19, 1929, as Acadia National Park

VISITORS 3,40,000+

ELEVATION 1,530 feet (466.3 m) at Cadillac Mountain

GEOLOGY Medium-grained granite and fine-grained black diabase

WHAT TO LOOK FOR

The park offers a variety of views and historic sites.

> Cadillac Mountain on Mount Desert Island and its amazing vistas

> Jordan Pond, near the town of Bar Harbor, one of the park's 14 Great Ponds

> Crashing waves at Thunder Hole, a small inlet naturally carved out of the rocks

> Iconic Maine lighthouses at Bass Harbor, Baker Island, and Bear Island

> The rugged coastline on the Schoodic Peninsula

> The Islesford Historical Museum tells the story of the Town of Cranberry Isles

Acadia provides a feast for the senses, with its dense piny woodlands, craggy cliff faces, pebbled beaches, and dramatic ocean views. There are 26 significant mountains in the park, including the famous Cadillac Mountain, the park's highest point. Wildlife, plant life, and sea life abound, enticing visitors to capture special moments with cameras, cell phones, or sketchpads.

EARLY HISTORY

This region of North America was inhabited for at least 12,000 years by Native American tribes, mainly members of the Algonquian Wabanaki Confederacy. They paddled canoes out to the island to fish, hunt, gather berries, collect grasses for baskets, and to trade with other nearby tribes. Eventually they began trading with European fur traders for European goods. By the 1620s, European diseases, along with tribal warfare, led to the decimation of nearly 90 percent of native populations from Mount Desert Island down to Cape Cod.

MODERN ERA

President Woodrow Wilson first established the Maine park as Sieur de Monts, a National Monument, in July 1916. In 1919 it became Lafayette National Park, the first such park east of the Mississippi. It gained its official name of Acadia in 1929.

The modern park consists of three main sections, the largest of which is located on Mount Desert Island; the next in size is located to the northeast on the mainland at Schoodic Peninsula. The third section, to the southwest—and accessible only by boat—is Isle Au Haut. Park land is also found on Baker Island (southeast coast) and Bar Island (north side of Bar Harbor).

DID YOU KNOW?

Acadia National Park was the first of its kind to be created from private lands gifted to the public. When landscape architect Charles Eliot first had the idea for the park, the plan was supported by donations of land and political advocacy by George B. Dorr, "the Father of Acadia National Park," and by his father, Charles W. Eliot.

"THE PARKS ARE THE NATION'S PLEASURE GROUNDS AND THE NATION'S RESTORING PLACES."

— J. Horace McFarland, American master printer and horticulturist

► **An osprey swoops** above the waters of Acadia with its catch clutched in its talons.

PARK FEATURES

The landscape of Acadia displays a wide diversity—from rocky shorelines to granite mountains, to countless lakes and ponds. Here towering evergreens and carpets of moss welcome many examples of New England wildlife. The margins of the park feature picturesque coastal villages like Somesville, Northeast Harbor, and Bass Harbor. A number of local landowners have placed easements on their properties to discourage development and preserve the pristine character of the region. Visitors often remark on how impressed they are by a park that combines a wilderness of woodlands with crashing seaside waves.

Recreational activities abound throughout the calendar year. Warm-weather visitors may enjoy car or bus tours, guided boat tours, and ranger tours, as well as well as hiking, biking, horse riding, bird watching, rock climbing, canoeing, kayaking, fishing, and swimming. Winter activities include cross-country skiing, snowshoeing, snowmobiling, and ice fishing.

There are two campgrounds on Mount Desert Island and a third on the Schoodic Peninsula. The main visitor center is located at Hulls Cove, near Bar Harbor.

The cliffside **Bass Harbor Head Lighthouse** marks the entrance to Bass Harbor and Blue Hill Bay on the southwest corner of Mount Desert Island.

A gorgeous sunset view draws park-goers to the top of Cadillac Mountain.

LIGHTHOUSES OF ACADIA

The jagged Maine seacoast can be treacherous, and so Maine lighthouses were an important maritime aid in the days before sonar. Today they stand as historic reminders of the state's seagoing heritage. Baker Island Light Station, Bass Harbor Head Light Station, and Bear Island Head Station are all currently managed by Acadia National Park.

WILDLIFE AND PLANT LIFE

This park is home to 40 species of mammals, more than 330 species of birds, 30 species of fish, 7 reptiles, and 11 amphibians, along with untold numbers of invertebrates. Among the most frequent animal sightings are red fox, snowshoe hare, mink, bat, beaver, and white-tailed deer. Due to territory limitations, however, it is rare to see either moose or black bear in the confines of the park. Bird sightings include bald eagle, hawk, falcon, osprey, plover, common loon, snowy owl, eider duck, and numerous songbirds and woodpeckers. As part of the Atlantic flyway, the park is also a crucial refuge for birds migrating to or from South America, such as warblers and raptors. There are 29 freshwater fish species, including landlocked salmon, shiners, and brook trout, and introduced species like smallmouth bass and river herrings called alewives.

Marine wildlife in and around the park includes finback, humpback, and Minke whales, harbor porpoises, and gray and harbor seals, as well as intertidal creatures like lobsters, hermit crabs, barnacles, sea stars, and sea anemones. Saltwater fish species include the giant ocean sunfish, mackerel, bluefish, striped bass, skate, halibut, shark, and winter flounder.

At first glance, the park may seem to be a vast panorama of pine trees, but a deeper look reveals a wide range of flora—trees, shrubs, wildflowers, and grasses. The coniferous forests feature pines and spruces, but balsam fir, ash, blueberry, eastern hemlock, hobblebush,

▲ **The Somesville Bridge** on Mount Desert Island is one of the most-photographed landmarks in Acadia.

THE NAME GAME

There are several possible sources for the park's name. It may stem from Arcadia, a region of Greece that explorer Giovanni Verrazano thought resembled this deep-green Eden, which he first saw in 1524. The native Wabanaki Indians called the region *akadie*, or "piece of land," which French explorers appropriated as *l'Acadie* and translated into the English "Acadia."

Aerial view of Bear Island Lighthouse. Bear Island and the Bear Island Lighthouse are located in the community of Cranberry Isles.

and mountain holly thrive here too. The deciduous woods include ash, aspen, beech, birch, cherry, laurel, maple, oak, sarsaparilla, Solomon's seal, starflower, violet, and white cedar. Roadsides and meadows offer blue-eyed grass, dogbane, fireweed, meadowsweet, rose, strawberry, and willow. Bogs feature aster, bog rosemary, chokeberry, cotton grass, huckleberry, iris, larch, laurel, and pitcher plant. Edging marshes and ponds, find arrowhead, bladderwort, blueberry, lobelia, pickerel weed, turtlehead, water lily, white cedar, and winterbury. Alpine regions offer aster, bearberry, bush honeysuckle, fern, gray birch, huckleberry, jack pine, juniper, laurel, pitch pine, oatgrass, red raspberry, sandwort, sweetfern, and wild raisin.

▲ **Barred owlets** peek at park visitors from their perch on a pine branch.

◄ **Sand Beach** is nestled between the granite mountains and rocky shores of Mount Desert Island. This popular spot allows visitors to swim in the frigid water or just explore the unique sand, which is composed of shell fragments.

► **A hiking path** curves through autumn foliage along the shore of Jordan Pond.

OHIO

CUYAHOGA VALLEY

Conservation helped bring back this polluted river valley.

LOCATION Summit County and Cuyahoga County, OH

CLOSEST CITY Cleveland and Akron, OH

AREA 32,572 acres (131.8 km²)

ESTABLISHED October 11, 2000

VISITORS 2,755,000+

ELEVATION 1,170 feet (357 m)

GEOLOGY Cuyahoga Formation of shale, sandstone, and siltstone over Berea Sandstone

WHAT TO LOOK FOR

The park is rich in natural beauty and history.

> Brandywine Falls and other water features

> Boston Mill Visitor Center

> Canal Exploration Center and historic homes

> Hale Farm & Village

▼ A male wood duck displays his distinctively colored spring plumage in one of the park's wetland areas.

The mission of this recently established park in northeastern Ohio was to reclaim, restore, and preserve the river valley that stretches between Akron and Cleveland.

Unlike other national parks, CVNP is traversed by numerous roadways and lies adjacent to two major metropolitan areas. Despite its urban bookends, the park offers plenty of scenic wonders: the winding Cuyahoga River, impressive waterfalls, dense forests, rolling hills, and spacious farmlands. It also provides a refuge for wildlife, resident and migrating birds, and native plants.

EARLY HISTORY

This region of Ohio was originally inhabited by Native American tribes like the Wyandot, Iroquois, Ottawa, Ojibwa, Munsee, Potawatomi, Miami, Catawba, and Shawnee. The Lenapés (the Delaware Nation) who settled here were known as the "grandfathers" of many nations of the upper Ohio River Valley. Originally a hunting and farming culture, the Lenapés turned to fur trapping after exposure to European traders—resulting in a massive population decline in beaver, fox, and other fur-bearing animals. By the late 1800s, the scenic valley had become a favored destination for urban families who desired a rural outing. During the early 20th century both the Cleveland and Akron park districts began formal development. In the 1930s the Civilian Conservation Corps worked on the park's infrastructure, including the creation of Happy Days Lodge, numerous trails, and a number of shelters. Later in the century, concern grew that urban sprawl would overwhelm the green belt between the two cities; the fact that the Cuyahoga River was so polluted with factory waste that it caught fire in 1952 and 1969 was not encouraging. In 1974, President Ford established the Cuyahoga National Recreation Area in an effort to preserve the region.

► Cascading water spills into the basin below at Brandywine Falls, one of the Cuyahoga Valley's top attractions. The mammoth waterfall is set amid dense foliage and river rock.

DID YOU KNOW?

Cuyahoga Valley is the only national park that was first designated as a National Recreation Area.

PARK FEATURES

The park offers plenty of outdoor activities—hiking (explore the Towpath Trail, the Ledges, and Brandywine Falls), biking, fishing, birding, backpacking, horse riding, canoeing, golfing, and winter sports—as well as educational experiences at the Boston Mill Visitor Center, the Canal Exploration Center at Lock 38 of the Erie and Ohio Canal, the nearby Brecksville Nature Center, and several historic homes and mills.

WILDLIFE AND PLANT LIFE

Animal inhabitants include raccoons, mink, opossum, chipmunks, beavers, muskrats, river otters, woodchucks, white-tail deer, coyotes, and 7 species of bats. Cuyahoga Valley is home to 250 species of birds, including songbirds, waders, waterfowl, raptors, and visitors' favorites like the bald eagle, peregrine falcon, great blue heron, and wood duck. Reptiles break down to 11 snakes, 8 turtles, and 1 skink. Park amphibians include 9 species of salamanders, 8 of frogs, and 1 toad. Insects in the park include 580 species of spiders, a host of butterflies (including migrant monarchs), moths, dragonflies, and damselflies.

More than 900 species of plants flourish in the forests, older fields, wet meadows, and wetlands. Tree pairings in the fragmented forest areas include oak-hickory, maple-oak, oak-beech-maple, maple-sycamore, pine-spruce, and hemlock-beech. The 21 state-listed rare species include sedges, grasses, wildflowers, shrubs, and 1 tree.

▼ **The Fritch Cabin** is one of the attractions of Hale Farm & Village, a living history museum within the boundaries of the park.

MISSOURI

GATEWAY ARCH

The soaring arch allows visitors to gaze westward—
like the early pioneers once did.

LOCATION St. Louis, MO
AREA 90.9 acres (0.14 km²)
ESTABLISHED February 22, 2018
VISITORS 2,055,300+
ELEVATION 630 feet (193 m) at top of Arch
GEOLOGY St. Louis limestone with scattering of chart beds

WHAT TO LOOK FOR

This park is famous for its soaring monument.

> Panoramas from the top of the Arch

> Visitor center exhibits on St. Louis, pioneers, and Indian life

> The historic Old Courthouse

This national park, situated along the west bank of the Mississippi River, includes the famous Gateway Arch as well as a surrounding memorial park. The site, which ignited controversy because it required the demolition of some historical buildings, still includes the Old Cathedral and the Old Courthouse.

The memorial reflects President Thomas Jefferson's role in the Louisiana Purchase, as well as the departure of the Lewis and Clark expedition in 1803, events that stimulated the westward migration of explorers and settlers. The park also commemorates the first civic government west of the Mississippi and the highly publicized Dred Scott court case of 1846, when two slaves, Dred and Harriet Scott, sued for their freedom in the courthouse. The 1857 decision by the U.S. Supreme Court, which overturned the Missouri Compromise and determined that no African-Americans were entitled to citizenship under the Constitution, hastened the onset of the Civil War. A poignant sculpture of the Scotts by Harry Weber stands on the south lawn of the Old Courthouse.

THE FAMOUS ARCH

The steel catenary arch, which rises 630 feet in the air—and is the tallest point in Missouri—has become the iconic emblem of the city of St. Louis. A tram carries visitors to the top of the arch, where they can view the city and river panorama. A live webcam on ground level also offers views from the summit. The park recently underwent a $380 million renovation that included enlarging the museum and visitor center, which are located beneath the arch and surrounded by manicured greenery. Here, immersive exhibits feature the history of St. Louis from its earliest settlement, including a riverfront model that recreates the fire of 1849, where the steamboats along the levy were destroyed. There are also recreations of historic facades, Native American exhibits such as a tipi and a river canoe visitors can paddle, and videos on the importance of bison to Plains culture. There is also a short film on the Scotts' long bid for freedom. Ranger tours cover the Arch itself and the Old Courthouse. The visitor center also houses a cafe and a store.

DID YOU KNOW?

The "Gateway to the West" Arch is the tallest human-made monument in the United States. To lend stability, its foundations were sunk 45-feet deep in limestone.

▼ **A view from Kiener Plaza Park**, with the Olympic Runner Statue, shows the Old Courthouse framed by the Gateway Arch.

"LET US HOPE THAT THE ARCH SOMEHOW SURVIVES—THAT IT BECOMES, FAR IN THE FUTURE, A MYSTERIOUS STRUCTURE LIKE THE GREAT PYRAMIDS OR STONEHENGE, THAT LEADS ONLOOKERS TO WONDER ABOUT THE PEOPLE WHO PRODUCED IT AND ASK THEMSELVES WHAT STRANGE COMPULSIONS LED TO ITS CREATION."

— *Tracy Campbell*

The elegant Gateway Arch is reflected in the serene blue waters below. Built as a monument to America's westward expansion, the judges in the competition for who would build it called it a "profoundly evocative and truly monumental expression."

DESIGN COMPETITION

In 1947, as work began on a monument and park that would both revive the blighted riverfront and stimulate the city's economy, city officials promoted a design competition for architects. The ultimate winner was Finnish-American Eero Saarinen. His sleek, graceful arch impressed all seven judges. The arch officially opened on June 10, 1967. The tram that carries visitors to the summit, designed by Dick Bowser, is something of a marvel itself. A combination elevator, escalator, and Ferris wheel, it keeps occupants vertically aligned as the car angles upward.

MORE TO EXPLORE

NATIONAL WILDLIFE REFUGES

▲ *A pair of ospreys tend their nest at Edwin B. Forsythe.*

National Wildlife Refuge Systems are natural habitats that the government deems worthy of federal protection. There is at least one refuge found in every state.

According to the National Wildlife Refuge System Improvement Act of 1997, the agency administers a national network of lands and waters for the conservation, management, and, where appropriate, restoration of fish, wildlife, and plant resources for the benefit of present and future generations. The system is to maintain the biological integrity, diversity, and environmental health of these natural resources, while allowing public access when compatible with federal conservation efforts. Established in 1903, Pelican Island National Wildlife Refuge in Florida was the first refuge established.

Today there are 568 refuges and 38 wetland management districts overseen by the United States Fish and Wildlife Service. The system comprises wetlands, prairies, and coastal and marine regions, as well as temperate, boreal, and tundra forests. Refuge maintenance includes controlling invasive species, using fire judiciously, ensuring adequate water sources, and assessing environmental threats like contamination or development.

Refuges host almost 50 million visitors yearly and include more than 700 bird species, 220 mammal species, 250 reptiles and amphibians, and more than 1,000 species of fish. Sixty sites were set up primarily to protect 280 endangered species. The system also manages six wildlife-dependent recreational uses in accordance with the Improvement Act of 1997: fishing, hunting, birding, photography, environmental education, and environmental interpretation.

Here is a representative sampling of refuges from around the nation.

▲ Edwin B. Forsythe National Wildlife Refuge

Location Atlantic County and Ocean County, New Jersey
Established 1984
Area 47,437.17 acres (192 km²)

Situated along the Atlantic Coast of southern New Jersey north of Atlantic City, this refuge combines two existing refuge parcels—Barnegat Division in Ocean County on Barnegat Bay and Brigantine Division, at the mouth of the Mullica River. The preserve protects more than 40,000 acres of tidal wetland and shallow bay habitats, while a 6,000-acre wilderness area limits public access, encouraging piping plovers and other shore birds to nest. The refuge is located beneath an active path of the Atlantic Flyway, so thousands of ducks, geese, waders, and shorebirds stop over during migration. Upland residents include woodcock, songbirds, white-tailed deer, and box turtles.

▲ *An aerial view of the refuge shows its serpentine waterways winding though marshy wetlands.*

▶ Rachel Carson Wildlife Refuge

Location Cumberland County and York County, Maine
Established 1966
Area 9,125 acres (37 km²)

Named for the well-known conservationist and author of *Silent Spring*, this refuge protects ten Maine estuaries that offer critical resources to waterfowl and other migratory birds. Habitats range from barrier beach and dune to salt marsh and rocky coastline. In winter, the marshes provide food, water, and cover when inland waterways are frozen. Birds that shelter here include piping plover, least tern, peregrine falcon, and bald eagle. Many recreationally and commercially valuable fish and shellfish use the wetlands for spawning.

▶ *A pair of white ibises wade in the waterways of the Rachel Carson Wildlife Refuge.*

▲ *Swans take flight over Red Rock Lake.*

▲ Red Rock Lakes National Wildlife Refuge

Location Southwest Montana
Established 1932
Area 65,810 acres (266 km²)

Perhaps best known for helping to bring the trumpeter swan back from near extinction in the 1930s, this remote, high-altitude Montana refuge has also had sightings of endangered whooping cranes. Bald eagles and peregrine falcons nest here, sharing the cold-water marshlands with black bears, Rocky Mountain elks, pronghorns, mule deer, beavers, mink and badgers, and possibly grizzlies and wolverines. The site is also a National Natural Landmark, ensuring few further human "improvements."

► *A ruddy turnstone stands in the muddy marshland at Chincoteague.*

► Chincoteague National Wildlife Refuge

Location Virginia and Maryland
Established 1943
Area 14,000 acres (57 km²)

This 14,000-acre wildlife preserve is primarily located on the Virginia half of Assateague Island, with portions on the Maryland side, as well as Morris Island and Wildcat Marsh. One of the most visited in the country, this refuge protects beaches, sand dunes, marshes, and maritime forests. It provides habitat for waterfowl, wading birds, shorebirds, and songbird, as well as the bands of small wild horses for which this location is famous.

▲ *Every year, visitors flock to Chincoteague National Wildlife Refuge to get a chance to see the famous Assateague ponies.*

▲ *A pair of Canada geese forage through the autumn's remains in Horicon's cattail marsh.*

▲ Horicon National Wildlife Refuge

Location Dodge and Fond du Lac counties, Wisconsin
Established 1941
Area 21,400 acres (87 km²)

This shallow, peat-filled lake bed—the largest freshwater cattail marsh in the country—was carved out of limestone by the Green Bay lobe of the vast Wisconsin glacier. The refuge was created as a sanctuary for migratory birds and waterfowl including the gregarious redhead duck; other denizens include fish, frogs, snakes, turtles, muskrats, insects, and plants. Here, visitors connect with nature through wildlife observation, photography, environmental education and interpretation, and fishing and hunting.

▶ Ash Meadows National Wildlife Refuge

Location Nye County, Nevada
Established 1984
Area 23,000 acres (93 km²)

This desert oasis represents southwestern Nevada's portion of Death Valley National Park's ecosystem. Located in Amargosa Valley—90 miles northwest of Las Vegas—Ash Meadows offers timeless desert landscapes, surprising green foliage, and a cave system. Boardwalks wander among aquamarine springs, and visitors may glimpse 27 plants and animals found nowhere else. Early on, the gushing water attracted both Southern Paiute and Timbisha Shoshone American Indians. In 1952, several species of the intriguing desert pupfish were discovered. President Truman declared the Devil's Hole desert pupfish and its habitat as protected, the first species listed as endangered. This propelled the oasis toward National Wildlife Refuge status in 1984.

▲ *A boardwalk trail to leads to the Longstreet Cabin and Spring. The old stone cabin was built by gunslinger Jack Longstreet in the 1890s.*

◀ *A roseate spoonbill, with its feathers showing lovely pink shading, feeds in the waters off Sanibel Island.*

▶ *The endangered Amargosa toad finds a safe place in Ash Meadows.*

▲ J. N. "Ding" Darling National Wildlife

Location Sanibel Island, Florida
Established 1976
Area 5,200 acres (21 km²)

This refuge is found on beautiful Sanibel Island, a beachcomber favorite, and was established to protect one of the largest mangrove ecosystems in the country. It was named after "Ding" Darling, a cartoonist and conservationist who won two Pulitzer Prizes. The refuge is home to raccoon, bobcat, river otter, alligator, marsh rabbit, manatee, loggerhead turtle, pelican, and flamingo, as well as large populations of migratory birds.

▶ Vieques National Wildlife Refuge

Location Vieques Island, Puerto Rico
Established 2001
Area 17,771 acres (72 km²)

This scenic Puerto Rican refuge is part of the Caribbean Islands National Wildlife Refuge Complex. Habitats include beaches, coastal lagoons, mangrove wetlands, and upland forests. The island's waters contain coral reefs and sea grass beds and are home to Antillean manatee, blue whale, fin whale, and four species of sea turtle—leatherback, green, hawksbill, and loggerhead. At least 190 species of bird, both migratory and resident, are found here.

▲ *Visitors to Vieques National Wildlife Refuge have adopted the habit of stacking the plentiful coral and conch shells found on the beautiful beaches. This one is draped with a Get Your Goose On towel. GYGO! is a national campaign created by the Mountain-Prairie Region of the U.S. Fish and Wildlife Service to encourage support of these kind of refuges.*

◀ *A black-tailed prairie dog leaves its colony at Wichita Mountains to find a snack.*

◀ Wichita Mountains Wildlife Refuge

Location Southwest Oklahoma
Established 1901
Area 59,020 acres (239 km²)

Situated between two granite mountain ranges, this site is a refuge in the truest sense. The rocky walls and shadowed canyons once protected Native Americans from the U.S. Cavalry. More recently the refuge helped save the American bison from extinction—importing bulls and cows from the Bronx Zoo. Other inhabitants, some restored to the area, include Rocky Mountain elk, white-tailed deer, armadillo, river otter, ring-tailed bassarisk, and prairie dog. A herd of Texas longhorn cattle are kept here in order to preserve the cultural legacy of the breed.

◀ *Longhorns and American bison graze together in the Wichita Mountains of Oklahoma.*

▲ A colorful orange, pink, and blue sunrise highlights the beauty of Sachuest Point's rocky coastline.

◀ **Sachuest Point National Wildlife Refuge**

Location Newport County, Rhode Island
Established 1970
Area 242 acres (1 km²)

Located on a peninsula between the Sakonnet River and Rhode Island Sound, Sachuest Point, although fairly small, features a variety of habitats, including salt marsh, beach strand, and upland shrub. Here more than 200 species of birds find refuge, and visitors might also catch glimpses of notable occasional visitors, such as peregrine falcons, northern harriers, or snowy owls.

▲ A snowy owl makes a visit to Sachuest Point.

◀ **Arctic National Wildlife Refuge**

Location Northeast Alaska
Established 1980
Area 19,286,722 acres (78,050 km²)

The largest national wildlife refuge in the United States is also the nation's biggest and least-tamed chunk of public land. First protected by President Eisenhower as a national wildlife range, the site wisely encompassed an entire Arctic ecosystem. Due to the burgeoning plant and insect life of the Arctic summer, millions of birds from six continents migrate here to feed, breed, and raise their young. It is also a haven for caribou, Dall sheep, wolf, grizzly bear, polar bear, golden eagle, and gyrfalcon. Currently, oil interests await a court ruling on Trump-issued drilling rights.

◀ The golden eyes of the arctic fox stand out against its stark white coat.

◀ Polar bear cubs tussle in the vast icy tundra of the Arctic National Wildlife Refuge.

▶ **Hart Mountain National Antelope Refuge**

Location Southeast Oregon
Established 1936
Area 270,720 acres (1,090 km²)

Hart Mountain National Antelope Refuge protects more than 422 square miles of high-desert habitat, overseeing the conservation of animal and plant life and restoring native ecosystems. Home to more than 300 species, the refuge harbors 239 bird species, 42 mammals, and at least eight reptiles. Wildlife includes pronghorn antelope, bighorn sheep, mule deer, marmot, bobcat, coyote, sage grouse, and Great Basin redband trout. Visitors enjoy photography, camping, hiking, on-road biking, limited fishing, and very limited hunting.

▲ A pronghorn antelope at Hart Mountain. The pronghorn is North America's fastest land animal, capable of speeds up to 45 miles per hour.

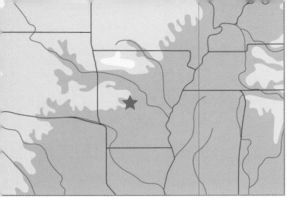

ARKANSAS

HOT SPRINGS

Thermally heated waters invite therapeutic bathing at the historic "American Spa."

LOCATION Garland County, AR
CLOSEST CITY Hot Springs, AR
AREA 5,550 acres (22.5 km²)
ESTABLISHED March 4, 1921
VISITORS 1,507,000+
ELEVATION 784 feet (239 m)
GEOLOGY Sedimentary sandstone, shale, and chert; porous tufa near the mineral springs

WHAT TO LOOK FOR:

This park combines natural wonders with elegant architecture.

> Historical buildings on Bathhouse Row

> Hot Springs Tower observation deck

> Hiking trails with natural hot springs

▲ **Hot Springs** lies nested in the Ouachita Mountains at the center of the oldest natural reserve in the United States.

As home to 47 naturally heated springs, Hot Springs, Arkansas, is unique. Once, this phenomenon drew ailing people from around the world to "take the baths," and an entire industry sprang up. Today, Hot Springs continues to attract visitors seeking to explore both its history and its national park.

Hot springs form when subsurface magma (molten rock) heats groundwater, creating steam and hot water that rises to the surface through fissures and cracks. This thermal activity also creates geysers, fumaroles, and mud pits. In the continental United States, hot springs occur most frequently in the West, but similar springs are also found in New York, Virginia, and Georgia. The Arkansas hot springs arise from the western slope of Hot Springs Mountain, part of the Ouachita Range, with a flow of well over half a million gallons a day and an average water temperature of 143 degrees Fahrenheit.

EARLY HISTORY

For more than 8,000 years humans have visited these springs, which numerous indigenous peoples believed to have medicinal properties. The thermal pools even became the subject of Native American legends. The area was called "Valley of the Vapors" when Spanish explorer Hernando de Soto arrived in 1591; he was likely the first European to view the springs. Around the 1700s the region was settled by the Caddo, then the Choctaw, Cherokee, Quapaw, and other Southeastern tribes. They reputedly put aside tribal disputes or territorial differences while bathing in the healing waters.

  The region was initially claimed by Spain, then France, then Spain, then France again. It finally became part of the United States territories after the Louisiana Purchase of 1803. The Quapaw initially ceded their land to the government through a treaty but were eventually removed to Oklahoma as the hot springs began to attract more and more settlers. In an effort to preserve the springs for the future, Congress designated them as Hot Springs Reservation in 1832. Well before the concept

► **The hot spring,** with an average temperature of 143 degrees F, flows over rocky terrain. The heat from the hot spring provides a misty and picturesque scene, which is particularly beautiful in the morning.

of national parks existed, this was the first time the government set aside any land for recreational use. This federal protection allowed the town of Hot Springs to grow and prosper until it was a destination on a par with elite European spas like Baden-Baden in Germany.

But by the 1920s, the springs were not the only "hot" things in the town. During Prohibition it was known for speakeasies and illegal gambling, horse racing at Oaklawn Park, and visits from gangsters like Al Capone. It was also an early home to Major League Baseball's spring training and the birthplace of 42nd president Bill Clinton. In 1921 the site's name was officially changed to Hot Springs National Park. The

▶ **The Hot Springs Mountain Tower** provides sweeping vistas of the surrounding area.

goes to the U.S. Treasury.) The remaining buildings are either being renovated or used for other purposes.

Across from the Row on Central Avenue lie shops, restaurants, and attractions such as A Narrow Escape, with its themed escape rooms and the Gangster Museum of America. For families with kids, other attractions in the area include an alligator farm and petting zoo and Magic Springs Theme and Water Park.

WILDLIFE AND PLANT LIFE

The park's animal life consists of rodents, bats, and small mammals along with white-tailed deer and an occasional black bear. The underbrush is home to 22 species of frogs, toads, and salamanders

◀ A natural hot spring empties into the steaming pool below the rocks.

government acquired more land, including Hot Springs Mountain, North Mountain, Sugarloaf Mountain, and Whittington Lake Park, eventually expanding the site to more than 5,000 acres. In spite of this increase, Hot Springs is the second-smallest national park after Gateway Arch National Park in St. Louis.

PARK AND LOCAL ATTRACTIONS

The park includes portions of downtown Hot Springs, making access to the park quite easy. The forested areas include 26 miles of trails for hiking, biking, swimming, and birding, plus campgrounds for backpackers.

On the trails, one can look for thermal pools and briefly touch the steaming water. The 216-foot Hot Springs Mountain Tower offers panoramic views from its observation deck, while a lower deck contains exhibits that

trace the area's history and note the many celebrities who have visited the springs. The surrounding area also provides opportunities for boating, and fishing.

The section of the town known as Bathhouse Row is now a designated National Historic Landmark. It features a collection of large, elegant bathhouses, where visitors once bathed in the mineral-rich water piped from the springs, experienced other water-related treatments, and socialized. These impressive buildings, unique in America, include outstanding examples of Gilded Age architecture. The Fordyce Bathhouse acts as the visitor center, while Buckstaff (c. 1912) and Quapaw (c. 1922) are the only bathhouses still in operation, with the latter featuring a natural steam cave in the basement. (The money collected from the bathing concessions and also fence lizards and box turtles. Arkansas's mild climate attracts many varied species of birds, including a wide range of songbirds, plus wild turkey, raptors, herons, bitterns, swans, geese, sandpipers, plovers, cuckoos, swifts, hummingbirds, woodpeckers, kingfishers, and migratory species. Every year there is a Christmas bird count manned by volunteers, which has tallied as many as 9,000 birds from 113 species.

The terrain is primarily oak-hickory-pine forest, but also includes many other tree and shrub species. The park's grasses, mosses, and liverworts aid in soil stabilization and regulate moisture and temperatures. The numerous wildflowers and blooming trees make an especially beautiful display in spring, while autumn brings bright foliage along with cooler temperatures for hiking.

WATER MANAGEMENT

The hot springs have not been preserved in their unaltered state as natural surface phenomena. Rather, they have been managed to conserve the production of uncontaminated hot water for continued public use. The park's mountains are also managed using this same conservation philosophy in order to preserve the hydrological system that feeds the springs.

► **An aquatic-themed stained-glass** skylight looks down on the Hernando de Soto fountain in the impressive Men's Bath Hall of the restored Fordyce Bathhouse. This grand bathhouse operated from 1915 to 1962.

▼ **Built in 1922** at a cost of $93,000 in the Spanish Colonial Revival style, the Ozark Bathhouse is one of the architectural gems of Bathhouse Row.

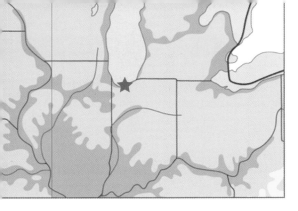

INDIANA

INDIANA DUNES

Explore the unique sand dunes and thriving wetlands of this mixed-habitat beachfront park.

LOCATION Porter, Lake, and LaPorte counties, IN

CLOSEST CITY Beverly Shores and Porter, IN

AREA 15,349 acres (62.12 km²)

ESTABLISHED February 15, 2019

VISITORS 2,293,000+

ELEVATION 900 feet (274 m)

GEOLOGY Wind-blown sand, peat bogs

WHAT TO LOOK FOR

This park offers hidden gems amid the sand and marshes.

> Mount Baldy, the wandering sand dune

> The Great Marsh and quaking bogs

> "Homes of Tomorrow" from 1933 Chicago World's Fair

DID YOU KNOW?

Mount Baldy, a 126-foot sand dune at the east end of the park is actually a wandering dune, or "living dune," that travels about four feet every year.

▼ **Mount Baldy** and its beach along Lake Michigan are top attractions of the park.

Indiana Dunes is a diverse patchwork of scenic beaches, grassy dunes, woody shrub dunes, pine- and oak-forested dunes, oak savannas, bogs, wetlands, and prairies. It became the 61st national park in 2019 after being designated a National Lakeshore in 1966.

Running for 15 miles along the south shore of Lake Michigan, it is among the most biologically rich parks in the country—rated fourth among the national parks—with more than 1,500 native plants, 46 species of mammals, 18 amphibians, 23 reptiles, 71 fish, 60 butterflies, and 60 dragonflies. The more than 350 species of birds provide first-class birdwatching.

PRESERVING THE DUNES

As early as 1899, when a publication extolled the virtues of the lakeshore's unique flora, locals were concerned about conserving this region's multiple habitats, but especially the dunes. One large dune, the Hoosier Slide, actually disappeared when glass manufacturers carried its sand away by the wagonload to make canning jars. By 1926, a state park had been created. A Save the Dunes Council in the 1950s spurred the purchase of more land and federal protection, resulting in the area's 1966 designation as a National Lakeshore.

PARK ACTIVITIES

Visitors to the park can enjoy swimming, boating, fishing, canoeing, kayaking, hiking, biking, horse riding, birding, camping, and cross-country skiing. There are 8 beaches, more than 10 hiking trails, several biking trails, and one equestrian trail. Indiana Dunes offers both a visitor center and the Paul H. Douglas Center for Environmental Education.

Nature-lovers can explore Cowles Bog and quaking Pinhook Bog, two national natural landmarks; Miller

A boardwalk twists its way through the park, allowing visitors to enjoy the dunes without harming their fragile structure.

Woods, with its rippling ridge-and-swale topography, and Calumet Prairie State Nature Preserve. The Great Marsh is home to coot, mallard, wood duck, kingfisher, green heron, tree swallow, beaver, and sedge. Hobart Prairie Grove on Lake George features wetlands, prairie remnants, white oak flatlands, and a rare bur oak savanna. Historic sites include pioneer trading post Bailly Homestead, Chellberg Farm, Swedish Farmsteads Historic District, and the Century of Progress Architectural District, a collection of five "homes of tomorrow" transported by barge from the 1933 Chicago World's Fair.

WILDLIFE AND PLANT LIFE

The park is located in the central forest-grasslands transition ecoregion, habitats that support a wide range of animals and plants. These include rarities like Mead's milkweed, pitcher's thistle, Virginia snake root, shooting star, the Indiana bat, rufa red knot, and piping plover. Animals found in the park include coyote, white-tailed deer, flying squirrel, red fox, muskrat, beaver, raccoon, and three types of bat. Birds include migrating hawks, wetlands waterfowl, shorebirds, waders, woodpeckers, and countless songbirds.

▼ **A raccoon** wriggles itself into the hollow of a tree in a forested section of the park.

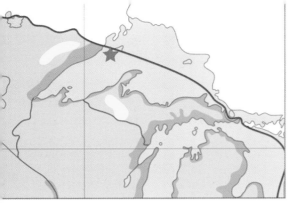

MICHIGAN

ISLE ROYALE

Experience the thrill of true wilderness on these remote Lake Superior islands.

LOCATION Keweenaw, MI

CLOSEST CITY Thunder Bay, ON

AREA 571,790 acres (2,314.0 km²)

ESTABLISHED April 3, 1940

VISITORS 25,800+

ELEVATION 1,394 feet (425 m) at Mount Desor

GEOLOGY 85% Portage Lake lava, 15% Copper Harbor conglomerates

WHAT TO LOOK FOR

This remote island park offers wilderness at its best.

> The Windigo Area with its harbor and amenities

> Sunken vessels for scuba diving exploration

> Day or night ranger programs

▲ **A calypso orchid** in full bloom at Isle Royale. This delicate pink flower, also known as fairy slipper or Venus's slipper, favors the sheltered areas on conifer forest floors.

This Michigan-based national park consists of Isle Royale and more than 400 smaller islands in Lake Superior. The park's northern boundary is adjacent to the Canadian Lake Superior National Marine Conservation Area, located along the international border of the two countries. Isle Royale, the largest island found in the Great Lake, is roughly 45 miles long and 9 miles across at its widest point. The island contains several interior lakes, with clear, cold Siskiwit being the largest. Siskiwit, in turn, boasts several islands, including Ryan Island.

EARLY MINING HISTORY

Isle Royale and its sister islands were formed by igneous rock layers that folded as a result of tectonic plate movement. The folded rock layers curved downward, creating the Lake Superior basin, and then curved up again to form the Keweenaw Peninsula. Due to the presence of copper on Isle Royale, early inhabitants began mining the island—and nearby Keweenaw Peninsula—for the malleable metal more than 6,500 years ago. Large quantities of copper tools and implements have been found in Indian mounds and settlements dating from 3000 BCE. Some researchers estimate that more than 750,000 tons of copper were taken from the region. Around 1669, a Jesuit missionary named Dablon wrote of "an island called Menong, celebrated for its copper." Menong, or Minong, was indeed the indigenous people's term for Isle Royale. Once the Chippewa gave up claim to the island in 1843, intensive prospecting began, especially in the ancient open pits, but also in the island's first modern mines. The endeavor ended in 1855 due to a lack of productive ore seams. Interest in mining rose again in 1873 with the opening of the Minong and Islands Mines, but they too petered out by 1881.

A treaty with Great Britain in 1783 gave the island to the United States, but the British maintained control until after the War of 1812. The local Ojibwa also considered the island their territory. They finally ceded the land to the United States in 1842 with the Treaty of LaPointe. Between the construction of mine shafts and the depredations of the logging industry, much of the

DID YOU KNOW?

Due to its remote location, this national park is the least visited within the contiguous United States. Only Gates of the Arctic in Alaska has fewer visitors per year.

Rock Harbor Lighthouse marks the southwest entrance to Rock Harbor at the Middle Islands Passage. Completed in 1855, it features a 50-foot white round brick tower with a black lantern. The attached keeper's house now serves as a museum.

▲ **The Lake Superior shoreline** gives a spectacular view of the deep blue water and lush green islands of Isle Royale.

island was deforested. It was not until the islands became a national park and the exploitation ceased, that the forests began to regenerate. Commercial fishing, primarily for whitefish, lake trout, and siskowit, was also an important industry for nearly two centuries, and disused fishing shanties and wharves still dot the island.

PARK ACTIVITIES

The waters around the park islands could be considered a boater's paradise, providing many bays and coves to fish in or explore, all accompanied by spectacular scenery. There are even sunken ships—protected by the park system as cultural treasures—for scuba divers to

investigate. The deepwater wrecks in chilly temperatures require experienced divers familiar with the decompression process. Once ashore, visitors can enjoy day hikes, birding, backpacking and camping, ranger programs, and special programs for children. Boat rentals can be found at the marina of Rock Harbor along with a hotel and cabins.

The Windigo Area is a popular destination located on the southwest end of Isle Royale; it is accessible by park vessels, private boat, or seaplane. There is a harbor with seaplane landing zone, visitor center, showers, laundry, gas station, store, potable water, several campgrounds, multiple nature trails, and several scenic overlooks.

WILDLIFE AND PLANT LIFE

Today, Isle Royale contains a number of habitats. The predominant one is boreal forest, similar to those found in neighboring Minnesota and Ontario. This consists of coniferous forests of pine, spruce, and larch. Other habitats are upland ridges, or "balds," which support scrubby trees, hardy grasses, and blueberry bushes; wetlands or marshes created by beaver activity; and lakes that often have boggy shores. The overall climate is affected by the cold water found in Lake Superior.

The floral habitats of the islands are within a Laurentian Mixed Forest Province, also known as North Woods, a habitat found in eastern North America—around the Great

six types of bat. Gray wolves, which are found in remote parts of Minnesota and Ontario, remain the apex predator on Isle Royale. Birders should look out for ruffled grouse, spruce grouse, bald eagle, red-tailed hawk, osprey, common loon, wild turkey, and pileated woodpecker. Lake fish include dace, chub, pike, muskellunge, minnow, lake sturgeon, alewife, perch, bass, walleye, Chinook salmon, and sculpin.

▲ A beaver nibbles on the shoots of a water lily in the waters of Isle Royale.

TRAVEL RESTRICTIONS

The islands of this park are only accessible by passenger ferry, boat, or seaplane. Isle Royale has no roads, so motorized wheeled vehicles are not allowed. Rock Harbor, however, allows wheeled carts for transporting luggage and equipment from the marina to the hotel and cabins. The park service uses tractors and utility terrain vehicles to move items in the developed areas and to perform maintenance.

▲ A simple board serves as a walkway for visitors to teeter through the wetlands.

▼ Moose antlers are arranged around the sign for Windigo. One of the park's two developed areas, Windigo gives visitors a change to enjoy camping, hiking, and stalking the moose, along with boating and trout fishing.

Lakes, New England, and northern New York. This temperate broadleaf mix forest biome acts as a transition zone between the boreal forests of the north and the Big Woods, the temperate hardwood habitats to the south. Conifers include jack pine, black and white spruce, balsam fir, and eastern red cedar. Deciduous trees include quaking aspen, red oak, paper birch, American mountain ash, red, mountain, and sugar maple.

A limited number of mammals are found on the island—most of which had to swim there originally. These include deermouse, eastern chipmunk, muskrat, moose, beaver, red squirrel, river otter, American marten, ermine, mink, snowshoe hare, red fox, and

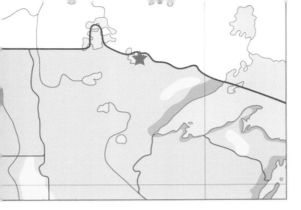

MINNESOTA

VOYAGEURS

Retrace the routes of French-Canadian trappers in this scenic, watery preserve.

LOCATION St. Louis County and Koochiching County, MN

CLOSEST CITY International Falls, MN

AREA 218,200 acres (883 km²)

ESTABLISHED April 8, 1975

VISITORS 240,000+

ELEVATION 1,227 feet (374 m)

GEOLOGY Schist and gneiss in west-central region, granitic rocks in east and southeast (limestone and dolomite)

WHAT TO LOOK FOR

This park offers visitors activities whether spring, summer, winter, or fall.

> Remains of 13 gold mines

> Ellsworth Rock Gardens, a complex, terraced garden "showplace" on a prominent rock outcrop

> Northern lights displays that often glow in the night sky

Marked by transitional ecosystems, this park features aquatic and land habitats and boasts both southern boreal and northern hardwood forests. Renowned for its water resources, the park is named for the French-Canadian fur traders, called *voyageurs*, who were among the first Europeans to travel these waterways. The park encompasses the entire Kabetogama Peninsula, which is accessible only by watercraft—or snowmobile, snowshoes, or skis in winter.

A BRIEF HISTORY

Voyageurs is located in northern Minnesota on the Canadian Shield geological plateau, which stretches up beyond the Great Lakes and encircles Hudson's Bay. The rocks in the Shield average between one and three billion years in age. In many places glacial scraping has left only a thin layer of soil. For more than 10,000 years the region was occupied by humans, who likely followed animal prey to the lakesides. Fish soon became a food staple, with wild rice added around 100 BCE. Tribes in the area included the Cree, Monsoni, and Assiniboine.

European explorers passed through in the late 1600s, then fur trappers appeared, drawn by the large beaver populations. By 1780 the Ojibwa were the dominant tribe at Rainy Lake, providing food, furs, and canoes. Later, heavy logging drastically altered the composition of the forest. Today, there are few stands of mature trees remaining in the park. In 1891 the Minnesota Legislature petitioned the president to make the area a national park, but it took another 80 years for the idea to become a reality.

ACTIVITIES AND AMENITIES

Understandably popular with boaters and fisherfolk, the park provides several visitor centers and boat ramps on its periphery. Canoes and small boats are also available for rent. Four major lakes make up 40 percent of the park—Rainy Lake, Kabetogama, Namakan, and Sand Point. The park's southern boundary is the north shore of Crane Lake. The Kettle Falls Hotel is the sole lodging within Voyageurs and is only accessible by water. The campsites, also accessible only by water, are rated as front-country and backcountry tents, houseboats, and day-use sites. Anglers can fish for walleye, northern pike, muskellunge, smallmouth bass, largemouth bass,

DID YOU KNOW?

In 1893, a gold rush occurred at Rainy Lake after George Davis discovered a gold-bearing quartz vein near Black Bay. A small town called Rainy Lake City sprang up, but the mines went bust in 1898, and the city was gone by 1901.

The Northern lights put on a colorful show over the lakes and forests of Voyageurs.

crappie, lake trout, bluegill, and yellow perch. In fall, lake whitefish may be netted in the shallows where they come to spawn. This four-season park remains open in winter, where cold-weather enthusiasts can enjoy lake driving, snowmobiling, cross-country skiing, ice fishing, snowshoeing, and winter camping. An ice road on Rainy Lake is plowed and marked for visitors; snowmobile trails are restricted to frozen lake surfaces and the Chain of Lakes Trail through the center of the peninsula.

WILDLIFE AND PLANT LIFE
The park is home to white-tailed deer, black bear, beaver, fox, muskrat, snowshoe hare, and weasel. In winter, visitors may observe more reclusive animals, like timber wolf and moose, crossing the ice. Bird sightings include bald eagle, loon, owl, double-crested cormorant, and many warblers. Park habitats include conifer and hardw0ood forests, bogs, swamps, marshes, rocky outcrops, and lakeshores. It supports more than 50 tree and shrub species, 200 grass, sedge, and rush species, and over 400 wildflowers.

◄ **Trees stud** one of the park's tiny, rocky islands.

▲ **Summertime canoers** paddle through the island-studded water of Voyageurs as dusk falls.

CHAPTER TWO

PARKS of THE SOUTH

The American South is known for its mild climate, its elegant historic homes, and its culture of hospitality, plus a landscape that includes the Appalachian Mountains and many outstanding beaches and shorelines. The Southern parks include the system's most popular site, Great Smoky Mountains National Park, as well as a massive cave, several Florida keys, Virginia's scenic beauty queen in the Shenandoah Valley, and the imperiled waterways and marshlands of the vast Everglades. These Southern parks are inviting and often exciting . . . and they make ideal destinations during the colder winter months, when their temperatures rarely go below a tolerable 50 degrees.

◀ **Great Smoky Mountains National Park, North Carolina and Tennessee**

FLORIDA
BISCAYNE

Mangroves and manatees lure visitors to this protected marine habitat.

LOCATION Miami-Dade County, FL
CLOSEST CITY Homestead, FL
AREA 172,971 acres (700 km²)
ESTABLISHED October 18, 1968 as National Monument; June 28, 1980 as National Park
VISITORS 708,000+
ELEVATION 9 feet (2.7 m) on Totten Key
GEOLOGY Oolitic Miami limestone and coral-based Key Largo limestone

WHAT TO LOOK FOR

The park is home to four separate ecosystems, each with its own character.

> Shoreline mangrove swamps—home to wading birds, waterfowl, and numerous species of fish, which shelter among the trees' underwater root systems

> The shallow bay—an estuary serving as a nursery for marine life

> Coral limestone keys— home to salt-tolerant plant life, as well as small mammals, reptiles, and hundreds of insects

> Florida Reef—one of the largest coral reefs in the world; supports hundreds of varieties of fish and invertebrates, including snapper, grouper, tarpon, bonefish, and spiny lobster

This national park, which is 95 percent water, highlights the mangrove forest coastline and coral reef islands of serene and shallow Biscayne Bay. These islands, the northernmost of the true Florida keys, include Soldier Key, Ragged Keys, Sands Key, Elliott Key, Totten Key, and Old Rhodes Key. A narrow strip of the mainland forms the park's western boundary and is home to the Dante Fascell Visitor Center at Convoy Point. A museum offers a virtual journey through the park; an art gallery showcases the work of local artists.

Biscayne Bay's islands have been home to human settlements for 10,000 years, starting with prehistoric tribes, followed by the Glades Culture (beginning around 500 BCE) and the Tequesta people. Next came the Spanish explorers, European colonists, pirates, pineapple farmers, America's wealthy elites, and even U.S. presidents and foreign dignitaries. In the 1930s, Biscayne saw the construction of Stiltsville, a small community of fishing shacks built on pilings above the bay. Over time, most were lost to hurricanes and fires; today, the unoccupied remainders are preserved within the park.

► **An American alligator** basks on a rock near the fresh waters found farther inland in the park; crocodiles, however, thrive in the warm and saltier estuarine waters.

◄ **A great blue heron on Elliot Key.** The largest island in the park, this key offers visitors abundant recreational opportunities, including camping, wildlife watching, picnicking, and a hiking trail.

Soldier Key is covered by grass and shrub vegetation. This tiny island lies on the Safety Valve, a sandbar that separates Biscayne Bay from the Atlantic Ocean, and it is the northernmost exposure of the Key Largo Limestone that forms the "true" Florida Keys.

SHIPWRECK ALLEY

Biscayne National Park's Maritime Heritage Trail allows scuba divers to explore the remains of the park's numerous shipwrecks—and the teeming marine life that congregates around them. The dive spots include wooden vessels from the 19th century, along with more modern steel ships.

· The *Attatoon Apcar* ran aground in 1878 close by the nearly completed Fowey Rocks Lighthouse.

· The *Eri King*, sunk in 1891, reflects the transition period from sailing ships to steamships.

· The loaded cargo ship *Alicia* ran aground during a storm in 1905. The ensuing battle between 70 groups of wreckers resulted in permanent revisions to the U.S. salvage laws.

· The *Lugano*, which went down in 1913, was the largest ship to sink in the Keys up to that time.

· The sleek *Mandalay*, a steel-hulled schooner outfitted with a teak and mahogany deck, sadly sank in 1966.

◄ **The Hicks House** is one of seven remaining stilt houses standing on the sand banks of the Safety Valve on the edge of Biscayne Bay in an area known as Stiltsville.

▼ **Red mangroves,** with their impenetrable tangle of roots, form a watery maze that provides habitat for tarpons and manatees.

PROTECTING THE KEYS

During the 20th century, the islands attracted many tycoons and celebrities, who built elaborate vacation homes and clubs. The creation of the park was initially proposed to protect the bay from land developers who envisioned a hotel-filled "paradise" on the pristine land. Conservation advocates like journalist Juanita Greene, politician Hardy Matheson, and vacuum-cleaner magnate Herbert W. Hoover, Jr. eventually won over the public and earned their support. With this groundswell still gaining momentum, President Lyndon B. Johnson officially established Biscayne National Monument in October 1968.

ACTIVITIES

Divers love exploring the park's sparkling waters and its barrier reefs that teem with fish, as well as its 44 documented shipwrecks. Landlubbers can take in the lush island scenery and terrestrial wildlife or just relax and enjoy the shore breezes.

Besides scuba diving and snorkeling, park activities include boating, kayaking, windsurfing, fishing, birding, and hiking. There are also a number of guided tours available.

WILDLIFE AND PLANT LIFE

Island wildlife includes gray fox, bobcat, river otter, raccoon, opossum, flying squirrel, white-tailed deer, and giant blue land crabs, while marine denizens include humpback, right, and sei whale, bottlenose dolphin, and false killer whale. Birders can view pelicans, waterfowl, shore birds, waders, raptors, and upland gamebirds, along with the songbirds and parrots that flood the islands with sound and color. And keep an eye out for alligators and crocodiles lurking in lakes or brackish wetlands. The park also offers refuge to 16 threatened species, such as gentle manatees, green and hawksbill sea turtles, eastern indigo snakes, and Schaus' swallowtail butterfly.

The park's wide assortment of trees, shrubs, and grasses include black, red, and white mangrove; Australian pine; yucca;

▲ **The iconic Boca Chita Key Lighthouse** was built in the 1930s. The 65-foot ornamental structure has become a park emblem.

bay cedar; coconut, cabbage, Senegal date, key thatch, and silver palm; wild lime; West Indian mahogany; gumbo limbo; tangerine; St. Augustine grass; seagrape; sea rosemary; saffron plum; paradise tree; monk orchid; bristlegrass; papaya; and lemon. Wildflowers that dot the islands include hibiscus, orchid, daisy, jute, periwinkle, morning glory, Queen Ann's lace, spiderlily, and tansy. Perhaps the rarest plant in America—the semaphore prickly pear cactus—is found here along with examples of the threatened buccaneer palm.

CROCODILE NURSERIES

Over time, the miles of cooling water canals built close to shore behind the Turkey Point power plant have become a favored nesting site for the park's population of American crocodiles. These large reptiles, which typically range along the mainland coast and northern islands, are comfortable navigating Biscayne's somewhat salty estuarine (brackish) waters. The park's alligators are less commonly seen, preferring the fresh water sources found near the interior of the islands.

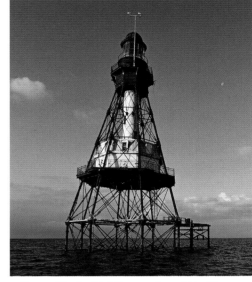

▲ **Fowey Rocks Lighthouse** lies within Biscayne National Park, but it is maintained by the U.S. Coast Guard as the "Eye of Miami."

◀ **Buttonwood trees** line a trail through the park that leads out toward the waters of the bay.

▼ **Black Creek Canal** is a shoreline trail that offers stunning vistas of the bay.

DID YOU KNOW?

In the early 1960s, the CIA used Elliott Key to train Cuban exiles in preparation for the ill-fated Bay of Pigs invasion of Cuba.

SOUTH CAROLINA
CONGAREE
Record-breaking "champion" trees crown this old-growth forest.

LOCATION Richland County, SC

CLOSEST CITY Eastover, SC

AREA 26,276 acres (106.34 km²)

ESTABLISHED October 18, 1976 as National Monument; November 10, 2003 as National Park

VISITORS 146,000+

ELEVATION 140 feet (43 m)

GEOLOGY Alluvial floodplain with deposits of sand, silt, and clay

WHAT TO LOOK FOR

Congaree's wilderness forests are a haven for hikers.

> Harry Hampton Visitor Center

> Boardwalk Loop hiking trail and canoe trail on Cedar Creek

> "World Champion" trees, among the tallest in the world

With more than half its acreage designated as a wilderness area, this park preserves a large part of the Middle Atlantic coastal forests ecoregion and boasts some of the tallest trees in the eastern United States. These in turn form one of the highest temperate deciduous forest canopies left in the world. Although this park was formerly referred to as Congaree Swamp, in reality it is an old-growth bottomland hardwood forest that occasionally floods.

LOGGING WOES
Commerce in the Congaree River region during the late 19th century centered on cypress logging, when the Santee River Cypress Logging Company began to harvest timber from what is now park land. One of the company's owners, Francis Beidler, made sure the

▲ **A circle of loblolly pines** reach for the sky in the dense forest of Congaree National Park.

DID YOU KNOW?

Congaree National Park is home to both the tallest (169 feet) and largest (42 cubic meters) loblolly pines (*Pinus taeda*) in the world; there are also several cypress trees that are more than 500 years old.

property would stay in his family through several generations. In the 1950s, however, newspapermen Harry R. E. Hampton and Peter Manigault fought to preserve the Congaree floodplain. When the Beidlers again began logging the forest in 1969, Hampton formed Congaree Swamp National Preserve Association, which, along with the Sierra Club and various state politicians, helped effect the establishment of the Congaree Swamp National Monument in October 1976.

ACTIVITIES

This unique national park also has the distinction of being a designated wilderness area, a UNESCO biosphere reserve, a recognized bird area, and a national natural landmark. Activities for visitors include hiking, canoeing, kayaking, and birding. For backpackers, primitive campsites are located throughout the park. Hiking trails include, in order of length, Bluff Trail, Weston Lake Loop, Oakridge Trail, and King Snake Trail. There is also the Boardwalk Loop, an elevated walkway through swampy terrain that provides closer looks at plant life and fungi. Current trail conditions can be accessed at the Harry Hampton Visitor Center. For water sport enthusiasts, there is a 20-mile canoe trail on Cedar Creek.

WILDLIFE AND PLANT LIFE

Animal sightings inside the park include bobcat, white-tailed deer, feral swine, feral dogs, coyotes, and otters. The rivers,

► **Bald cypress knees.** These large trees produce "knees" that rise up from the forest floor.

creeks, and wetlands contain turtles, snakes, occasional alligators, various amphibians, and many species of fish, including bowfin, alligator gar, and catfish. Notable birdlife consists of red-cockaded and pileated woodpecker, cuckoo, wood stork, American woodcock, roseate spoonbill, and white ibis, as well as a variety of songbirds, waders, waterfowl, shorebirds, gamebirds, and raptors.

As an old-growth forest, the park contains one of the largest concentrations of "world champion" trees, including the tallest examples of 15 different species. Among these titans are a 169-foot 361-point loblolly pine; a 157-foot, 384-point sweetgum; a 154-foot, 465-point cherrybark oak; a 135-foot, 354-point American elm; a 133-foot, 356-point swamp chestnut oak; a 131-foot, 371-point overcup, and a 127-foot, 219-point common persimmon. (Points combine a tree's circumference, height, and quarter-crown spread.)

Other flora includes lily, magnolia, tulip tree, eastern prickly pear, jessamine, dwarf palmetto, milkweed, pawpaw, fern, cardinal flower, holly, bamboo, honeysuckle, violet, privet, passion flower, waterlily, beauty berry, and horrid thistle.

► **A cottonmouth snake** drapes itself in the fork of a tree. These venomous semiaquatic snakes are often called water moccasins.

▲ **A whimsical sign** in Congaree's old-growth area lets visitors know what to expect from the park's abundant mosquito population.

◄ **The cypress forest and swamp** of Congaree preserves the largest expanse of old-growth bottomland hardwood forest remaining in the southeastern United States.

FLORIDA
DRY TORTUGAS
A massive fort awaits visitors to the westernmost Florida Keys.

LOCATION Monroe County, FL

CLOSEST CITY Key West, FL

AREA 47,125 acres (580,000 km²)

ESTABLISHED January 4, 1935, as Fort Jefferson National Monument; October 26, 1992, as Dry Tortugas National Park

VISITORS 60,000+

ELEVATION 10 feet (3 m)

GEOLOGY Platform of carbonate rocks (limestone and dolomite)

WHAT TO LOOK FOR

The park provides attractions both historical and aquatic.

> Former naval base Fort Jefferson

> Living coral reefs that teem with exotic fish

> Numerous shipwrecks and sealife for scuba divers

Located 68 miles west of Key West in the Gulf of Mexico, this national park is accessed by ferry, chartered boat, or seaplane. The park is home to the former naval base, Fort Jefferson, located on Garden Key and focuses on preserving the ecology of the seven Dry Tortugas Islands, the westernmost and most isolated of the Florida Keys. The six remaining keys are called Loggerhead, Bush, Long, East, Hospital, and Middle. The park is renowned among divers for its azure waters, coral reefs, assortment of fish species and other marine life, and the many shipwrecks in the area.

FORT JEFFERSON, THE GHOST FORT

In 1825, only five years after Spain sold Florida to the United States, American Navy Commodore David Porter evaluated Bush Key (Garden Key) for use as a naval base to suppress Caribbean piracy, but he turned it down. In 1826 the island became home to the Garden Key Light. Another naval expedition in 1829 found the island more promising, and in 1846 construction of the fort began around the existing lighthouse. Named Fort Jefferson, it was composed of 16-million bricks and remains the largest brick-masonry structure in the western hemisphere.

At the start of the Civil War, Union forces took command of the fort to keep it out of Confederate hands. It was used as a military prison for captured Confederate soldiers and Union deserters, and after the war it housed Samuel Mudd and the other three men convicted of conspiracy in the assassination of Abraham Lincoln.

The fort eventually deteriorated and by 1934 was a crumbling ruin. Then in 1935, President Franklin D. Roosevelt designated the area as Fort Jefferson National Monument. For three years the Works Progress Administration performed structural renovation and historic preservation work on the site. It was listed on the National Register of Historic Places on November 10, 1970, and it was eventually established as a National Park in October 1992.

◀ **A seaplane** arrives in the waters of the Dry Tortugas. The park is accessible only by air or by boat.

ACTIVITIES

In addition to scuba diving and snorkeling, visitors to Dry Tortugas enjoy boating, kayaking, paddleboarding, fishing, birding, hiking, and swimming. Some even endeavor to swim completely around Garden Key. There are also guided tours for fishing, diving, and viewing wildlife and tours of the fort itself, which includes a museum and bookstore.

◄ **Garden Key Light,** also known as the Tortuga Harbor Light, stands alongside a cannon atop the battlements of Fort Jefferson.

WILDLIFE AND PLANT LIFE

Animal sightings in the park are mostly of the marine variety, and you might see sharks, living coral, squid, octopus, lobsters, reef fish, and grouper. Explorer Ponce de Leon named the islands *Las Tortugas,* or "the Turtles," due to the green, hawksbill, leatherback, and loggerhead turtles he found there in 1513—and which still bury their eggs on the keys. Birders enjoy viewing the large colonies of sooty tern, brown noddy, masked boobie, and magnificent frigatebird that nest there, along with a frequent number of vagrant birds.

The low and irregular keys feature thin growths of mangrove trees and small patches of grass. Some keys have no vegetation at all. Rising from deep water, the individual islands sometimes disappear, but then several new ones may take their place, depending on geomorphology and severe weather incidents.

▼ **A magnificent frigatebird,** displaying his bright red inflated throat patch, flies over the waters of Dry Tortugas.

DID YOU KNOW?

Because there is no fresh water source on Garden Key, earlier inhabitants had to gather rainwater in underground cisterns or use steam condensers to distill fresh water from sea water.

An aerial view of Dry Tortugas National Park shows the outline of the sprawling Fort Jefferson surrounded by aquamarine waters.

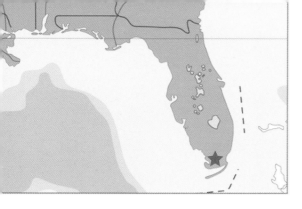

FLORIDA

EVERGLADES

Alligators and crocodiles dwell side-by-side
in this vulnerable Eden.

LOCATION Miami-Dade, Monroe,
and Collier counties, FL

CLOSEST CITY Florida City, Everglade
City, FL

AREA 1,508,970 acres (6,106.6 km²)

ESTABLISHED May 30, 1934

VISITORS 597,000+

ELEVATION 8 feet (2.4 m)

GEOLOGY Early deposits of calcium
carbonate in sand, shells, and coral were
converted into limestone

WHAT TO LOOK FOR

*This fragile park offers much
for the eco-minded visitor.*

> Wetlands and mangrove
  swamps on the 10,000
  Islands Cruise

> Florida Pioneer Museum

> Miccosukee Cultural Center

> Buttonwood Canal tour for
  families with children

The Everglades is more than a forested swamp, more than a park.
To many it embodies a rare and unique resource, one full of myth and
mystique; it is almost a state of mind. The wetlands are fed by the
overflow that rises in Lake Okeechobee and eventually drains into
Florida Bay. Site of the largest mangrove ecosystem in North America,
the region is a major breeding ground for tropical wading birds. It is also
rich in culture, home to Seminole Indians and other tribes that lived for
centuries along its many waterways.

This esteemed wetlands preserve at
the tip of the Florida peninsula, with
its long, vivid history, nonetheless once
teetered on the brink of ecological ruin.
The government agencies meant to
safeguard it left behind a dubious record
of environmental stewardship. Many early
Floridians considered the area worthless,
and so from the 1880s onward, plans
were made to drain the wetlands for
use in agriculture and residential
construction. The waterways that fed the
swamp were increasingly controlled and
even diverted. In the 20th century, the

ongoing South Florida sprawl sent
land-hungry developers even deeper
into pristine wilderness.

According to author Tommy Rodriguez
in *Visions of the Everglades*, "complete
restoration of Florida's Everglades could
take approximately 30 years and 7.8
billion dollars. There's a lot of work to be
done—but the damage is not irreversible.
Together, through conservation and public
awareness, we may be able to correct
many of these unfortunate trends. Today, it
is not enough to just appreciate nature—we
have to actively work to protect it."

**The subtropical wetland
ecosystem** of the Everglades
spans 2 million acres across central
and south Florida and is home to a
vast array of flora and fauna.

"THE EVERGLADES HAVE A SINISTER, BEGUILING BEAUTY,
SHADOWS DARK AND MYSTERIOUS, A HOLOCAUST OF SECRETS
UPON SECRETS UPON SECRETS; AND YOU CAN'T HELP
BUT WONDER HOW MANY LAYERS THERE ARE,
HOW MANY ARE YET TO COME."

— Foster Kinn, *Freedom's Rush II*

The National Park Service is now part of that endeavor, guarding the southern 20 percent of the Everglades against habitat destruction. In fact this was the first national park established specifically to preserve a fragile ecosystem, as opposed to those created to protect geological features. Yet, even today, the preservation and restoration of the 'Glades is still a hotly debated political trigger in much of South Florida.

EARLY INHABITANTS

Rich in animal, plant, and marine life, the Everglades has attracted human habitation for tens of thousands of years. The early Tequesta people lived on the eastern side of the wetlands, a natural boundary, and the Calusa were found in even greater numbers on the western side. In the 18th century, the Creeks

▶ **A Florida panther** skulks through the Everglades brush as it stalks its prey. This protected North American cougar has seen a rise in population, from 20 wild individuals in the 1970s to an estimated 230 by 2017. Since 1982 it has been the Florida state animal.

DID YOU KNOW?

Florida was once part of the African portion of the supercontinent known as Gondwana.

invaded and absorbed the remaining Tequesta, while the Calusa had also disappeared by 1800, their presence signified only by the shell mounds they left behind. In the early 19th century the Seminole nation formed from a mixture of Creeks, escaped African slaves, and members of other tribes from North Florida , but after the Seminole Wars with the U.S. military, many tribe members were relocated to Oklahoma. To escape the forced emigration, some bands of hunters and scouts settled in the area of today's Big Cypress National Preserve. Along with the Miccosukee tribe, the Seminoles lived in isolation, trading to survive. Members of

both tribes are still found within the park's bounds. New policies and procedures in the park are submitted for approval by tribal representatives.

ACTIVITIES

The Everglades National Park is considered the largest surviving subtropical wilderness in the contiguous United States, and it contains a wealth of important habitats. Guided tours of the parkland and boat tours provide different perspectives of these habitats. Offerings include a two-hour narrated tram tour along a 15-mile loop trail and the 90-minute 10,000 Islands Cruise through the park's mangrove islands. There

are also exciting airboat tours available from several local businesses. Other activities include fishing, boating, biking, hiking, birding, backpacking, camping, canoeing and kayaking, and horse riding.

FAMILY ADVENTURES

For families with children, there is plenty here to engage young imaginations. The Buttonwood Canal tour, a 2-hour boat trip along a artificial watercourse, features manatees, alligators, and even dolphins. Eco Pond is home to roseate spoonbills, ospreys, and many other feathered favorites, as well as numerous exotic butterflies. The Florida Pioneer Museum, a

An airboat taking tourists through the maze of Everglades waterways is on course to meet a swimming alligator.

FLORIDA · EVERGLADES | 51

▲ **An alligator** suns itself on a grassy bank. No visit to the Everglades would be complete without a sighting of these ubiquitous Floridian reptiles.

▲ **A striking purple gallinule** uses its large feet to walk across lily pads. This big and noisy bird lurks in marshes and other wetlands.

UNWELCOME VISITORS

The Everglades is currently home to several invasive reptiles that are altering the ecological balance. Burmese pythons, with an estimated population of 100,000, are decimating many species of small native mammals; bigger specimens are even tackling deer and crocodilians. The tegu, a large lizard sold as a pet, is another interloper—it endangers rare birds and reptiles by feeding on their eggs. The monitor lizard preys on mammals, reptiles, fish, and birds. As an egg eater, it has been damaging to populations of burrowing owl, sea turtle, and crocodile. These three scaled menaces possibly started as abandoned pets or escapees from reptile-themed attractions hit by hurricanes, but now they are breeding and proliferating.

real restored pioneer home, houses Native American artifacts, farm tools, archival photos, and memorabilia from the early 20th century. Shark Valley is short on sharks but long on other wildlife. It is located within the park's freshwater marsh, and a tram trip or bike ride along the wetlands trails provides sightings of alligators, dozens of birds, and many mammals. For history buffs of all ages, consider the Miccosukee Indian Village, an attraction with a museum and open-air chickee huts that show how this tribe lived, including demonstrations of basket weaving, patchwork, doll-making, and beading. The center also has a restaurant and gift shop. The free Museum of the Everglades is located in Everglades City and housed at a historic site. It offers film clips, photographs, and artifacts that highlight the area's past.

▲ **Many of the grass species** in the Everglades form "hammocks," small island refuges found in swampy areas.

◀ **Man versus alligator** at the entry to the Miccosukee Indian Village. The Miccosukee tribe is a federally recognized Indian tribe residing in the Florida Everglades. The village hosts demonstrations of Miccosukee tribal arts and culture, with crafts, airboat rides, and alligator shows.

▼ **In the heart of the Everglades** is the Shark Valley Visitor Center and its Observation Tower viewing platform, the highest accessible point in the entire park. It allows visitors to climb to the top for miles-wide panoramic views.

WILDLIFE AND PLANT LIFE

The Everglades contains many odd lifeforms, some occurring in unusual locations. According to Michael Grunwald, author of *The Swamp*, "it had carnivorous plants, amphibious birds, oysters that grew on trees, cacti that grew in water, lizards that changed colors, and fish that changed genders." It is also one of the only spots in the world where alligators and crocodiles share the same waterways. It is home to 36 threatened or protected species like the Florida panther, snail kite, and West Indian

manatee and the only place to look for Everglades mink, Okeechobee gourd, and Big Cypress fox squirrel.

Among the park's more than 40 species of mammals are white-tailed deer, black bear, river otter, nine-banded armadillo, southern flying squirrel, opossum, marsh rabbit, Eastern cottontail, bobcat, red and gray fox, long-tailed weasel, eastern spotted and striped skunk, feral pig, and five species of bats. Marine mammals include short-finned pilot whale, Atlantic bottlenosed dolphin, and Rice's whale.

Reptiles found here include caiman, indigo snake, corn snake, eastern hognose snake, rat snake, eastern coral snake, Florida water snake, Florida and scarlet kingsnake, brown anole, island glass lizard, ground skink, Florida softshell turtle, gopher tortoise, Florida box turtle, striped mud turtle, diamondback terrapin, snapping turtle, and five species of sea turtles: loggerhead, green, Atlantic hawksbill, Atlantic leatherhead, and Atlantic ridley.

Fish have always formed a key link in the Everglades' food chain, and recreational fishing is now one of the most popular activities in the park. Freshwater inhabitants include bowfin, bluegill, largemouth bass, peacock bass, garfish, crappie, sunfish, warmouth, and freshwater golden clam; saltwater species include speckled trout, redfish, pompano, black drum, moray eel, tarpon, grouper, barracuda, and snook. Marine invertebrates include several species of crab,, blue shrimp, white-leg shrimp, zebra mussel, winkle sea snail, and oyster.

The park is home to plenty of "bucket list" birds like white ibis, roseate spoonbill, wood stork, great egret, bald eagle, Indian peafowl, and American flamingo. The wetlands/grasslands combo also attracts an enormous range of avian residents and migrants, including duck, goose, grebe, wild turkey, pigeon, dove, ani, cuckoo, goatsucker, swift, hummingbird, crane, rail, loon, gull, tern, shore birds, petrel, booby, gannet, cormorant, anhinga, pelican, bittern, heron, vulture, accipiter, falcon, owl, kingfisher, woodpecker, parrot, parakeet, and a multitude of songbirds.

Located between temperate North America and tropical Caribbean, Everglades National Park can boast flora found in both climates. The frequency of flooding and the favorable growing conditions also influence the types of plants found here. As some native species died off due to drainage, farming, or natural causes, they were replaced by introduced species, mainly tropical escapees used by landscapers. This has resulted in a mix of vegetation that is unique and hardy. Trees include black and red mangrove, soldierwood, cockspur, slash pine, loblolly, willow bustic, West Indies mahogany, live oak, ironwood, royal palm, gumbo-limbo, wild tamarind, strangler fig, bald cypress, mastic, pitch apple, and inkwood.

Wildflowers abound, with 39 separate species of orchids, including the elusive ghost orchid, a frequent quest of nature photographers. Visitors will also find bromeliads, cacti and succulents, lichens, mosses, and marine plants, including algae.

▲ The sun rises on the pine rocklands on Long Pine Key Nature Trail. One of the most threatened habitats in Florida, the Everglades' pine rocklands is home to a variety of animal species, including birds like woodpeckers and grackles, as well as black bears and Florida panthers.

An anhinga spreads its wings, ready for flight across the wetlands.

MORE TO EXPLORE
NATIONAL WILD AND SCENIC RIVERS

The National Wild and Scenic Rivers System was created by Congress in 1968 and signed into law by President Lyndon B. Johnson. These exceptional rivers have been "designated to protect their free-flowing condition, water quality, and outstanding natural, cultural, and recreational values for the enjoyment of present and future generations." This visionary system was conceived at a time when Americans were becoming more ecologically active. It was the result of advocacy by citizens and lawmakers concerned over maintaining free-flowing rivers in the face of extensive national dam-building initiatives and water diversions. Today the system oversees more than 13,400 miles of U.S. rivers and streams.

Initially, 8 rivers were earmarked for protection—the Clearwater (ID), Eleven Point (MO), Feather (CA), Rio Grande (TX/NM), Rogue (OR), St. Croix (MN), Salmon (OR), and Wolf (WI). Today, there are 226 wild and scenic rivers within the system, representing 41 states and Puerto Rico. All were chosen for their "outstandingly remarkable scenic, recreational, geologic, fish and wildlife, historic, cultural, or other similar values" or their ORVs.

River segments are sorted into three classifications—wild, scenic, and recreational— based on the river's accessibility and surrounding development.

- Wild rivers are primitive, undeveloped, and unpolluted, typically accessible only by trail or small plane. They represent vestiges of primeval America.
- Scenic rivers are rivers or sections of rivers that are free of impoundments, with shorelines or watersheds still largely primitive and shorelines largely undeveloped, but accessible by roads in places.
- Recreational rivers can be easily reached by car or train and may have shoreline or watershed development.

There are currently 56 exclusively wild rivers, 21 are exclusively recreational, and 24 are exclusively scenic. The remainder have multiple classifications. Management strategies vary according to type, but will always strive to protect and enhance the value of the waterways and their surroundings.

Most of these rivers are managed by one of the following agencies: National Parks Service (NPS), U.S. Army Corps of Engineers (USACE), Bureau of Land Management (BLM), U.S. Forest Service (USFS) and U.S. Fish and Wildlife Service (USFWS). Some individual states monitor their own rivers.

Here is a representative sampling of the 226 designated rivers.

TOP STATES

The following states can boast the most rivers in the federal system.

- Oregon: 57 rivers totaling 1,839 miles
- Alaska: 25 rivers totaling 3,210 miles
- California: 23 rivers totaling 1,714 miles

▶ *Colorful hot-air balloons take flight over the Rio Grande.*

▼ **Rio Grande Wild and Scenic River**

Location In and downstream of Big Bend National Park, Texas/New Mexico
Established 1968
Length 260 miles (420 km)
Type Wild/scenic
Agency NPS

This principle southwestern river allows visitors to experience three rugged canyons—Boquillas can be reached via an RV campground; Mariscal Canyon requires high-clearance 4-wheel drive vehicles, and Lower Canyon, due to the size of its rapids, requires a National Park Liability waiver.

▼ *With its majestic length, the Rio Grande runs through diverse landscapes. In one of its wilder sections in south Texas, two javelinas make their way to its banks.*

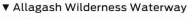

▼ Allagash Wilderness Waterway

Location Aroostook County to Piscataquis County, Maine
Designated 1970
Length 92.5 miles (148.9 km)
Type Wild
Agency Maine Bureau of Parks and Lands

This remote northeast-flowing waterway is composed of a ribbon of lakes, ponds, streams, and rivers that traverse Maine's North Woods. Here, along the Allagash River, outdoors enthusiasts can enjoy canoeing, fishing, hunting, and camping. In the Abenaki language, the word *allagash* means "bark stream."

▲ Buffalo National River

Location Newton, Searcy, Marion, Baxter counties, Arkansas
Designated 1992
Length 153 miles (246 m)
Type Wild/scenic
Agency NPS

This north Arkansas river was the very first to be designated a National River. It has become a popular camping, hiking, and fishing destination and offers dramatic karst scenery that features caves, sinkholes, springs, and waterfalls along with 500-foot sandstone and limestone bluffs.

▲ *A view from atop the Tie Slide overlook captures the muted autumn colors of the foliage that covers the banks and hillsides surrounding the Buffalo National River.*

▶ *A canoe sits poised for launching on the riverbank on a journey from Scofield Point to Ledges along the Allagash Wilderness Waterway in Maine.*

▲ *A pair of intrepid kayakers navigate whitewater rapids along the Chattooga Wild and Scenic River.*

▲ Chattooga Wild and Scenic River

Location South Carolina and Georgia
Designated 1974
Length 57 miles (92 m)
Type Wild/scenic/recreational
Agency USFS

The Chattooga River, the "crown jewel of the southeast," was the first river east of the Mississippi to gain wild and scenic status. Visitors can thrill to whitewater rafting through its legendary rapids or enjoy a swim in the placid pools downstream.

▼ Delaware River

Location Pennsylvania, New Jersey, New York, and Delaware
Established 1978
Length 301 miles (484 m)
Type Wild/scenic/recreational
Agency NPS

Rising in the Catskills, the Delaware forms a boundary between Pennsylvania and two adjoining states, New Jersey and New York, and between New Jersey and Delaware. The Upper River was once home to the Lenapé Indians. The Middle and Lower Delaware were settled by Dutch and Swedish colonists, while commerce in the river's navigable tidal region supported the rise of Philadelphia, Camden, and Trenton. Today the river, designated in two sections—the Upper Delaware Scenic and Recreational River and the Lower Delaware Wild and Scenic River—is a favorite for boating, canoeing, fishing, and camping.

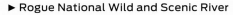

▲ A view from Mount Tammany in New Jersey gives a bird's-eye view of the Delaware as it snakes around Mount Minsi on the Pennsylvania side of the Delaware Water Gap.

◄ A steel truss bridge crosses the Delaware River at Dingman's Ferry, Pennsylvania. This bridge, connecting New Jersey and Pennsylvania, is one of the few remaining privately owned toll bridges in America.

► Rogue National Wild and Scenic River

Location Southwest Oregon
Designated 1968
Length 215 miles (346 km)
Type Wild/scenic/recreational
Agency BLM/USFS

One of the original eight Wild and Scenic Rivers, the Rogue is renowned for its salmon runs, rugged scenery, and whitewater rafting. Humans have lived along its shores for more than 8,500 years. It begins near Oregon's famous Crater Lake and flows through the geologically young High Cascades and the older Western Cascades.

▼ Autumn colors reflect off a calm South Fork Eel River within the evergreen redwood forest of Humboldt Redwoods State Park along the Avenue of the Giants just north of Weott, California.

▲ Rafters face a placid stretch of the Rogue River wilderness.

◄ Eel Wild and Scenic River

Location Northwestern California
Designated 1981
Length 196 miles (315 km)
Type Wild/scenic/recreational
Agency BLM/USFS/local government

This major river and its tributaries form the third-largest watershed in California. It also provides a municipal, industrial, agricultural, and recreation water source. Flowing north through the Coast Ranges, the Eel basin supports rich forest lands—including groves of the world's largest trees, *Sequoia sempervirens*—as well as important salmon and steelhead trout runs.

► Nashua River

Location Hillsborough County, New Hampshire and Middlesex County, Massachusetts
Established 2019
Length 27 miles (43 km)
Type Scenic
Agency NPS, local government

For many decades this "Cinderella" river, a scenic tributary of the powerful Merrimack, was polluted with industrial waste from paper mills and dye factories. In the mid-1960s civic leaders led by activist Marion Stoddert initiated a clean-up that included treatment plants, restoring many parts of the river and making it safe for recreation. It is part of the Nashua, Squannacook, Nissitissit Wild and Scenic Rivers designation.

▲ *Factories along the Nashua River once dumped waste into the water before a 1960s clean-up effort.*

▲ *The now-clear waters of the Nashua River flow through the green New Hampshire summer countryside.*

◄ Niobrara National Scenic River

Location North-central Nebraska
Established 1981
Length 76 miles (120 km)
Type Scenic/recreational
Agency NPS/USFWS

Considered an outstanding example of a Great Plains river, Nebraska's Niobrara watercourse offers cliffs, canyons, woodland scenery, wildlife, waterfalls, fishing, tubing, camping, fossil resources, and birding. It is also one of the country's top-rated canoeing rivers with class I and II rapids.

▲ *A tributary of the Missouri River, Niobrara River is a favorite with paddlers, anglers, and wildlife enthusiasts.*

► Alagnak Wild River

Location Southern Alaska
Designated 1980
Length 64 miles (103 km)
Type Wild
Agency NPS

This river's headwaters rise within the Aleutian Range in neighboring Katmai National Park. Wending westward across the Alaska Peninsula and toward the Bering Sea, the Alagnak offers an unparalleled wilderness experience that includes viewing brown bear, caribou, and moose. Outdoor activities include salmon and sport fishing, hunting, and whitewater canoeing.

► *A brown bear splashes through the shallows as it fishes in Alaska's Alagnak River.*

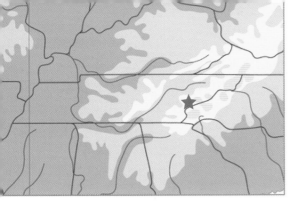

NORTH CAROLINA AND TENNESSEE
GREAT SMOKY MOUNTAINS

America's most-visited National Park offers both beauty and history.

LOCATION Swain County and Haywood County, NC; Sevier, Blount, and Cocke counties, TN

CLOSEST CITY Cherokee, NC, Townsend and Gatlinburg, TN

AREA 522,419 acres (2,114.15 km²)

ESTABLISHED June 28, 1980

VISITORS 12,000,000+

ELEVATION 6,643 feet (2,025 m) at Clingmans Dome

GEOLOGY Late Precambrian rocks including metamorphosed sandstone, phyllites, schists, and slate

WHAT TO LOOK FOR

There is so much to see and do in America's favorite park.

> Sugarlands Visitor Center

> Clingmans Dome

> Chimney Tops

> Roaring Fork Motor Nature Trail

> The Elkmont ghost town

This ancient Appalachian mountain range, with its blanket of blue-gray haze, has been a popular tourist destination for many decades. Now the most visited of all the national parks, it provides tourist dollars to the tune of $2.5 billion annually to bolster the local economy. Other attractions in the area include Dollywood, one of the top tourist destinations in Tennessee. In addition to the towering Clingmans Dome, the park features sixteen mountains that exceed 5,000 feet. The Great Smoky Mountains were also designated a UNESCO World Heritage Site in 1983 and an International Biosphere Reserve in 1988.

HISTORY OF THE SMOKIES

For thousands of years these weathered mountains were occupied by a series of indigenous peoples. The Cherokee, a populous Southeast Woodland tribe, created villages in the river valleys on either side of the Appalachians. Although the Indians bartered with European traders from the Carolinas or Virginia, Europeans did not really settle the area until the late 18th and early 19th century. Due to the settlers' need for land in the Deep South, in 1830 President Andrew Jackson signed the Indian Removal Act, which forced the removal of all Indian tribes located east of the Mississippi River to "Indian territory," now the state of Oklahoma. This mandatory migration resulted in the Trail of Tears, an arduous 5,000 mile journey west, where many Native Americans died. Although the majority of the Cherokee were displaced by the edict, several bands eluded the authorities by settling in the Smokies, in the region of the current national park. Their descendants still inhabit parts of Tennessee and North Carolina and comprise the federally recognized Eastern Band of Cherokee Indians.

THE BEGINNINGS OF THE PARK

As towns sprang up, logging became a major industry in the Smokies. The construction of the Little River Railroad to haul timber from the remote mountains

▲ **"Daisy Town."** This row of abandoned holiday cabins is part of the Elkmont ghost town.

DID YOU KNOW?

Since 1934, there have been more than a half billion visitors to this park, with autumn, when leaves burst into brilliant color, the most popular season for a trip here.

to large hub cities ended up spurring other companies to invest in local logging. By 1920, two-thirds of the park's area had been stripped of timber—via the brutalizing "cut-and-run" method of clearcutting—or burned out by logging operators. Alarmed locals formed an organization to raise money to preserve their mountain heritage. And even though the National Park Service desired an eastern park, they had few funds to purchase land. Finally, John D. Rockefeller, Jr. contributed $5 million, the US government added

another $2 million, and private citizens pitched in what they could to purchase the land, piece by piece. Loggers, miners, homesteaders, and farmers were eventually evicted from the park land. The park was chartered by Congress in June 1934 and dedicated by President Franklin D. Roosevelt in 1940. During the Great Depression, both the Civilian Conservation Corps and the Works Progress Administration were employed in the park, creating trails and watchtowers, and making infrastructure improvements.

The fog settles in on Craggy Garden Trail on an autumn day. All the colors combined with the misty evening gives this scene an eerie yet magical feel.

▲ **Sunrise at Clingmans Dome.** This observation tower, with its winding walkway, provides visitors with breathtaking views of the mist-shrouded mountains.

▼ **The Cable Mill In Cades Cove.** Built in 1867, this grist mill is located on park lands, and the Great Smoky Mountain Association operates the mill from April to October.

ACTIVITIES AND SIGHTS

The park is renowned for its rugged beauty, wildlife, and cultural and historic sites. Top visitor draws include Cades Cove, a valley containing preserved buildings—log cabins, barns, and churches—that offer a glimpse into life in early Appalachia. The Cataloochee area offers late 19th-century homesteads, the Roaring Fork Motor Nature Trail featuring Noah Ogle's settler cabin and other old dwellings, and Elkmont's "ghost town" that showcases the remains of an old resort. The mountain farm museum and Mingus mill are located outside the Sugarlands Visitor Center. Outdoor enthusiasts can enjoy hiking, biking, horse riding, camping, and fishing, as well as viewing stunning waterfalls along wooded trails (Grotto Falls), and experiencing strenuous climbs (Clingmans Dome or Chimney Tops). The less-adventurous can take a scenic drive along Roaring Fork Motor Nature Trail.

Hikers get a peek at Chimney Tops from an opening in one of the park's rugged backcountry trails

"CLIMB THE MOUNTAINS AND GET THEIR GOOD THINGS. NATURE'S PEACE WILL FLOW INTO YOU AS SUNSHINE FLOWS INTO TREES. THE WINDS WILL BLOW THEIR OWN FRESHNESS INTO YOU, AND THE STORMS THEIR ENERGY, WHILE CARES WILL DROP AWAY FROM YOU LIKE THE LEAVES OF AUTUMN."

— *John Muir*

Sunrise at Mills Overlook highlights the smoke-like mist that the park is famous for.

WILDLIFE AND PLANT LIFE

The park is almost 95 percent forested, and an estimated 36 percent of the land is old-growth forest—that is, a forest that has attained great age without significant disturbance and that exhibits unique ecological features. The park contains one of the largest blocks of deciduous temperate forest and many trees that predate European settlement of the area. The multiple elevations, abundant rainfall, and established woodlands lend the park a rich selection of biota. Roughly 19,000 species of organisms are known to live here, as well as many thousands of undocumented species.

▶ **Black bears** make their home in the park.

For those seeking wildlife, there are more than 200 species of birds, 50 fish species, 39 reptiles, and 43 amphibians. Mammals include deer, black bear, squirrel, opossum, coyote, chipmunk, two species of skunk, and a number of bats.

More than 100 species of trees are found in the park, including yellow buckeye, yellow poplar, basswood, eastern hemlock, white ash, sugar maple, yellow birch, American beech, black cherry, and northern red oak. There are also 1,400 flowering plants and 4,000 nonflowering plants.

UNDER THE MIST

The blanket of bluish haze that hovers over the mountains inspired the Cherokee to name this sacred place *Shaconage* (Sha-Kon-O-Hey), or "land of the blue smoke." Early settlers, perhaps borrowing from the Indians, coined the name Smoky Mountains. The haze or fog likely arises from vegetation—plants exhalating VOCs or volatile organic compounds, give off scents and odors and can easily form vapors at warmer temperatures. The blue color occurs when the molecules that make up the gas scatter blue light from the sky.

KENTUCKY
MAMMOTH CAVE

Underground or above ground, this park offers natural wonders galore.

LOCATION Edmonson, Hart, and Barren counties, Kentucky

CLOSEST CITY Brownsville, Kentucky

AREA 53,000 acres (213.8 km²)

ESTABLISHED July 1, 1941

VISITORS 530,000+

ELEVATION 853 feet (260 m) at Brooks Knob Mountain

GEOLOGY Mississippian-era limestone strata capped by sandstone

WHAT TO LOOK FOR

Bove or below ground the park has plenty to offer.

> Tours of the cave's many formations

> Ranger-led talks

> Visitor center and surrouding attractions

> Green and Nolin Rivers

This unique park features not only the longest known cave system in the world—a 400-mile maze of passages, cavernous domes, pits, and underground rivers—but also scenic rolling hills and deep river valleys aboveground. The region boasts a history of human occupation for thousands of years and offers a wide range of plant and animal life. This rare combination of assets has earned Mammoth Cave recognition as both a UNESCO World Heritage Site and an International Biosphere Reserve.

A HISTORY LESSON

Approximately 350 million years ago, Kentucky lay beneath the seas of the Mississippian era, which deposited layers of limestone on the seabed. The early passages of the cave were created around 10 million years ago, when rainwater started to dissolve the limestone. A million years ago, the largest passages

▲ **A steep and winding stairway** leads visitors in and out of the depths of the cave.

"I SAW OR SEEMED TO SEE THE NIGHT HEAVEN THICK WITH STARS GLIMMERING MORE OR LESS BRIGHTLY OVER OUR HEADS, AND EVEN WHAT SEEMED A COMET FLAMING AMONG THEM."

— *Ralph Waldo Emerson, on the Star Chamber in Mammoth Cave*

Frozen Niagara, one of the most famous sections of Mammoth Cave, serves as the last stop for a many of the cave's guided tours.

Greetings FROM **MAMMOTH CAVE** *NATIONAL PARK* **KENTUCKY**

▲ **Sunlight streams** into a shallow cave in the parkland grounds of Mammoth Cave.

▲ **The blue waters** of the River Styx emerge from the cave before this subterranean waterway flows onward to join the Green River.

that gave the "mammoth" cave its name began to form. From 5000 to 2000 BCE, indigenous peoples discovered the cave, and they eventually began to mine it for minerals.

Europeans eventually settled the eastern seaboard, and in 1790, after the War of Independence, John Houchin moved from Virginia and settled near the Green River. He was possibly the first European to enter the cave. Not long after, Kentuckians were making gunpowder from the "niter" found in cave dirt.

Land containing two saltpeter (potassium nitrate) caves was eventually purchased by Valentine Simons in 1798; he then sold them to John Flatt, who lent his name to the largest of the two caves. By 1810, seven hoppers were processing saltpeter, and the cave system was first labeled Mammoth Cave in a Richmond, Virginia, newspaper. During the War of 1812, enslaved men mined vast amounts of saltpeter for the production of gunpowder.

In the 1840s, several stone buildings were erected inside the cave to house tuberculosis patients. Five patients ultimately died there. During the 1840s and 1850s, an African-American slave,

Stephen Bishop, acted as a cave guide; he made extensive maps of the system and named many of the cave's features.

During the late 19th and early 20th century, the cave was owned by the Croghan family, but in 1941, thanks to public donations, Mammoth Cave was formally made a National Park in order to protect, preserve, and study its unusual geological and biological aspects.

MUMMIES OF MAMMOTH CAVE

In 1815, prosperous landowner Nahum Ward was so impressed by the cave, he wrote a long description, including that of a mummy, and drew a new map. These accounts made the cave famous. As for the mummy, in 1812 the body of an elderly Native American woman was discovered in Short Cave, home to at least six burial sites. Known as Fawn Hoof, she was dressed in coarse clothing and wrapped in deer skin and was originally displayed in the Rotunda near the entrance. Ward petitioned to have the American Antiquarian Society take possession, but when the AAS refused, Ward ended up touring the country with the remains. "Little Alice" was another mummy found in 1875. The crushed body of an early Native American miner was found in 1935. After being displayed to visitors for decades, the body was respectfully interred in the cave during the 1970s.

WILDLIFE AND PLANT LIFE

Above Mammoth Cave lies a diverse parkland ideal for hiking, fishing, canoeing, kayaking, and watching wildlife. Within the park grounds, including Big Woods—an old-growth forest of 300 acres with massive 100-foot tree specimens—lie hemlock groves, wetlands, and rounded sinkholes. Examples of wildlife, such as white-tailed deer, raccoon, owl, opossum, gray squirrel, rabbit, woodchuck, muskrat, beaver, bat, red fox, coyote, and wild turkey, are also found here.

Endangered creatures found in the park include the Kentucky cave shrimp, the Indiana brown bat, and seven species of freshwater mussels. In Mammoth's darkest reaches dwell blind beetles, spectral white spiders, and eyeless fish. Fossils commonly found in the cave include crinoids, blastoids, and gastropods.

HIGHLIGHTS OF THE CAVE

Some noteworthy cave formations, many with fanciful names, include the Grand Gallery (aka Broadway), Mammoth Dome (192-feet high), Bottomless Pit (105-feet deep), Edna's Dome, Gorin's Dome, Grand Avenue, Gothic Avenue, Tall Man's Misery, Fat Man's Misery, River Styx, Crystal Cave, Flint Ridge, the Church, Standing Rocks, Grand Arch, Giant's Coffin, Dante's Gateway, Wooden Bowl, Scotchman's Trap, the Dog-Hole (or Steeps of Time), and the Labyrinth.

▲ **The historic Mammoth Cave Baptist Church** stands within the park's grounds. The original structure was built in 1827, but after a tornado destroyed it, it was rebuilt in 1927.

▶ **Pathways lead park-goers** past the drooping stalactites and rising stalagmites that form the stunning formations of the extensive cave system.

▼ **The park is set** in the beautiful rolling hills of Kentucky's Green River Valley.

WEST VIRGINIA
NEW RIVER GORGE

Travel along an ancient whitewater river that flows through mature forests.

LOCATION Fayette, Raleigh, and Summers counties, WV

CLOSEST CITY Beckley, WV

AREA 70,000 acres (294.64 km²)

ESTABLISHED November 10, 1978

VISITORS 1,129,000+

ELEVATION 2,431 feet (741 m)

GEOLOGY Exposed sandstone, Nuttal sandstone (98 percent quartz) and shale above the Appalachian Plateau

WHAT TO LOOK FOR:

Nature and history meet here for a memorable experience.

> Sandstone and Canyon Rim Visitor Centers

> Ancient rock walls along the river gorge

> Peregrine falcons that are being restored to the park

> Thurmond ghost town

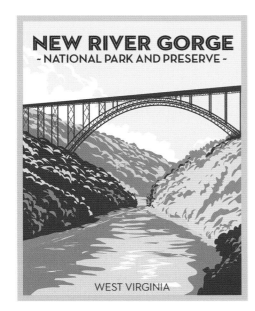

Despite its name, New River is among the oldest rivers in America, a powerful waterway that runs north through deep canyons in southern West Virginia. This river gorge is not only rich in natural and cultural history, but it also offers spectacular scenery and a range of recreational activities. The park itself lies within a globally important forest and contains the most diverse plant life of any river gorge in this region of Appalachia. The rock walls exposed by the river's course are quite ancient, with the oldest found in the lower gorge around Batoff Mountain.

HISTORY OF THE REGION

Originally settled by Paleo-Indians, who left behind artifacts dating from 11,000 years ago, the area was later home to the Moneton, Tutelo, Cherokee, and S'atsoyaha people. Many Indians were forced to migrate as Europeans encroached on their lands. Timber harvesting and the New River Coalfield brought industry to the region in the early 1800s, augmented by the arrival of a railroad in 1873. (The coal found in the gorge is still exceptional for its purity and quality.) The remains of early farming hamlets and homesteads are still located around the park.

RECREATIONAL ACTIVITIES

New River National Park and Preserve is a well-known site for whitewater enthusiasts, with whitewater rafting in the lower gorge and canoeing in the milder rapids of the upper gorge. This park is also one of the most popular rock-climbing sites in the country, with more than 1,400 established climbs. Other activities include fishing, hiking, and biking on old railroad grades. Year-round visitor centers are located at Sandstone and Canyon Rim.

WILDLIFE AND PLANT LIFE

With its diverse terrain—including continuous forest, cliff and rimrock, seeps and wetlands, and mature bottomland forests—the park provides habitats for at least 65 species of mammals like raccoon, opossum, deer, bear, river otter, groundhog, beaver, and mink. Abandoned mine

▲ **Whitewater rafters** head to a patch of rocky rapids on the New River.

"NATIONAL PARKS ARE THE BEST IDEA
WE EVER HAD. ABSOLUTELY AMERICAN,
ABSOLUTELY DEMOCRATIC,
THEY REFLECT US AT OUR BEST
RATHER THAN OUR WORST."

— *Wallace Stegner*

DID YOU KNOW?

The flowing force of the New River continues to sculpt the longest and deepest river gorge found in the Appalachian Mountains.

The New River winds its way through the canyons of the Appalachian Mountains.

portals provide shelter for rare species of bats and the Allegheny woodrat, a species in decline. The many waterways and shaded glades are home to 48 species of amphibians, including black-bellied and cave salamanders, and endangered eastern hellbenders. Nearly 40 species of reptiles live here, including eastern box turtles, five-lined skinks, black rat snakes, timber rattlesnakes, and copperheads. Venomous snakes are only occasionally seen and are not normally aggressive.

The park offers a refuge to many native and migratory birds. Wood warblers, vireos, and thrushes may winter in the tropics, but they breed in the wide swathes of forest found in New River Gorge. In fall, thousands of migrating hawks fill the skies above the park. The park service and West Virginia Department of Natural Resources are currently attempting to restore the fierce

and beautiful peregrine falcon to the gorge. Visitors can sometimes spy them soaring and hunting near the cliffs.

Anglers can fish for bass, walleye, carp, muskellunge, crappie, bluegill, or catfish. Nightcrawlers and hellgrammites are the bait favored by the locals.

There are more than 1,300 species of plants found in the gorge, 54 of them endangered. Flora includes white pine, spruce, hemlock, poplar, aspen, cottonwood willow, white oak, American chestnut, beech, honeysuckle, rhododendron, peach, black raspberry, sweetbrier, and chokeberry.

▲ **Remnants of the region's past** lie tucked away in the forest, such as this sloping mining bridge that recalls the days when this was the New River Coalfield, home to more than 60 coal towns.

◄ **The New River Gorge Bridge** stretches from ridge to ridge 876 feet above the river

▼ **A former train depot** stands in the abandoned Thurmond ghost town.

VIRGINIA
SHENANDOAH

Virginia's distinctive "blue" mountains rise above forests, wetlands, and waterfalls.

LOCATION Warren, Page, Rockingham, Augusta, Rappahannock, Madison, Greene, and Albemarle counties, VA

CLOSEST CITY Front Royal, VA

AREA 199,173 acres (806.02 km²)

ESTABLISHED December 26, 1935

VISITORS 1,666,000+

ELEVATION 4,051 feet (1,234.7 m) on Hawksbill Summit

GEOLOGY Gneisses and granitoids under the lowlands and some rugged peaks; metabasalt under the highlands; siliciclastic rocks under linear ridges

WHAT TO LOOK FOR

This premier park offers visitors the best of the Blue Ridge Mountains.

> Big Meadow, perfect for picnicking by day or stargazing after dark

> Skylands Lodge with accommodations, dining, a gift shop, and amazing views

> Park wildlife—ranger programs offer safe close encounters

One of the most captivating showpieces of a famously beautiful state, Shenandoah National Park lies within the Blue Ridge Mountains of north-central Virginia. The park's major thoroughfare is the winding and scenic Skyline Drive, which was constructed in the mid-1930s atop the spine of the mountain range. The park is mainly forested, with occasional wetlands, waterfalls, and jagged peaks, such as Hawksbill Summit and Old Rag Mountain. Many exposed rocks are over a billion years in age, making them some of the oldest rocks in Virginia. Shenandoah features an intertwining network of trails, more than 500 miles worth, including a 101-mile stretch of the historic Appalachian Trail, which runs from Tennessee to Maine.

EARLY HISTORY

The Blue Ridge Mountains were created by tectonic activity from 1.1 billion to 250 million ago. They are believed to be one of the ten oldest ranges in the world, with the oldest being South Africa's Barberton Greenstone Belt. Their distinctive bluish coloration is the result of trees emitting isoprene into the atmosphere. The mountains were at one time the boundary that separated colonial settlers from Native American territories. The earliest inhabitants began to congregate in this area some 16,000 years ago. The major tribe of Southern Appalachia was the Cherokee, who lived along the Blue Ridge with the Iroquois, Powhaten, and Shawnee people. The first enslaved Africans arrived some time during the 16th century, another group that helped shape the region's culture.

Colonists from Europe first began to form communities here around 1700. They began what is now known as Appalachian culture, which eventually spread beyond the original 13 colonies to the lately opened lands to the west. As settlers poured into Virginia, the majority of native inhabitants were forcibly evicted from their ancestral lands by the US military and marched to Oklahoma along the brutal "Trail of Tears."

ESTABLISHING THE PARK

Interest in creating a national park along the Blue Ridge Mountains was high at the turn of the 20th century, yet even though President Theodore Roosevelt backed the plan, Congress failed to pass the legislation. Decades

◀ **Dark Hollow Falls** is the closest to Skyline Drive and is accessed by the Dark Hollow Trail, one of the park's most popular trails.

"IF YOU DRIVE TO … SHENANDOAH NATIONAL PARK … YOU'LL GET SOME APPRECIATION FOR THE SCALE AND BEAUTY OF THE OUTDOORS. WHEN YOU WALK INTO IT, THEN YOU SEE IT IN A COMPLETELY DIFFERENT WAY. YOU DISCOVER IT IN A MUCH SLOWER, MORE MAJESTIC SORT OF WAY."

— Bill Bryson

later, when the park seemed more likely to progress, the Commonwealth of Virginia began to acquire land through eminent domain, although many tenant farmers and squatters were not happy to lose their homes. (A number of individuals were "grandfathered" in and allowed to live out their lives in the park.) Meanwhile, building the infrastructure of Shenandoah created thousands of jobs through the Civilian Conservation Corps. The park was finally established on December 26, 1935, and officially opened by Franklin D. Roosevelt on July 3, 1936. Sadly, park facilities were segregated, a concession made

▶ **Iron Mike** stands outside Byrd Visitor Center. This statue honors the young men of the Civilian Conservation Corps who in the 1930s built much of the park's infrastructure, which is still in use today.

The late-summer landscape of the **Blue Ridge Mountains is awash in verdant greens and blue-green teals.**

The boulder-covered summit of Blackrock offers breathtaking views over the Shenandoah Valley as the sunset paints the Blue Ridge Mountains with pinks, purples, and oranges.

by the State of Virginia, which initially wanted black Americans excluded from the park. In 1945, the parks department mandated that all park properties would be desegregated.

ACTIVITIES

This popular destination for hikers, campers, and backpackers offers five major campgrounds. Rangers warn backcountry overnighters to hang leftover food in bear-proof bags or pack it in canisters provided by the park. The local black bears are habituated to being fed by humans, which makes them dangerous. Venomous snakes may also be encountered on the trails. All wildlife is protected by law. Other activities include fishing, biking, birding, attending ranger programs, viewing exhibits, or gazing at the night sky, including the Milky Way, from Big Meadow or the Skyland amphitheater.

WILDLIFE AND PLANT LIFE

There are more than 50 documented species of mammals found in the park, including bobcat, coyote, white-tailed deer, skunk, gray squirrel, and big brown bat. A number of species that had disappeared from the Southern Appalachians have been re-established in the region, including beaver, elk, peregrine falcon, and river otter. Wild turkey and black bear, once threatened, are also making a strong comeback. Birdlife includes more than 190 species of native and transient birds, with roughly half that number breeding in the park—among them are 18 different types of warbler. Year-round residents include red-tailed hawks, barred owls, Carolina chickadees, and downy woodpeckers.

The forests of Shenandoah are generally classified as oak-hickory, but that label only tells a fraction of the story. Within the park's multiple habitats can be found chestnut oak, red oak, tulip poplar, and cove hardwood, along with fir-spruce zones. Vegetation of the understory includes numerous herbs, ferns, and shrubs such as lady's slipper, trillium, jack-in-the-pulpit, azalea, and blueberry bushes. Wetlands support blue flag iris, marsh willow herb, and cardinal flower. The region supports a bounty of wildflowers—862 species—including hepatica, bloodroot, violets, pink lady's slipper, wild geraniums, bluets, touch-me-nots, black cohosh, columbine, aster, goldenrod, wild sunflower, ox-eye daisy, Turk's cap, and milkweed. A wide array of grasses, sedges, rushes, mosses, lichen, liverwort, mushrooms, and fungi are also found throughout the park.

DID YOU KNOW?

The Blue Ridge Parkway, America's longest linear park at 469 miles, connects Shenandoah to Great Smoky Mountains National Park in Tennessee and North Carolina.

▲ **Skyline Drive,** famous for its scenery and impressive views, runs the length of the park along the ridge of the mountains.

◄ **Elkwallow Trail** meanders through a serene forest setting.

►► **A white-tailed deer** peers out through the trees.

▶ **Vintage postcard of Skylands,** located on Skyline Drive. Founded in 1888, this historic summer retreat sits at 3,680 feet, giving guests amazing views of the Shenandoah Valley.

Skyland Resort in Shenandoah National Park. Virginia

THE APPALACHIAN CULTURE

This geographic region gave rise to a cultural movement that has come to include music, arts and crafts, folklore, food, and multiple ethnic influences (German, Celtic, African, and Native American). Along with its positive attributes, unfortunately, there also arose a negative stereotype of the suspicious, insular mountain hick or "hillbilly." Yet the culture created by these hard-working, self-reliant backcountry people went on to define a large part of what we call Americana and is still vital and influential today.

CHAPTER THREE

PARKS OF THE SOUTHWEST

America's Southwest can boast some of the world's most dramatic scenery—pale ocher deserts with bristly sagebrush and stately saguaros, purple mountain peaks rising abruptly from vast flatlands, ruddy buttes, deep arroyos, amazing rock formations carved by wind and water, bubbling hot springs, Indian petroglyphs, and massive caves. Many of these parks present sharp geological contrasts—arid deserts traversed by whitewater rivers with lush riparian belts; deep canyons with eroded rock formations rising up to sheer cliffs. This landscape is entwined with the culture; Native American and Mexican influences flavor the cuisine, but also the architecture and the décor, which both echo the colors and textures of the terrain.

Visitors to the Southwest's national parks also arrive seeking unusual or endangered wildlife, like ocelot, jaguarundi, pupfish, California condor, or sandhill crane, and many species of cacti and other succulents. The deserts, as with any extreme habitat, demand a specific set of adaptations for animal and plant life to thrive.

◄ Bryce Canyon National Park, Utah

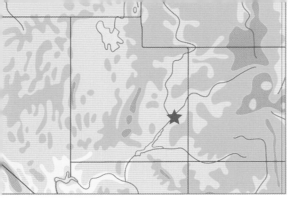

UTAH
ARCHES

Monumental rock sculptures in shades of russet and ocher draw visitors to this Utah site.

LOCATION Grand County, UT

CLOSEST CITY Moab, UT

AREA 76,679 acres (310.31 km²)

ESTABLISHED April 12, 1929, as National Monument; November 12, 1971, as National Park+

VISITORS 1,235,000+

ELEVATION 5,653 feet (1,723 m) at Elephant Butte

GEOLOGY Water-soluble mineral deposits over Nevada sandstone

WHAT TO LOOK FOR

One of Utah's amazing "Big 5" national parks, Arches has much for visitors to observe.

> Delicate Arch

> Balanced Rock

> Ancient Native American petroglyphs

> Wolfe Ranch homestead

Native Americans and early settlers to Moab were among the first to wonder at the breathtaking sandstone formations that have since made this Utah landmark famous. Arches National Park, a semi-desert region adjacent to the Colorado River, contains in excess of 2,000 natural sandstone arches, the highest density of such phenomena in the world. The mission of the park is "to protect extraordinary examples of geologic features including arches, natural bridges, windows, spires, balanced rocks, as well as other features of geologic, historic, and scientific interest, and to provide opportunities to experience these resources . . . in their majestic natural settings." And as any park veteran will tell you, the scenery and setting are indeed majestic.

Notable geologic features include Balanced Rock, Delicate Arch, Landmark Arch, and Double Arch. Some formations have evocative names, such as Elephant Butte, Dark Angel, Park Avenue, Courthouse Towers, and Fiery Furnace. The Petrified Dunes are remnants of sand dunes blown from the shores of an ancient lake that once covered the park. Just off the Delicate Arch hiking trail, visitors are greeted by a wall of Ute petroglyphs—symbols carved into rock—consisting of stylized horse-and-rider figures in the midst of bighorn sheep and doglike animals. Dating from the mid-1600s, these are among the park's unique treasures.

EARLY RESIDENTS

This region of southeast Utah was first settled by humans around the time of last ice age, 10,000 years ago. Fremont people and Ancestral Puebloans inhabited the region until about 1300 CE. Four centuries later, Spanish missionaries reported meeting Ute and Paiute

◄ **The Balanced Rock,** visible from the road leading to the park, is one of Arches most recognizable attractions. To offer a sense of perspective, this formation is the size of three school buses.

Delicate Arch has becomes a symbol of this national park.

"THESE ARCHES ARE OF THRILLING BEAUTY. CAUSED BY THE CUTTING ACTION OF WIND-BLOWN SAND (NOT STREAM EROSION), ONE MARVELS AT THE INTRICACIES OF NATURE."

— *Frank Bethwick, leader of a 1933–1934 scientific expedition*

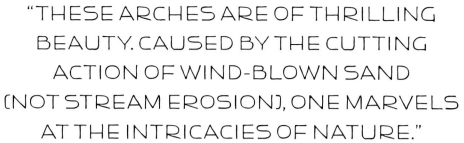

DID YOU KNOW?

Delicate Arch was the subject of the third 2014 quarter in the U.S. Mint's America the Beautiful quarters program honoring national parks and historic sites. The Arches quarter had the highest production run of the five national park quarters from that year—more than 465 million.

Indians as they passed through the area. The Mormons attempted to establish a mission here in 1855, but it did not last.

By the 1870s, local ranchers, farmers, and prospectors understood the special appeal of the natural rock formations. Frank A. Wadleigh, a passenger traffic manager for the Denver and Rio Grande Western Railroad, was invited to view the site by prospector Alexander Ringhoffer in 1923. Wadleigh brought along railroad photographer George L. Beam. They were both impressed by what they saw, and Wadleigh contacted Park Service director Stephen T. Mather to suggest he make the area a national monument.

Confusion as to the exact location of the formations led to a number of government investigators assessing the area. On maps, the name "Devils Garden" ended up applied to a different area of the site. Shortly after his inauguration in 1929, new president Herbert Hoover declared the creation of Arches National Monument. In 1938, Franklin D. Roosevelt expanded protection to the rock features, and some development of the site was finally approved to encourage tourism. President Lyndon B. Johnson substantially enlarged the area, and Richard Nixon upgraded its status to national park.

ACTIVITIES AND GUIDELINES
Recreational activities in the park include auto touring, hiking, mountain bicycling, birding, astronomy, and camping at the Devils Garden campground. Backpacking, canyoneering, and rock climbing are allowed, but require permits. Guided commercial tours and ranger programs are also available to visitors. Climbing any of the arches is strictly prohibited. Visitors arriving from April 3 to October 3, need to secure advance reservations. Most hiking trails and campgrounds remain open all year.

WILDLIFE AND PLANT LIFE
Much of the wildlife here has adapted to desert conditions. Some animals are nocturnal, coming out at night to avoid daytime temperatures or predators. Some prey animals are crepuscular, meaning they seek food at dusk and dawn, when they are less visible. The park's inhabitants include red fox, desert bighorn, mule deer, cougar, antelope squirrel, and kangaroo

▼ **The North Window** frames a view of Turret Arch.

▲ **The Windows Section,** a bit more than two square miles and containing a large concentration of arches, including North Window, Turret Arch, and Double Arch, is a favorite with park-goers.

▶ **A rock panel of petroglyphs** stands just off the Delicate Arch hiking trail. These petroglyphs were carved sometime between 1650 and 1850.

rat, along with scrub jay, peregrine falcon, many sparrow species, spadefoot toad, midget faded rattlesnake, western rattlesnake, collared lizard, and the pollinating yucca moth.

Among the many desert plants found in Arches are prickly pear cactus, Indian ricegrass, bunch grass, cheatgrass, Utah juniper, Mormon tea, blackbrush, cliffrose, saltbrush, pinyon pine, sand verbena, yucca, liverwort, and sacred datura, which produces the largest flower in canyon country. A knobby black biological soil crust is found in this region of Utah. Composed of cyanobacteria, lichens, mosses, green algae, and microfungi, this layer aids in keeping soil particles together and helps prevent erosion.

▶ **A desert cottontail,** also known as Audubon's cottontail, makes a stop in the sands of Arches.

LASERS TO THE RESCUE

In 1980, when vandals used abrasive kitchen cleanser to deface the ancient petroglyphs in Arches, horrified park officials contacted physicist John F. Asmus, who had used lasers to restore works of art, to help repair the damage. The physicist "zapped the panel with intense light pulses," which removed most of the cleanser.

TEXAS
BIG BEND

Spectacular limestone canyons and weathered rock formations contrast with rugged desert landscapes.

LOCATION Chihuahuan Desert, TX
CLOSEST CITY Alpine, TX
AREA 801,163 acres (3,242.19 km²)
ESTABLISHED June 12, 1935
VISITORS 463,800+
ELEVATION 7,832 feet (2,387 m) at Emory Peak
GEOLOGY Marine sedimentary, volcanic, and continental sedimentary rocks

WHAT TO LOOK FOR
The park offers visitors a wealth of breathtaking sights.

> The Balanced Rock
> Ross Maxwell Scenic Drive
> Petroglyphs along Chimneys Trail

This spectacular west Texas park forms an international boundary between the United States and Mexico. It also comprises the largest protected area of the desert habitats and topography of the Chihuahuan Desert in America. Named for a large bend in the Rio Grande/Rio Bravo waterways, the park abuts two protected sites in Mexico—Cañón de Santa Elena and Maderas del Carmen.

EARLY HISTORY
This culturally rich area has a long history of human settlement—with archaeological sites dating back 10,000 years. During the 1500s, the Chisos tribe lived at Big Bend, with the nomadic Jumanos trading in the same region. Around 1700 the Mescalero Apaches inhabited

▲ **A wild Mexican jay** perches on a branch in the Chisos Basin of Big Bend. This lovely blue bird is relatively common in the cool pine-oak-juniper woodlands of western Texas.

Big Bend's Chisos Mountains are the only American mountain range to be located entirely within a national park. This isolated park is one of the least visited, but there are so many unique features here to appreciate.

the canyons; later the Comanches were one of the last tribes to use Big Bend. During the 19th century the discovery of mineral deposits brought settlers to the area, and by the 1930s many ranchers and farmers wanted the beautiful canyons and desert preserved for future generations. As a result, the park was designated in 1935 and officially opened on July 4, 1941.

ACTIVITIES AND SIGHTS

Hiking and backpacking are the park's two main draws. Favorite trails include Chimneys, with its soaring rock formations and Indian petroglyphs; Marufo Vega, with scenic canyons en route to the Rio Grande; South Rim and Outer Mountain Loop, both in the Chisos Mountains; and Dodson, which descends into the desert. Other sites include Santa Elena Canyon, Balanced Rock in Grapevine Hills, and Mule Ears, two upright rock towers. Geological features include hot springs, sea fossils, and dinosaur bones.

The park service oversees 118 miles of the Rio Grande for recreational activities. Commercial outfitters offer river tours, and private boats are allowed with a permit. Because the southern portion of the riverbed is technically in Mexico, boaters are considered to have left the U.S. and need a valid ID to return to the park.

DID YOU KNOW?

Designated an International Dark Sky Park, Big Bend has the darkest skies in the contiguous United States. On clear nights, park-goers can view thousands of twinkling stars, bright planets, and the magnificent Milky Way.

WILDLIFE AND PLANT LIFE

Due to its remote location, Big Bend is one of the least visited national parks, but it is nevertheless a worthwhile destination for wildlife lovers and birdwatchers. Visitors thrill to glimpses of javelina, black bear, coyote, elk, and bobcat. There are at least 450 bird species, both resident and migrant, represented here, plus Big Bend is home to more types of bats, butterflies, ants, and scorpions than any other national park. Desert-loving reptiles include 31 species of snake and 22 species of lizard.

Desert landscapes support many plants, even flowering ones awaiting a rainstorm to bloom. Big Bend offers more than 1,200 species, from wild orchids and yuccas to oaks, sumacs, and willows.

▼ **The Balanced Rock** on Grapevine Hills Trail is a favorite with photographers.

► **Canoeists prepare to paddle** down the Rio Grande River through the limestone cliffs of the imposing Cañón de Santa Elena.

COLORADO
BLACK CANYON OF THE GUNNISON

This park encompasses one of America's most rugged, steep, and beautiful—as well as challenging—canyons.

LOCATION Montrose County, CO

CLOSEST CITY Montrose, CO

AREA 30,750 acres (124.4 km²)

ESTABLISHED March 2, 1933, as National Monument; October 21, 1999, as National Park

VISITORS 309,000+

ELEVATION 8,000 feet (2,400 m)

GEOLOGY Precambrian gneiss and schist

WHAT TO LOOK FOR

The park offers scenic trails and magnificent views.

> South Rim Road

> East Portal Road

> Gunnison River trails

> Painted Wall

Located in southwest Colorado, this steep, narrow canyon, with its craggy walls rising thousands of feet in places, was formed over the course of two million years as the Gunnison River cut through soft volcanic deposits. Although the terrain may seem intimidating to some, it can evoke a sense of intimacy as visitors get up close to wilderness landscapes and southwestern wildlife.

REGIONAL HISTORY

The Ute Indians and other tribes were aware of the canyon long before European settlers discovered it. Yet these indigenous peoples only ever camped on its rim, never inside the somewhat forbidding gorge, perhaps for superstitious reasons. Fur trappers in search of beaver arrived in the 1800s, but the first written account concerning the area was by Captain John Williams Gunnison, the head of a surveying expedition. He noted that the terrain was "the roughest, most hilly, and most cut up" he'd ever seen. After the captain was killed in a Ute attack, the river he originally named the Grand was rechristened the Gunnison in his honor.

In 1882, the Denver and Rio Grande Railroad was improbably routed through 15 miles of the Black Canyon, creating a link between Denver and the gold and silver mines in the San Juan Mountains. According to the editor of the *Gunnison Review-Press*, this was "the largest and

DID YOU KNOW?

The canyon gets its name from its black-stained, lichen-covered rock walls, which intensify the darkness of the deep chasm.

▲ **A park service signboard** compares the heights of the tallest human-made structures in the world to that of the Painted Wall.

The steep-walled gorge of the Black Canyon of the Gunnison includes the Painted Wall, Colorado's highest cliff.

most rugged canyon in the world traversed by the iron horse." The winding, narrow-gauge railway route remained in use up until the early 1950s.

In the 1890s construction on a tunnel began between the canyon and the arid Uncompahgre Valley. It was meant to bring much-needed irrigation water to local farmers, many of whom had moved to Colorado to take advantage of the Homestead Act of 1862. Yet they lacked a reliable supply of water, and without it, their land was useless. Planning and creating the Gunnison tunnel was a massive undertaking, requiring workers to blast their way through a mountain. Eventually the teams carved an opening through the cliffs that was 12 feet in height and 6 miles in length. The Gunnison ended up providing enough water to support the valley; a town called East Portal actually sprang up inside the canyon near the tunnel entrance. Due to lobbying efforts by local citizens in the 1930s, the canyon was designated a national monument on March 2, 1933.

ACTIVITIES AND AMENITIES
The popular scenic drive along the South Rim Road offers views of the striated Painted Wall, the tallest sheer cliff in Colorado at 2,250 feet, as well as Gunnison Point and Sunset View. The East Portal Road winds steeply down to the Gunnison River and has a campground and picnic area at the bottom. Hikers will find trails for all skill levels, from Rim Rock and Uplands for the novice to more advanced trails within the canyon itself that require a permit. The park has also become a center for rock climbers who prefer traditional climbing methods, which employ protective gear and tackle to arrest any falls. The climbs are difficult and should only be attempted by experienced climbers.

The park headquarters are located on the South Rim. There are no accommodations or dining facilities inside the park, but the town of Montrose is 20 minutes away and has numerous amenities, including chain hotels.

▲ **An overlook** on the edge of a cliff allows visitors to get a sense of the canyon's awesome depth.

WILDLIFE AND PLANT LIFE

A variety of animals and plants are found here—pronghorn, elk, mule deer, cougar, coyote, black bear, beaver, river otter, and bobcat, along with six species of lizard. Notable birds include American dipper, bald and golden eagle, great horned owl, eight types of hawk, and Steller's jay. Migrants like mountain bluebird, peregrine falcon, white-throated swift, magpie, and canyon wren also take refuge here.

Much of the park's landscape features Gambel oak and serviceberry. Other vegetation includes aspen, ponderosa pine, sagebrush, desert mahogany, and Utah juniper. Among the many shrubs and smaller plants is Black Canyon gilia, a wildflower found only in this park.

▲ **At the mouth of Cimarron Creek** stands the Cimarron Canyon Rail Exhibit. The exhibit includes Locomotive #278, its coal tender, a boxcar, and a caboose, which perch atop the last remaining railroad trestle along the Black Canyon of the Gunnison route.

◀ **A lazy black bear** relaxes on a rocky outcrop overlooking the gorge.

▲ **A lone juniper tree,** with its twisted trunk, stands near the canyon rim

◀ **The Gunnison River** cuts through the Black Canyon gorge. The Ute Indians who once settled along the canyon rim, described the river as "much rocks, big water."

UTAH

BRYCE CANYON

This astonishing assemblage of giant multicolor amphitheaters and hoodoo rock spires leaves an indelible mark upon the visitor's imagination.

LOCATION Garfield County and Kane County, UT

CLOSEST CITY Tropic, Panguitch, UT

AREA 35,835 acres (145.02 km²)

ESTABLISHED June 8, 1923, as National Monument; February 25, 1928, as National Park

VISITORS 2,679,500+

ELEVATION 9,124 feet (2,778 m) at Rainbow Point

GEOLOGY Sedimentary and volcanic rock

WHAT TO LOOK FOR

These "Big 5" Utah park offers amazing sights and memorable experiences.

> Bryce Amphitheater

> Hoodoo rock pillars

> Native American art and artifacts

> Rainbow Point

Despite its name, Bryce Canyon is not technically considered a canyon. Rather it encompasses a number of awe-inspiring natural amphitheaters, the largest known as Bryce Amphitheater. The vast open space was most likely sculpted by headward erosion, the widening of a gorge or chasm by erosion at its upper edge. The "breaks" in the pinnacle walls—unforested exposed areas—are known as the pink cliffs.

The park is situated along the eastern side of the Paunsaugunt Plateau in southwestern Utah. Visitors may arrive on the well-vegetated plateau and look over its edge to the arid valley below, which contains the Paria River (called Muddy Water or Elk Water by the Paiute).

▲ **The Bryce Amphitheater.** This bowl-shaped area is one of a series of "breaks" eroded into the eastern slope of the Paunsaugunt Plateau. Even visitors who come to the park for just a few hours can view this magnificent amphitheater, which can be seen from Bryce Point, Inspiration Point, Sunset Point, and Sunrise Point.

The late-afternoon sun lights up Thor's Hammer, one of the park's towering hoodoos. This massive stone spire can be seen from Navajo Loop Trail and Queen's Trail, among others.

DO YOU HOODOO?

The park's famous hoodoos are tall, narrow spires of rock that rise up from arid drainage basins or badlands . . . like clustered minarets out of the *Arabian Nights*. Often reaching 200 feet in height, they are typically softer rock at the bottom and harder rock at the top, which protects the upper part of the pillars from erosion. Hoodoos form when ice and rainwater combine with carbon dioxide to create carbonic acid, which slowly dissolves the pink limestone. Bryce Amphitheater contains the largest collection of hoodoos in the world.

EARLY HISTORY

Starting 10,000 years ago, many different cultures were enthralled by the natural phenomena in the valley. The winters can be so severe on the rim, however, that few settled down permanently. Still, based on archaeological evidence, Paleo-Indians hunted the oversize mammals of the last Ice Age near here; Pueblos later sought game in the forests and open meadows of the plateau, the same places Paiutes gathered pine nuts and conducted large-scale rabbit hunts, while creating a mythology about the origins of the hoodoos, which they called "painted red faces." Artifacts from the Fremont culture have also been found.

In 1850, the area was settled by Mormon pioneers, who routed water from the plateau down into the dry valley in order to establish flourishing farms. The town of Tropic rose up as a result. The region was named for Mormon homesteader Ebenezer Bryce who arrived in 1875.

This unique area was first declared a national monument by President Warren Harding in 1923 and then designated a national park by Congress in 1928. Ultimately, the Union Pacific Railroad and improvements made by the Civilian Conservation Corps both helped popularize remote Bryce Canyon for tourists.

ATTRACTIONS AND ACTIVITIES

The park's numerous scenic drives allow visitors to view such park mainstays as Aquarius Plateau, Bryce Amphitheater, the Henry Mountains, the Vermilion Cliffs, and the White Cliffs. Rainbow Point, the park's highest elevation, lies at the end of an 18-mile scenic drive. Yellow Creek, in the northeast, is the lowest point in the park at 6,620 feet. Although Bryce is full of natural wonders and can take days to explore, visitors with only four or so hours to spend can get a good sense of the park by driving to Sunrise, Sunset, Inspiration, and Bryce viewpoints. These four overlooks furnish the prime visual experiences Bryce is known for.

In addition to sightseeing, hiking is the main activity in the park, with trails for novice, intermediate, or experienced hikers that wend through rocky desert terrain or spruce and fir forests. Hikers wishing to overnight in the park need permits. Visitors also enjoy photography, birding, ranger-led programs, and wrangler-guided horseback tours to the amphitheater. In winter there is snowshoeing and cross-country skiing atop the plateau, with equipment rentals available outside the park.

Park amenities include a visitor center with maps, museum exhibits, a bookstore, and a short, award-winning film; accommodations at the historic Lodge at Bryce Canyon, and two campgrounds. Nearby towns offer restaurants, chain hotels, motels, B&Bs, vacation rentals, and additional campsites.

ALTERNATE ROUTES

Many national parks, including Bryce Canyon, have designated scenic backways—paved or dirt roads that allow visitors to access more remote, often beautiful, areas. Check weather conditions locally or at the visitor center, and be sure to have enough gasoline, food, and water if you decide to venture along the "road less taken."

◄ **Snow-covered Natural Bridge.** This example is only one of several natural arches in Bryce Canyon.

▼ **A pair of common ravens** looks annoyed as their peaceful gaze over Black Birch Canyon is disturbed.

WILDLIFE AND PLANT LIFE

With its diverse habitats, Bryce Canyon is home to a range of animal life—Rocky Mountain elk, pronghorn, mule deer, North American porcupine, Green Basin rattlesnake, common sage lizard, short-horned lizard (horny toad), and tiger salamander. Cougar do reside in the region but are rarely seen.

Bird sightings include red-tailed hawk, American coot, white-throated swift,

◄ **A pronghorn** finds a place for peaceful repose in one of the park's grassy meadowlands.

▼ **The setting sun** lights up a panorama of hoodoos and fairy spires as hikers wend their way through a park trail.

black-chinned hummingbird, western and mountain bluebirds, red-winged blackbird, and yellow-rumped warbler. The park's bigger birds—golden eagle (and bald eagle in the winter), turkey vulture, osprey, peregrine falcon, and various hawks—are always good for a thrill, especially glimpses of the endangered California condor, North America's largest bird.

The park transcends 2,000 feet of elevation and contains three distinct climatic zones. At the highest elevations are spruce/fir forests with bristlecone pine in the limestone knolls, followed by ponderosa pine forests with manzanita, and pinyon/juniper forests at the lower levels, which include Gambel oak, cactus, and yucca. The plateau gets more rainfall than the valley, resulting in a lush ecosystem compared to the arid badlands below. The rain also keeps temperatures down. More than 1,000 species of plants are found in the park—grassy and deciduous plants in the meadows and seeps, while drier terrain contains sagebrush and rabbitbrush and grasses. Wildflowers display a variety of colors, sizes, seasonalities, and locations; species include blue flax, western iris, mountain-death camas, wallflower, stoneseed, rock columbine, bush cinquefoil, and several types of penstemon and paintbrush.

▶ **The roots of a pinyon pine** seem to desperately clutch the rocks below to maintain the tree's precarious position on a cliff..

DID YOU KNOW?

Three examples of park wildlife are listed under the Endangered Species Act: the Utah prairie dog, California condor, and southwestern willow flycatcher. Condor populations are still making a recovery after facing extinction in the 1980s.

UTAH

CANYONLANDS

This "Big 5" park of Utah features spectacular eroded rock formations bisected by rivers.

LOCATION San Juan, Wayne, Garfield, and Grand counties, UT

CLOSEST CITY Moab, UT

AREA 337,598 acres, (1,366.21 km²)

ESTABLISHED September 12, 1964

VISITORS 750,000+

ELEVATION 7,120 feet (2,170 m) at Cathedral Point

GEOLOGY Eroded sedimentary rock carried from the Rocky Mountains and the Appalachians

The Colorado has proved itself a formidable river, if only for rendering the wondrous geometry of the Grand Canyon. But the river and its tributaries created another miracle of nature in southwestern Utah that is nearly as breathtaking as its big sister in Arizona. Canyonlands National Park, renowned for its endless red rock canyons and buttes, receives more than half a million visitors annually. The rugged, remote terrain is well suited to hikers, mountain bikers, backpackers, and four-wheelers, while its eye-popping scenery has attracted artists, photographers, and filmmakers for decades.

WHAT TO LOOK FOR

The park's districts appear close together on maps, but there are no roads that link them. Travel time between them ranges from two to six hours by car due to limited river crossings.

> Island in the Sky District scenic overlooks

> Needles District backcountry

> Remote Maze District

> Colorado and Green in Rivers District

> Upheaval Dome, possible meteor crater

> Horseshoe Canyon and Native American artifacts

Golden-lit needles seem to glow under the moody clouds over Elephant Canyon in the Needles District.

"… THE MOST WEIRD, WONDERFUL, MAGICAL PLACE ON EARTH —THERE IS NOTHING ELSE LIKE IT ANYWHERE."

— Edward Abbey, American author and former ranger at Arches National Park, on Canyonlands

▲ **False Kiva** is a human-made stone circle of unknown origin in a cave in a remote area of Canyonlands. This is one of the secret places in the park not marked on any map that requires some hiking knowledge or special directions to find.

HISTORY OF THE PARK

Indigenous Paleo-Indians visited these canyons more than 10,000 years ago, followed by hunter-gatherers from the Late Archaic Period (2000–1000 BCE). Apparently neither group settled here. About 2,000 years ago, the Ancestral Puebloans occupied areas of the Needles District, leaving behind stone and mud dwellings. At least 25 indigenous groups have been associated with or passed through this region, and the pictographs, artifacts, and murals that marked their time here are some of the oldest in America. Like the Indians before them, European settlers traveled through the area without homesteading.

It was during the 1950s, when Bates Wilson, superintendent of Arches National Monument, became an advocate for the scenic canyon landscapes southwest of his own park. He won over Secretary of the Interior Stewart Udall by offering jeep tours of Canyonlands. In 1964, President Lyndon Johnson established it as a national park. Wilson became the first park superintendent and is celebrated as the "father of Canyonlands."

RECREATIONAL ACTIVITIES

The park is divided into four districts, each offering a distinct wilderness experience.

- Island in the Sky is the most accessible district and accounts for roughly 76 percent of park visitors. It offers overlooks along a paved scenic drive, several hiking trails, and a moderate four-wheel-drive route called the White Rim Road (permit required).
- The Needles, in the southeast, provides a backcountry approach to hundreds of sandstone spires, but reaching it requires some serious hiking or four-wheel driving.
- The Maze lies west of the Colorado and Green rivers and is the most remote district. As one of the least accessible places in the United States, it is geared to experienced and self-reliant wilderness campers.
- The Rivers attract rafters and kayakers who want to experience the park's beauty up close. Visitors may enjoy tranquil flatwater trips on the Green or Colorado rivers and exciting whitewater raft excursions in Cataract Canyon. In years with heavy snowmelt, the Cataract Canyon stretch offers the largest whitewater in the country.

Horseshoe Canyon, northwest of the Maze, contains examples of American Indian rock art made by early hunter-gatherers. The drawings of horses, meanwhile, date from the 1500s, when Spanish explorers reintroduced horses to the continent.

Mesa Arch on the eastern edge of the Island in the Sky District is a spectacular pothole arch that provides visitors with amazing views of the La Sal Mountains, canyons, and formations like Monster Tower, Washer Woman Arch, and Airport Tower in the distance.

▲ **Cyclists face** a uphill stretch of White Rim Road, a 100-mile unpaved track that loops around and below the Island in the Sky mesa top, affording visitors stunning views of the canyons.

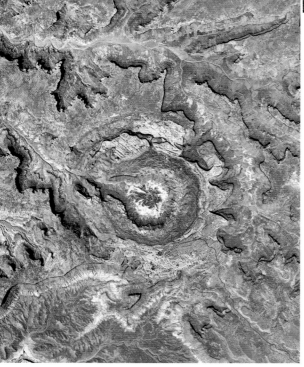

◄ **Aerial image of Upheaval Dome** impact structure. Upheaval Dome is a geological puzzle; it is perhaps the site of a meteor crater or possibly a collapsed salt dome.

WILDLIFE AND PLANT LIFE

Mammals found in here include black bear, coyote, bobcat, cougar, badger, skunk, bat, ring-tailed cat, pronghorn, and desert bighorn sheep. Most visitors can spot desert cottontails, kangaroo rats, and mule deer.

The more than 273 bird species include raptors like the golden eagle, bald eagle, Cooper's hawk, northern goshawk, red-tailed hawk, rough-legged hawk, Swainson's hawk, and northern harrier. Owls are represented by the great horned owl, northern saw-whet owl, western screech owl, and Mexican spotted owl. Other avian inhabitants include grebe, heron, duck, gull, osprey, falcon, quail, grouse, pheasant, raven, crow, woodpecker, flycatcher, bluebird, wren, warbler, oriole, goldfinch, swallow, and sparrow.

Among the desert-loving creatures are eight species of lizard and eight species of snake, including the side-blotched lizard, the northern whiptail lizard, and the rarely seen midget faded rattlesnake. Common kingsnake and prairie rattler have been reported but not confirmed. The park is home to six confirmed amphibian species—the red-spotted toad, Woodhouse's toad, American bullfrog, northern leopard frog, Great Basin spadefoot toad, and tiger salamander. Canyon tree frogs have been reported but not confirmed.

The park supports 11 cactus species, 20 moss species; liverworts; hardy grasses like Indian ricegrass, galleta, grama, and needle and thread; and trees like neatleaf hackberry, Russian olive, Utah juniper, pinyon pine, tamarisk, and Fremont's cottonwood. Shrubs include shadscale, Mormon tea, blackbrush, four-wing saltbush, and cliffrose. Cryptobiotic soil, a rich crust made up of living organisms, is the foundation of life here and provides nitrogen fixation and moisture for seeds. One misplaced footprint can destroy decades of growth, however.

▲ **The Chocolate Drops** rise over the magnificent land formations of the uncompromising terrain of the remote Maze District.

▶ **Holy Ghost panel** in the Great Gallery of Horseshoe Canyon. Horseshoe Canyon, in the remote Green River area of Canyonlands, contains spectacular examples of Barrier Canyon-style rock art, including pictographs and petroglyphs.

▼ **The warm salmon pinks and russets** of the Cedar Mesa Sandstone caprock stand out against the azure blue sky.

DID YOU KNOW?

Adding to the park's colorful history, the Robber's Roost hideout of Butch Cassidy's Wild Bunch gang was located not far from the Maze District of Canyonlands.

MORE TO EXPLORE
NATIONAL FORESTS

In 1897, Congress approved the Organic Act, allowing for the establishment of forest reserves in order to ensure a supply of timber, protect the forest from development, and secure water sources.

The first national forest was established as the Yellowstone Park Timber and Land Reserve in 1891 and was overseen by the Department of the Interior. In 1905, these forest reserves became the province of the Department of Agriculture. By 1907, President Theodore Roosevelt had more than doubled the forest-reserve acreage; a wary Congress responded by limiting a president's ability to create new reserves. In 1960, the Multiple-Use Sustained-Yield Act expanded the management goals of the Organic Act to include "outdoor recreation, range, timber, watershed, and wildlife and fish purposes" as well as the establishment of wilderness areas.

Today there are 155 national forests—and 20 national grasslands—in the United States, which are overseen by the National Forest Service. In spite of this "security blanket" of federal protection, many national forests are currently facing increased risk to their habitats from the development of private land on their boundaries. Only ten states lack national forests: Connecticut, Delaware, Hawaii, Iowa, Kansas, Maryland, Massachusetts, New Jersey, North Dakota, and Rhode Island.

The following is a representative sampling of national forests from around the country.

▼ Pisgah National Forest

Location Western North Carolina
Established 1916
Area 509,283 acres (2,061.0 km²)

Known for its recreational options and exquisite fall foliage, Pisgah was one of the first national forests in the East and site of the country's first forestry school. It contains 46,600 acres of old-growth forest, has several peaks over 6,000 feet, and contains three wilderness areas: Linville Gorge, Middle Prong, and Shining Rock.

▲ *Hikers pause on the trail to the summit of Silver Star Mountain in the Silver Star Scenic Area of the Gifford Pinchot National Forest, which affords visitors a breathtaking view of Mount St. Helens, an active stratovolcano.*

▲ Gifford Pinchot National Forest

Location Southern Washington
Established 1908
Area 1,312,274 acres (5,310.6 km²)

One of America's oldest national forests, Gifford Pinchot is located in a mountainous region of Washington State, with Mount Rainier National Park to the north, the Columbia River to the south, Mount Adams to the east, and Mount St. Helens to the west. Mount St. Helens National Volcanic Monument, with its tunnels and caverns formed by ancient cooled lava, is the showpiece of this forest. There are 1,475 miles of trails, 4,104 miles of roads, and several wilderness areas. Wildlife includes elk, black bear, mountain goat, and bobcat. For anglers, there are Chinook salmon, coho salmon, steelhead trout, cutthroat trout, and rainbow trout.

▲ *Gifford Pinchot National Forest sprawls beneath Mount Adams, the second-tallest volcano in the state.*

▶ *Sunlight bathes the tranquil woods near Lewis Falls in Gifford Pinchot National Forest.*

◀ *Looking Glass Falls, one of the most popular falls in western North Carolina, is located in Pisgah.*

NATIONAL GRASSLANDS

These are rangelands within the United States that are similar to national forests but consist of prairies. All but four designated grasslands are part of or on the edge of the Great Plains.

► Coconino National Forest

Location Northern Arizona
Established 1908
Area 1,852,201 acres (7,495.6 km²)

The diverse landscape at this popular recreational forest ranges from sculpted red rocks to alpine tundra, with wildlife that includes elk, javelina, and black bear. Other attractions include the ancient village of Sinagua at Elden Pueblo, the San Francisco Peaks, Oak Creek and Sycamore canyons, and Mogollan Rim. Humphrey's Peak, at 12,637 feet, is Arizona's highest point.

▲ *A fascinating variety of vegetation grows in the red rocks and red soil below Bell Rock in Coconino National Forest near Sedona in northern Arizona.*

▼ White Mountain National Forest

Location Eastern New Hampshire and western Maine
Established 1918
Area 761,687 acres (3,082.4 km²)

This spectacular reserve is crossed by both the Appalachian Trail and the White Mountain Scenic Byway. The forest includes Mount Washington, which at 6,288 feet, is the highest point in the Northeast and the site of the second-fastest wind speed recorded on earth, 231 miles per hour. The summit, with a visitor center and weather station, is a state park.

▲ *A young moose explores the springtime greenery of the White Mountain National Forest.*

▼ *The picturesque Albany Covered Bridge, along the Kancamagus Highway in White Mountain National Forest, is emblematic of an ideal bucolic New England landscape.*

▲ *An angler shows off a steelhead caught in Petersburg Creek, which flows outside the fishing town of Petersburg in Alaska's Tongass National Forest.*

► Tongass National Forest

Location Southeastern Alaska
Established 1907
Area 16,748,360 acres (67,778.2 km²)

America's largest national forest, Tongass spans 500 miles in southeast Alaska from the Canada-U.S. border to the Pacific Ocean. It is best known for its wide expanses of Sitka spruce, western hemlock, and cedar, as well as a geological and climatic diversity that includes supporting ice fields and glaciers. The forest includes Misty Fjords and Admiralty Island National Monuments, and nearly one-third is covered by 19 wilderness areas, such as the Kootznoowoo Wilderness.

► *An aerial view shows mist hanging over the Tongass temperate rainforest in the Misty Fjords National Monument Wilderness.*

▼ Bridger-Teton National Forest

Location Western Wyoming
Established 1908
Area 3,402,684 acres (13,770 km²)

Part of the Greater Yellowstone Ecosystem, Bridger-Teton straddles the Continental Divide. It features Wyoming's highest elevation, Gannet Peak at 13,804 feet, another 40 mountains exceeding 12,000 feet, the massive Gros Ventre Landslide, three wilderness areas, and 27 glaciers located in the Wind River Range.

▲ *Camel Rock, Shawnee's most famous rock formation, is a highlight of the Garden of the Gods wilderness area.*

▲ *A vantage point on the banks of the Little Wind River gives a stunning view of Buffalo Head Peak in Bridger-Teton National Forest.*

▲ Shawnee National Forest

Location Southern Illinois
Established 1933
Area 273,482 acres (1,106.7 km²)

Nestled between the Ohio and Mississippi rivers lies Illinois's only national forest. Shawnee contains seven wilderness areas, including the Garden of the Gods, known for its ancient sandstone cliffs and rock formations. Among its many hiking trails are the 160-mile River to River Trail and the Rim Rock Trail that circles an escarpment.

▶ *A winding trail leads to Shawnee's Garden of the Gods overlook.*

▼ *A view over the slopes of the Sierra de Luquillo Mountains shows the misty rainforest of the El Yunque National Forest.*

▲ *A gentle cascade breaks up the dense rainforest jungle of El Yunque.*

▶ El Yunque National Forest

Location Puerto Rico
Established 1903
Area 28,683 acres (116.1 km²)

The lone tropical rain forest in the National Forest System, El Yunque is located on the slopes of the Sierra de Luquillo Mountains. The higher elevations rise over 3,400 feet and receive nearly 200 inches of rainfall per year, creating lush foliage and cascading waterfalls. There are 240 tree species in this forest, 23 of which are found only in this spot.

▲ *A rustic sign in the classic style associated with America's national parks and forests directs visitors to Minnesota's Superior National Forest.*

▲ Superior National Forest

Location Northern Minnesota
Established 1909
Area 2,093,590 acres (8,472.5km²)

Superior National Forest is known for its boreal woodlands, pristine lakes, and rich cultural history. It is also home to Eagle Mountain, the highest point in Minnesota at 2,301 feet. The reserve includes the Boundary Water Canoe Area Wilderness—over 1,500 miles of canoe routes, 1,000 lakes, and 2,200 campsites. Here, visitors may glimpse gray wolf, lynx, black bear, and moose.

▲ *Late autumn colors stand out against the snow-covered evergreens along an Aspen creek in the White River National Forest.*

▲ White River National Forest

Location Northwest Colorado
Established 1902
Area 2,287,495 acres (9,257.2 km²)

White River is the ideal destination for the sports-minded vacation traveler. It is the most visited national forest in the country, likely due to its 12 ski resorts, which include Aspen, Vail, and Breckenridge. It also boasts eight wilderness areas, four large reservoirs, 2,500 miles of trails, 1,900 miles of roads, and 10 peaks above 14,000 feet in elevation.

▶ *A hiker takes in a gorgeous sunrise on the summit of Mount Whitney in Inyo National Forest.*

▼ *The magnificent Patriarch Tree stands in the Ancient Bristlecone Pine Forest of Inyo.*

▲ *An easy hike takes Green Mountain National Forest visitors to Moss Glen Falls. This waterfall empties into an open area of mixed forest growth and meadows.*

▲ Green Mountain National Forest

Location Western Vermont
Established 1932
Area 408,419 acres (1,652.8 km²)

This temperate broadleaf and mixed forest includes eight wilderness areas and supports beaver, moose, coyote, black bear, white-tailed deer, wild turkey, and ruffed grouse. Among the 900 miles of trails three are nationally designated: the Appalachian Trail, the Long Trail, and Robert Frost National Recreation Trail. There are also three alpine and seven Nordic ski areas.

▶ Inyo National Forest

Location California/Nevada
Established 1907
Area 1,957,264 acres (7,920.8 km²)

Located in both the Sierra Nevada and White Mountains, Inyo features Mono Lake, the Ancient Bristlecone Pine Forest, the Long Valley Caldera, nine wilderness areas, Boundary Peak—the highest elevation in Nevada—and Mount Whitney, which at 14,505 feet is the highest point in the contiguous United States.

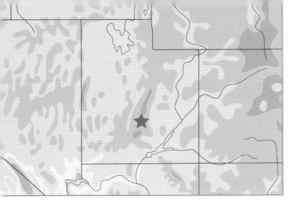

UTAH

CAPITOL REEF

Color and form combine here to create breathtaking high-desert tableaus and mountain panoramas.

LOCATION Wayne, Garfield, Sevier, and Emery counties, UT

CLOSEST CITY Torrey, UT

AREA 241,904 acres (978.95 km²)

ESTABLISHED August 2, 1937, as National Monument; December 18, 1971, as National Park

VISITORS 1,227,627+

ELEVATION 7,041 feet (2,146 m) at Golden Throne

GEOLOGY Sandstone cliffs, fossils

WHAT TO LOOK FOR

The park offers spectacular views, along with glimpses of the pioneer past.

> Cathedral Valley

> Waterpocket District

> Pictographs and petroglyphs

> Gifford Homestead and Fruita Schoolhouse

▼ **A panoramic view** of Capitol Reef's distinctive layered sandstone formations are viewed from a drive that follows the Waterpocket Fold, a monocline that extends nearly 100 miles.

Located in south-central Utah's scenic red rock country, Capital Reef casts a visual spell that few can resist. With peerless vistas at nearly every turn, the massive rock formations—with their varying hues, textures, and shapes—resemble a geological layer cake.

Unlike parks known for a few distinctive natural features, like arches or hoodoos, Capitol Reef offers arches, bridges, domes, spires, gorges, buttes, mesas, canyons, elongated "strike" valleys, dikes and sills, intrusive gypsum domes, massive landslides, fossilized oyster reefs, petrified logs, dinosaur bones, bentonitic hills, and unusual soft-sediment. In other words, something for everyone. As one of Utah's "Big 5" national parks, Capitol Reef is definitely worth discovering.

STEP BACK IN TIME

Early geologist Clarence Dutton, who studied the park in the 1800s, viewed the area as a fantasy land. Later geologists understood the irony that the arid desert terrain had been shaped by water—fresh water, rainwater, snow, ice, and saltwater.

For much of its long existence, this region remained at sea level, often tropical and forested, sometimes inundated by the sea. It was not until 65 million years ago, when the westward-moving Atlantic plate collided with the Pacific plate and forced an upheaval of huge masses of land, that the Colorado Plateau rose between four and seven thousand feet. Some chunks broke into sharp angles or folded into ridges far beneath the upper strata of rock. As many millions of years passed, water erosion wore down the upper layers, revealing the up-thrusts and warped, folded layers seen today.

The park's main feature, the hundred-mile Waterpocket Fold, is a one-sided ridge called a monocline and the largest example in the nation. The Fremont River contributed to the sculpting of the parklands and also moves sand toward the Gulf of California, a reminder this park has not stopped reshaping itself.

Nomadic Paleo-Indians began to settle here 13,000 years ago. By 1000 CE an agrarian community was living on the banks of the Fremont, which lent its name to this early culture. These people left behind odd pictographs and petroglyphs unlike those of other Indians. Their neighbors to the south and east, the crop-growing Ancestral Puebloans, were later followed by Ute and Paiute. They lived alternately in the mountains and the desert, depending on the season.

Temple of the Moon in the Cathedral Valley District. A dirt road leads to this remote, rugged region, which is a stark desert characterized by amazingly beautiful sandstone monoliths that some say resemble cathedrals.

"THE COLORS ARE SUCH THAT NO PIGMENTS CAN PORTRAY. SO LUMINOUS ARE THEY THAT THE LIGHT SEEMS TO SHINE OR FLOW OUT OF THE ROCK RATHER THAN BE REFLECTED FROM IT."

— *Clarence Dutton, pioneering geologist*

▲ **Bright tipis** echo the colors of the surrounding landscape. At the doorstep to the park, the Capitol Reef Resort offers tipis or Conestoga wagons as guest accommodations.

DID YOU KNOW?

The park got its name from the Capitol Reef ridge on Waterpocket Fold, a barrier to human travel the same way a coral reef impedes ship travel. "Capitol" came from the line of white sandstone domes that resembled the U.S. Capitol building.

Colorful bentonite hill in Cathedral Valley. Charles Kelly, the first caretaker and superintendent of Capitol Reef, gave the area its name because the eroded sandstone shapes reminded early explorers of ornate, Gothic cathedrals, with fluted walls, alcoves, and pinnacles.

In 1853 explorer John C. Fremont mapped the plateau, becoming one of the first outsiders to view this landscape. He was followed by prospectors and Mormon farmers, who labored to irrigate their fruit orchards. A restored schoolhouse and homestead from the Fruita settlement are among the park's features. In the 1920s local boosters publicized the area, which is partially in Wayne County, as "Wayne Wonderland." It was established as Capitol Reef National Monument in 1937 but did not open to the public until 1950. The park has expanded to six times its original size and now manages 75 percent of its land as wilderness.

▲ A fascinating petroglyph panel can be seen close to the visitor center on Highway 24. The early Fremont culture was known for its outlier petroglyphs of alien or spirit-like beings, some wearing elaborate horned headdresses that look like helmets with antennae.

◄ The Fruita Schoolhouse. This log building, which also served as a community meeting house and church, served as a school from 1900 to 1941.

▶ A horse grazes in the field of the Pendleton Barn, framed by Capitol Reef's red cliffs. This historic structure is part of the Gifford Homestead, which lies in the heart of the Fruita valley. The 200-acre Fruita Rural Historical District is listed on the National Register of Historic Places. The original home was built in 1908 by polygamist Calvin Pendleton.

▼ Campers enjoy a star show in the night sky. Capitol Reef is one of the national parks designated as an International Dark Sky Park and has taken measures to reduce light pollution and provides programs to inspire stargazing.

PARK PLEASURES

Visitors here enjoy hiking, biking, camping, picnicking, horse riding, ATV touring, fishing, birding, and wildlife watching. The many trails encourage hikers of all levels and offer instructive overviews of the region's skewed geology. The Tanks feature small potholes full of collected rainwater—and tadpoles and tiny shrimp—atop Waterpocket Fold, while expansive Cathedral Valley showcases colorful rocks and monoliths, and Hickman natural bridge frames distant Capitol Dome. The Capitol Reef Natural History Association operates the visitor center and attached bookstore as well as the Gifford House Store and Museum, which sells handmade pioneer-era items and fresh fruit pies.

Other nearby destinations include Hanksville-Burpee Dinosaur Quarry, Mars Desert Research Station, Horseshoe Canyon, Robber's Roost, and Canyonlands National Park.

WILDLIFE AND PLANT LIFE

The east section of the park has lower elevations and scant rainfall, creating a demanding climate that requires plants and animals with specialized abilities. Capitol Reef wildlife includes black bear, cougar, pronghorn, Utah prairie dog, porcupine, marmot, and kangaroo rat. There are also 83 bird species; larger residents include red-tailed hawk, black-billed magpie, and pinyon jay, along with dozens of smaller songbirds and several species of hummingbird.

During wet years, the sere desert can burst into a riot of color, as dormant grass and wildflower seeds begin to sprout. Plant life includes cottonwood, tamarisk, Gambel oak, Mormon-tea, Indian ricegrass, round-leaf buffaloberry, yucca, virgin's-bower, Utah serviceberry, squawbush, and box elder.

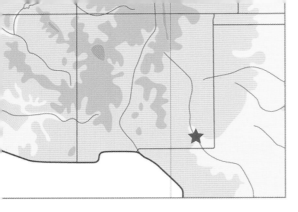

NEW MEXICO
CARLSBAD CAVERNS

The superb caverns at Carlsbad offer thrills, chills, and an unparalleled learning adventure for spelunkers of all ages.

LOCATION Eddy County, NM

CLOSEST CITY Carlsbad, NM

AREA 46,766 acres (189.25 km²)

ESTABLISHED October 25, 1923, as Carlsbad Cave National Monument; May 14, 1930, as Carlsbad Caverns National Park

VISITORS 440,700+

ELEVATION 3,596 feet to 6,368 feet (1,036 m to 1,941 m)

GEOLOGY Limestone

WHAT TO LOOK FOR

Although some of the named rooms are not open to the public because of inaccessibility and safety issues, there is more than enough to see in this unique national park.

> Big Room

> Queen's Chamber

> King's Palace

> Mirror Lake

> Crystal Spring Dome

> Slaughter Canyon Cave

> Spider Cave

> Bat Watch Amphitheater

> Chandelier Ballroom in Lechuguilla Cave

DID YOU KNOW?

In June of 1959 scenes from the hit movie *Journey to the Center of the Earth* starring James Mason and Pat Boone were filmed in the Kings Palace and the Boneyard.

Located in—and beneath—the Chihuahuan Desert, is New Mexico's most popular attraction. Consisting of 83 individual caves, these caverns are among the best preserved and most accessible in the world. They were declared a national monument in 1923, a national park in 1930, and a UNESCO World Heritage site in 1995. The city of Carlsbad, gateway to the caverns, lies in southeast New Mexico, straddling the Pecos River at the eastern edge of the Guadalupe Mountains.

DISCOVERY AND EXPLORATION

Carlsbad is one of more than 300 limestone caves existing in a Permian fossil reef created by an inland sea that covered the area 250 million years ago. Unlike the many caves formed by water-based erosion, these caverns were most likely formed by the sulfuric acid from underground deposits of petroleum.

Paleo-Indians lived in this area 12,000 years ago, leaving behind pictographs within the parklands. Though they surely knew the location of the entrance, there is no evidence they explored the inner caves. In the 1500s Spanish explorers passed through, likely encountering Mescalero Apaches in the Guadalupe Mountains. In 1849, American military expeditions crossed the region, inspecting lands acquired by the United States after the Mexican Cession. Between 1860 and 1880 ranchers and settlers arrived in increasing numbers. In 1898, a young cowhand named Jim White was purportedly the first person to enter the caverns . . . and he was astonished by what he found. Over the following decades White helped to explore and promote the site and became known as "Mr. Carlsbad Caverns."

► **The Lions Tail** formations are strange stalactites encrusted with popcorn-like rock shapes. They dangle from the ceiling along the west side of the Big Room.

"THE ENGLISH LANGUAGE IS TOO WEAK TO DESCRIBE THE CAVERN. …IN THE CAVERN NATURAL LAWS SEEM SUSPENDED; IT IS NATURE GONE MAD IN A RIOT OF FANTASY.…WE MOVED THROUGH A WONDERLAND OF FANTASTIC GIANTS WHOSE IMMEMORIAL ANTIQUITY WAS APPALLING TO CONTEMPLATE."

— Pulp fiction author Robert E. Howard's description of Carlsbad Caverns in the early 1930s

A series of switchbacks leads to the Natural Entrance of Carlsbad Caverns.

Photographs taken around 1915 by Ray V. Davis, and later published in the *New York Times*, helped stir public interest in Carlsbad Caverns.

Work on the infrastructure of the cave, including the 4.2 miles of trails, was begun in the 1920s. An elevator allowed the concrete and rocks used in the construction to be transported to the lower levels. Safety railings were added in the 2000s, as were non-slip surfaces underfoot. The Bat Flight Amphitheater outside the entrance, where visitors can watch bats leave the cave at sunset, was constructed in 1963.

GOING UNDERGROUND

Exploring the caves is top priority for most visitors. Some of Carlsbad's most beloved formations are the Whale's Mouth, the Baby Hippo, Iceberg Rock, Green Lake Pool, Frozen Waterfall, Eternal Kiss (where a stalactite and stalagmite nearly touch), New York, New York, the Keyhole, the Queen's Orchestra with its alien-looking musicians, and the Queen's Chamber. The King's Highway leads through the majestic King's Palace with its numerous stalactites. The Big Room, almost 4,000 feet in length, is North America's largest underground chamber. The temperature inside the caverns ranges from a constant 68 degrees F with high humidity at the lowest point in the cave, 1,034 feet underground, to an average of 56 cool, dry degrees in the Big Room.

AMENITIES

There are self-guided tours of the Big Room and ranger tours through scenic rooms. The visitor center provides a restaurant, a gift shop, and a bookstore, plus on weekends there is an underground snack bar inside the cavern. There are no campsites or lodging accommodations within the park, only backcountry camping with a permit. Campgrounds and other amenities are available in nearby White's City or in Carlsbad, 20 miles away.

WILDLIFE AND PLANT LIFE

The park supports 17 bat species. Roughly half a million Brazilian (or Mexican) free-tailed bats live in the caverns. At dusk, their flittering shapes fill the sky, as 5,000 per minute exit the caves on their way to consume several tons of insects. Meanwhile, Eastern red bats and hoary bats roost in trees, and Western pipistrelle bats roost on rock cliffs. Other denizens of darkness include three species of cave cricket, cave swallows, and most of the park's crustaceans, like the unusual copepods called *Cyclops vernalis* and branchiopods called water fleas (*Holopedium amazonicum*). Additional cave invertebrates include isopods, troglophilic beetles, millipedes, centipedes, and various spiders.

The parkland's wide diversity of fauna and flora is due to its location at the intersection of three biogeographic provinces—southern Rocky Mountain, northern Chihuahuan Desert, and southwestern Great Plains. There are 67 mammal species, 357 birds, 5 fish, and 55 amphibian and reptile species. Mammals includes cougar, coyote, black bear, elk, fox, wolf, bobcat, otter, weasel, and badger. Some native species, like the javelina and pronghorn, have been reintroduced. Studies of the park's rich insect life frequently turn up new species for the state, like the damselfly Lenora's dancer.

More than half the park is shrubland, and about a third is grassland. Smaller habitats include arroyo riparian woodlands and shrublands, scattered herbaceous wetlands, and the forested wetland at Rattlesnake Springs. Plants include Pinchot juniper, sandpaper oak, viscid acacia, ocotillo, mariola, prickly pear cactus, Mormon tea, creosote bush, tarbush, littleleaf sumac, claret cup cactus, agave, and mesquite. There are also abundant wildflowers, including many species of milkweed.

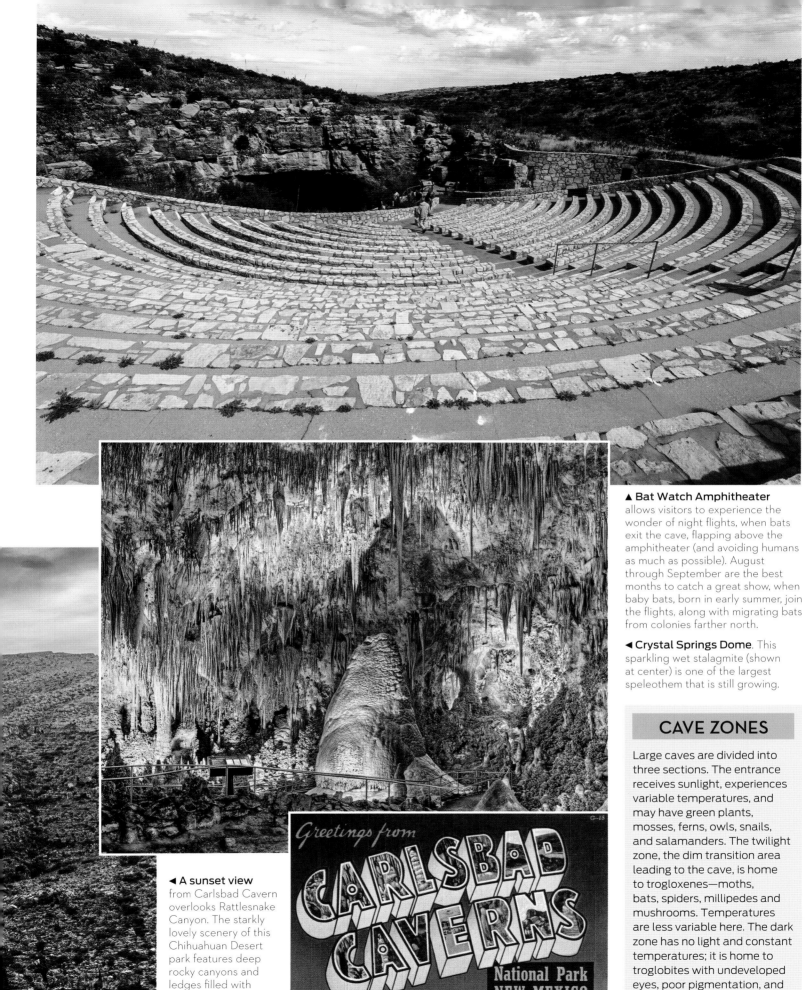

▲ **Bat Watch Amphitheater** allows visitors to experience the wonder of night flights, when bats exit the cave, flapping above the amphitheater (and avoiding humans as much as possible). August through September are the best months to catch a great show, when baby bats, born in early summer, join the flights, along with migrating bats from colonies farther north.

◄ **Crystal Springs Dome**. This sparkling wet stalagmite (shown at center) is one of the largest speleothem that is still growing.

CAVE ZONES

Large caves are divided into three sections. The entrance receives sunlight, experiences variable temperatures, and may have green plants, mosses, ferns, owls, snails, and salamanders. The twilight zone, the dim transition area leading to the cave, is home to trogloxenes—moths, bats, spiders, millipedes and mushrooms. Temperatures are less variable here. The dark zone has no light and constant temperatures; it is home to troglobites with undeveloped eyes, poor pigmentation, and long antennae.

◄ **A sunset view** from Carlsbad Cavern overlooks Rattlesnake Canyon. The starkly lovely scenery of this Chihuahuan Desert park features deep rocky canyons and ledges filled with flowering cactus and desert wildlife.

Greetings from **CARLSBAD CAVERNS** National Park NEW MEXICO

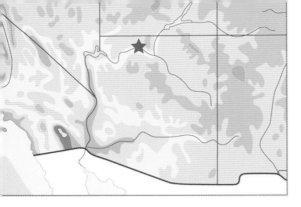

ARIZONA
GRAND CANYON

The Southwest's crown jewel possesses such massive scope and breathtaking beauty as to stagger the mind.

LOCATION Coconino County and Mohave County, AZ

CLOSEST CITY Tusayan, AZ, South Rim; Fredonia, AZ, North Rim

AREA 1,218,560 acres (4,931 km²)

ESTABLISHED January 11, 1908, as National Monument; February 26, 1919, as National Park

VISITORS 5,000,000+

ELEVATION 7,000 feet (2,100 m) at South Rim

GEOLOGY Sandstone showing angular unconformity (tilting)

It is instructive to picture the reaction of the first humans to view the Grand Canyon, whether indigenous peoples or the later European explorers who were crossing the continent bent on finding riches. It doubtless never entered their imaginations that such a wealth of beauty, such a natural wonder existed on earth. As a means of putting it into perspective for modern visitors, the canyon is larger in area than Rhode Island . . . larger than an actual state.

WHAT TO LOOK FOR

The Grand Canyon may truthfully be described as "a hole in the ground," but a visit to America's second-favorite park shows off its breathtaking beauty.

> Paved Rim Trail
> Bright Angel Trail to the base
> Grand Canyon Village
> Yavapai Point
> Rafting excursions on the Colorado River
> Nearby Horseshoe Bend and Antelope Canyon

A panoramic view of Grand Canyon from the South Rim. Over millions of years, the Colorado River carved out this convoluted gorge.

"IN THE GRAND CANYON, ARIZONA HAS A NATURAL WONDER WHICH IS IN KIND ABSOLUTELY UNPARALLELED THROUGHOUT THE REST OF THE WORLD."

— Theodore Roosevelt

The national park encloses the majority of the canyon, which shares boundaries with three federally recognized tribes—the Navajo, the Havasupai, and the Hualapai. In 2022, the park began construction of the Desert View Inter-tribal Cultural Heritage site, which recognizes the contribution of Native Americans to the stewardship of the canyon.

THE PARK'S INTRIGUING GEOLOGY

There is a long-held belief that the Colorado River began carving out the canyon around six million years ago, but recent research indicates the process may have started more than 70 million years ago. The fossils found in the canyon are not from dinosaurs, which appeared after the canyon's layers were formed, but of marine animals that date back more than a billion years. The canyon also displays a geological mystery called the Great Unconformity, where 250-million-year-old rock layers adjoin rocks that are 1.2 billion years old. The puzzle of the missing strata, representing hundreds of millions of years, keeps geologists awake at night. Although the canyon is home to an estimated 1,000 caves, only 335 are recorded and of those only one is open to the public.

Today the canyon reigns as the largest in the Western Hemisphere, 277 miles long, more than a mile deep in places, and 18 miles across at its widest point. The world-champion canyon, however, rated the longest and deepest, is likely the Yarlung Tsangpo Grand Canyon in the Himalayas.

EARLY HABITATIONS

Humans have been living in this area for at least 10,500 years and Native Americans

▶ **The North Rim.** The daunting landscape of this side of the Grand Canyon sees fewer visitors than the South Rim, but it is no less impressive.

▲ **A Navajo sweat lodge** at Eagle Point. The Native American Village here leads guests through a self-guided tour of an authentic Native American village featuring housing, ovens, and sweat lodges that highlight the unique architecture and functionality of the structures built by the Hualapai, Navajo, Plains, Hopi, Havasupai, and other Indian tribes who once roamed these lands.

▲ **Park rangers** lead a slow train of mules along the switchbacks to the bottom of the Grand Canyon. Since the first years of the park's history in the early 1900s, mules have ferried visitors, luggage, and supplies into the canyon.

for the past 4,000 years. The Basketmaker culture of the Ancestral Puebloans, who were later known simply as Pueblos, evolved from the nomadic Desert Culture as they began to depend on agriculture. They were among the first to create settlements in the canyon and its caves. Another agricultural group, the Cochimi, also dwelled nearby. In the late 13th century, these tribes all departed, possibly due to a great drought. The area was then settled by the Paiute, Cerbat, and Navajo. Sadly, these peoples were eventually displaced and forced onto reservations.

DID YOU KNOW?

Supai Village, administered by the Havasupai tribe, lies in Havasu Canyon within the Grand Canyon. With a population of around 200, this remote community has no access roads and gets mail delivered by mule.

The Pueblos considered the Grand Canyon a holy site, and made pilgrimages to it, while the Hopi see it as a gateway to the afterlife, believing the dead pass westward through a "place of emergence" upstream from the confluence of the Colorado and Little Colorado rivers.

In 1540, Spanish explorer García López de Cárdenas, attached to the expeditions of Francisco Vázquez de Coronado, was likely the first European to view the canyon. His men were unable to access the river below the rim, and so they turned back. A pair of Spanish priests wrote about the canyon 200 years later. In 1869, John Wesley Powell, American geologist, U.S. Army soldier, and explorer of the American West, led an expedition through the canyon via the Colorado River, opening the area to geologists. Mining companies were interested in copper and asbestos deposits, but the early residents saw more opportunities from tourism. By the early 20th century, the canyon was a popular destination. Grueling stagecoach journeys were replaced by train trips on the Grand

A desert bighorn ram stands at the edge of the Grand Canyon. The park provides a remote habitat for this sheep, the largest native animal in the park, with rams weighing up to 250 pounds.

Canyon Railway. The noted Fred Harvey Company opened a number of facilities including the posh El Tovar Hotel on the South Rim and the Phantom Ranch in the gorge, both still in operation.

By the early 1990s, an estimated 20,000 people a year were making the journey into the canyon by mule, 800,000 by hiking, 22,000 passed through the canyon by raft, while another 700,000 tourists flew over in helicopters and fixed-wing aircraft.

PARK ACTIVITIES AND AMENITIES

Hiking along new versions of former Indian trails is always popular. The overlooks encountered on these trails are not to be dismissed lightly—they provide a vivid impression of the canyon's size and the remarkable beauty of its gorges, ridges, and rock formations. Depending on the time of day, observers find that the colors of the cliffs change in hue and intensity. The South Rim is more manageable for most hikers than the rugged North Rim and offers more attractions. These include Grand Canyon Village, the park's most popular entry point, which provides lodging as well as an exceptional overlook called Yavapai Point. Mather Point Overlook is located near the visitor center. The six-mile Bright Angel Trail leads hikers to the bottom—though walking down and back in one day is not recommended—and there are also multi-day mule tours. Other park options include Hummer tours, rafting the Colorado River, and breathtaking helicopter excursions. Tent and RV camping is available along the South Rim, while a campground and guest ranch are located on the canyon's floor.

Nearby attractions include the striking Horseshoe Bend and Antelope Canyon, as well as the controversial Grand Canyon Skywalk. This large, semi-circular bridge has a transparent glass floor, allowing tourists to walk out 70 feet over the canyon and view the base from 4,000 in the air. It is located on the grounds of the Hualapai Indian Tribe.

◄ **Bright Angel Creek campground** at the Phantom Ranch sits deep in the Grand Canyon Colorado River Wilderness.

▼ **A curious rock squirrel**. As cute as this tiny animal is, it can be dangerous to get too close.

▲ **Grand Canyon Skywalk** at Grand Canyon West on the Hualapai Indian Reservation is a horseshoe-shaped cantilever bridge with a glass walkway that affords unparalleled canyon views.

WILDLIFE AND PLANT LIFE

There are plenty of wild creatures found in the canyon, but the most dangerous to visitors is the diminutive rock squirrel, which frequently bites overly friendly tourists. Less troublesome wildlife includes cougar, coyote, gray fox, beaver, the occasional black bear, mule deer, elk, bighorn sheep, pipistrelle bat, peregrine falcon, bald eagle, and California condor. There are 47 species of reptiles, including iguana, Gila monster, chuckwalla, gecko, desert tortoise, and desert-dwelling snakes.

Like many desert or semi-desert environments, the Grand Canyon supports a wide range of plants. Regional species include sagebrush, snakeweed, Mormon tea, Utah agave, banana and narrowleaf yucca, snakeweed, winterfat, Indian ricegrass, dropseed, and needlegrass. As visitors approach the canyon floor, the vegetation grows sparser; here are found pinyon pine and Utah and one seed juniper.

▶ **The Colorado River** cuts through the canyons to give rafters a phenomenal view of early-morning light illuminating the rugged cliff faces.

A bald eagle takes flight over the canyon.

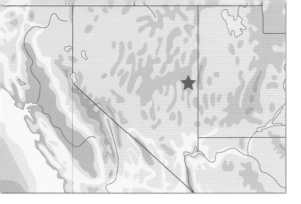

NEVADA
GREAT BASIN

This high-desert park boasts vast underground caverns, some of Nevada's tallest peaks, and its only remaining glacier.

LOCATION White Pine County, NV

CLOSEST CITY Ely, Baker, Border, NV

AREA 77,180 acres (312.3 km²)

ESTABLISHED January 24, 1922 as Lehman Caves National Monument; October 27, 1986 as Great Basin National Park

VISITORS 131,800+

ELEVATION 13,063 feet (3981.6 m) at Wheeler Peak

GEOLOGY Sandstone, shale, and limestone

WHAT TO LOOK FOR

This park offers a variety of landscapes and attractions.

> Lehman Caves

> Wheeler Peak Glacier

> Ancient bristlecone pines

> The 12-mile Scenic Drive

Located in east-central Nevada, the park derives its name from the dry mountainous region known as the Great Basin, which lies between the Sierra Nevada and Wasatch Mountains. The terrain can be rugged and challenging, but the awe-inspiring peaks and subterranean caves are worth the effort.

EARLY HISTORY

Paleo-Indians inhabited this region more than 12,000 years ago and hunted large ice age mammals, such as mammoth and ground-sloth. Three thousand years later hunter-gatherers known as the Great Basin Desert Archaic group occupied the area. They were followed by the Fremont culture, and then the Shoshone around 1300 CE. Their descendants in the area include the Duckwater Shoshone and the Skull Valley Band of the Gosiute.

Trappers and military expeditions crossed the region in the 1800s, but it was not until 1855 that the first ranchers settled here. In 1885, rancher Absalom Lehman discovered the limestone caverns that bear his name. These extensive caves, once a national monument, became a major tourist draw for the park.

ACTIVITIES AND AMENITIES

Favorite activities include hiking, picnicking, birding, fishing, exploring the caves, and camping. After-dark ranger-led astronomy programs are available May through September. There are visitor centers for both the park and Lehman Caves; the latter has a cafe and gift shop open from May to October.

▲ **A twisted bristlecone pine** stands on the slope of Mount Washington. These imposing trees are remarkable for their great age and their ability to survive adverse growing conditions. A need to protect these ancient trees was a driving force in the designation of Great Basin as a national park.

THE BRISTLECONE PINE TRAGEDY

Great Basin is known for its long-lived bristlecone pines. One particular bristlecone was thought to have lived for 5,000 years. This august tree was nicknamed Prometheus, after the Titan who stole fire from the other gods and gave it to humans. In 1964, a graduate student and U.S. Forest Service personnel cut down the pine in order to determine its age. It was only afterward that researchers realized that they had killed the oldest nonclonal organism on earth. Public outrage over the fate of Prometheus helped prompt the creation of the national park.

WILDLIFE AND PLANT LIFE

The park's great biodiversity is represented by 61 species of mammals, 18 species of reptiles, 238 species of birds, 2 amphibians, and 8 species of fish. Mammal inhabitants include yellow-bellied marmot, black-tailed jack rabbit, mountain cottontail, ground squirrel, pronghorn, kangaroo rat, packrat, coyote, kit fox, badger, and at least bat 10 species.

Eleven species of pine and more than 800 plants are found here, including hundreds of wildflower varieties. The visitor center landscape is dominated by sagebrush, saltbush, single-leaf pinyon, and Utah juniper, while mountain meadows support white fir, quaking aspen, Englemann spruce, and large ponderosa pine. At the treeline an alpine area displays low, delicate plants amid rocky outcroppings.

▶ **Yellow-bellied marmots** are commonly found among rock piles. Great Basin also engages in programs to increase the park's population of the critically endangered Vancouver Island marmot.

Brilliant autumn colors contrast with the somber tones of Wheeler Peak, which reaches higher than 13,000 feet in elevation.

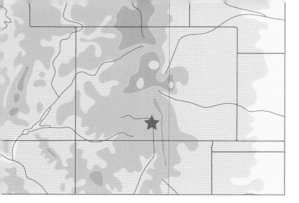

COLORADO
GREAT SAND DUNES

Towering sand dunes provide fun activities and a chance for exploration, along with a diverse habitat.

LOCATION Alamosa County and Saguache County, CO

CLOSEST CITY Alamosa, CO

AREA 149,028 acres (603.1 km²)

ESTABLISHED March 17, 1932, as National Monument; September 24, 2004, as National Park

VISITORS 527,500+

ELEVATION 750 feet (229 m) at Dunes

GEOLOGY Darker, fine-grained and lighter, coarse-grained sand dunes with black magnetite deposits

WHAT TO LOOK FOR

The park features a variety of views and activities.

> Star Dune

> Alpine lakes

> Medano Pass

> Primitive Road

▲ **Wild deer** forage in the park's grasslands.

This national forest and preserve in south-central Colorado is home to North American's highest sand dunes, which rise to 750 feet and cover an area of about 30 square miles. The relatively flat sand sheets that feed the towering dunes are actually the largest component of the dunes system, containing roughly 90 percent of the park's sand.

The site is located on the eastern edge of the San Luis Valley and an adjacent national preserve in the Sangre de Cristo Range. The wind blows the sand grains up into the mountains, and the Medano and Sand creeks carry them back down. In spring and summer, visitors must walk across wide, shallow Medano Creek to reach the dunes.

HISTORY OF THE REGION

The earliest evidence of human habitation dates back 11,000 years. The first occupants were likely nomadic hunter-gatherers following mammoth and prehistoric bison. More recent tribes, like the Southern Ute, settled here, as did the Apache and Navajo. The Utes called the dunes "sand that moves," while the Apaches simply said, "it goes up and down." In the late 1600s, the Spanish were the first Europeans to enter the valley. Explorers like De Anza, Zebulon Pike, John C. Fremont, and John Gunnison all crossed the region in subsequent centuries. Ranchers and miners followed; in fact the area was declared a national monument to protect it from gold mining and concrete manufacturing.

PARK FEATURES

Sandboarding—"surfing" down the dunes—and sand sledding are both popular activities. Equipment can be rented just outside the park entrance. Activities include swimming, fishing, backpacking, and camping, as well as hiking across the dunes. Four-wheelers may drive for 20-miles on the unpaved Medano Pass Primitive Road, which includes four miles of deep sand. The park is open all year. There is a visitor center that offers a short video and several exhibits, and a store. Park rangers are available to answer questions and provide trail conditions.

WILDLIFE AND PLANT LIFE

This biologically diverse area supports at least seven different habitats, from wetlands and grasslands, to salt plains, dunes, subalpine forest, and alpine tundra.

DID YOU KNOW?

The dark areas that appear in the dunes are deposits of magnetite, which has eroded out of the Sangre de Cristo mountains. Magnetite, the most magnetic mineral, is both attracted to a magnet and can also be magnetized to become a magnet.

The park is home to beaver, badger, pika, mule deer, elk, bighorn sheep, black bear, coyote, cougar, bobcat, white pelican, sandhill crane, and peregrine falcon, along with the endemic Great Sand Dunes tiger beetle. Amphibians are represented by tiger salamander and several frogs and toads. Reptiles include fence lizard, many-lined skink, bullsnake, and garter snake. The streams support Rio Grande cutthroat trout, Rio Grande sucker, and fathead minnow.

Among the hundreds of plant species are aspen, Douglas fir, bristlecone, pinyon, ponderosa, and bristlecone pine, dogwood, cottonwood, alpine phlox, fairy primrose, Indian paintbrush, penstemon, Indian ricegrass, prairie sunflower, prickly pear cactus, narrowleaf yucca, Indian ricegrass, and inland saltgrass.

▶ **A bull elk** stops for a drink at Big Spring Creek.

The Sangre de Cristo Range rises beyond the slopes of the Star Dune, while the Medano Creek flows at the base of the dune.

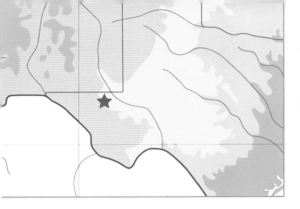

TEXAS
GUADALUPE MOUNTAINS

Mountain peaks and desert dune meet at the site of a massive ancient fossil reef that rises like a behemoth from the flatlands.

LOCATION Culberson County and Hudspeth County, TX

CLOSEST CITY Dell City, TX

AREA 86,367 acres (349.51 km²)

ESTABLISHED September 30, 1972

VISITORS 172,300+

ELEVATION 8,751 feet (2,667 m) at Guadalupe Peak

GEOLOGY Fossiliferous limestone

This West Texas park lies east of El Paso in the Guadalupe Mountains that rise above the Chihuahuan desert. These are the same mountains that shadow Carlsbad Caverns National Park to the west. These peaks are composed of the world's most extensive Permian fossil reef, an escarpment uplifted by tectonic activity during the late Cretaceous. The reef's southern terminus is a stark limestone monolith known as El Capitan. The park is also home to the four highest elevations in Texas, including Guadalupe Peak, the state's highest point. In 1978, Congress designated 46,850 acres of the park as a wilderness area.

WHAT TO LOOK FOR

The diversity of its landscapes, as well as its historical site, ensures park-goers will have a memorable experience.

> Guadalupe Peak

> El Capitan

> McKittrick Ranch and its small museum

> Dog Canyon

A BRIEF HISTORY

According to archaeological evidence, people have lived here for over 10,000 years in the many caves and alcoves. Hunter-gatherers followed large game and collected edible vegetation, leaving behind projectile points, baskets, pottery and rock art. They were followed by ancient Pueblo and Mogollon peoples. The early 16th-century Spanish explorers did not settle here, but they restored horses to the continent, which the Apache and other tribes quickly adapted for hunting and migrations. Various 19th century outlaws also hid out here. By the 1850s many immigrants were settling the West, and the Mescalero Apache were eventually driven onto reservations by the U.S. cavalry.

PARK ACTIVITIES

Visitors enjoy picnicking, hiking, backpacking, camping, and birding. There is camping at Dog Canyon on the Texas-New Mexico border, as well as at Pine Springs. There is even a corral for livestock. Sites include the ruins of a stagecoach station near the Pine Springs visitor center, and the restored Frijole Ranch, the first permanent ranch house and now a museum of local history. The Guadalupe Trail ascends more than 3,000 feet to the top of Guadalupe Peak and offers views of El Capitan and the desert. McKittrick Trail—Felix McKittrick was the first European settler in these mountains—leads to a 1930s stone cabin, vacation home of petroleum geologist Wallace Pratt, who donated part of the park land. Gypsum sand dunes are found in the far west of the park.

WILDLIFE AND PLANT LIFE

Mammals found here include elk, javelina, gray fox, black bear, cougar, coyote, bobcat, skunk, badger, mule deer, and 16 bat species. Park birdlife includes great horned owl, chickadee, woodpecker, grosbeak, hummingbird, turkey vulture, greater roadrunner, peregrine falcon, golden eagle, and many species of sparrow.

The are three major ecosystems for vegetation: Chihuahuan Desert, with salt flats, creosote bushes, and honey mesquite found to the west; and grassland, pinyon pine, and juniper to the east; canyon interiors, which exhibit bigtooth maple, velvet ash, chinkapin oak, and other deciduous trees; and alpine areas more than 7,000 feet in elevation, with forests of ponderosa pine, Arizona pine, southwestern white pine, Rocky Mountain Douglas fir, and alligator juniper, and stands of quaking aspen.

◄ **Campers greet the sunrise** after a night of camping in a flat shrubby area of the park.

El Capitan looms over the park's rugged terrain. This towering peak is notable for its distinctive exposed-limestone summit.

DID YOU KNOW?

El Capitan in Texas, a jutting, jagged monolith of fossilized limestone, is not to be confused with the more famous El Capitan in Yosemite National Park, a massive chunk of granite in the Sierra Nevada.

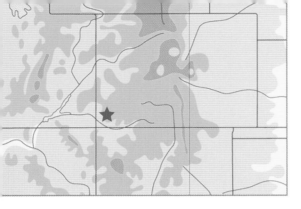

COLORADO
MESA VERDE

Visitors experience a slice of history as they follow in the footsteps of the Ancestral Puebloans at their incredible cliff dwellings on the "Green Mesa."

LOCATION Montezuma County, CO
CLOSEST CITY Cortez, CO
AREA 52,485 acres (212.40 km²)
ESTABLISHED June 29, 1906
VISITORS 563,400+
ELEVATION 8,572 feet (2,612 m) at Park Point Overlook
GEOLOGY Sandstone and limestone

Located near the Four Corners region of southwest Colorado, this park oversees some of the best-preserved archaeological sites of the Ancestral Puebloans. Containing more than 5,000 historic sites, including 600 cliff dwellings, Mesa Verde is the largest archaeological preserve in the country, while the Cliff Palace is considered the largest cliff dwelling in North America. The parkland is also a UNESCO World Heritage site.

WHAT TO LOOK FOR

This unique national park preserves centuries-old treasures that give visitors a glimpse of a long-ago way of life, while also offering amazing scenery and fun outdoor activities.

> Cliff Palace
> Sun Temple
> Sacred kivas
> Petroglyph Point
> Chapin Mesa Archeological Museum

The Cliff Palace, the largest cliff dwelling in Mesa Verde National Park. For more than 700 years, the Ancestral Pueblo people built thriving communities on the mesas and in the cliffs of Mesa Verde. These well-preserved ruins are now a UNESCO World Heritage Site.

"WHAT A COUNTRY CHOOSES TO SAVE IS WHAT A COUNTRY CHOOSES TO SAY ABOUT ITSELF."

— Mollie Beattie, Director of the U.S. Fish and Wildlife Service

STEP BACK IN TIME

Around 7500 BCE, nomadic Paleo-Indians known as the Foothills Mountain Complex seasonally visited this area, most likely to hunt mammoth and prehistoric bison based on the variety of projectile points left behind. Archaic Indians (6000 BCE– 750 CE) established semi-permanent rock shelters here, and by 1000 BCE the Basketmaker culture had evolved from the Archaic population. By 750 CE, the Ancestral Puebloans had emerged from the Basketmakers. This culture hunted, gathered, and grew subsistence crops such as corn, beans, and squash.

The first pueblos were built after 650 and by the end of the 12th century, construction had begun on the vast cliff dwellings, which would later make this site so valuable to archeologists. Yet by 1285 the Puebloans had vanished from the region—possibly due to social or environmental instability brought on by a number of extreme and prolonged droughts. Whatever the cause, they left their cliff homes en masse and moved south to Arizona and New Mexico. Some researchers believe they live on today as the Rio Grande Pueblo, Hopi, and Zuni Indians.

In 1776, missionaries Francisco Dominguez and Silvestre de Escalante, seeking a route from Santa Fe to California, came upon

▶ **The Long House,** located on Wetherill Mesa in the western portion of the park, is its second-largest archaeological site. Evidence suggests it was home to 150 to 175 people, and it features a formal plaza in the center of the site that was most likely a great *kiva,* or dance plaza.

DID YOU KNOW?

The Ancestral Puebloans were once known as the Anasazi, but that term has fallen from favor. Once thought to mean "ancient ones," the Navajo word *anasazi* actually means "enemy ancestors."

▲ **Petroglyphs on the Petroglyph Point Trail.** Rock art is found throughout the Mesa Verde region. This panel, according to one Hopi elder, might tell the story of the Mountain Sheep Clan and the Eagle Clan separating from other people and returning to their place of origin.

◄ **A rustic timber** ladder leads down to a circular kiva inside the Cliff Palace.

▼ **A yellow-headed collared lizard** skitters across a sandstone cliff.

the site and named it Mesa Verde for its forested plateaus. Yet they never got close enough to view the cliff dwellings. The Utes had long occupied the region, but when homesteaders settled in Colorado, the Utes were given a strip of land that included Mesa Verde. Photographs by William Henry Jackson from 1874 publicized the cliff dwellings, bringing geologists and archeologists to the site. Journalist Virginia McClurg, whose party rediscovered three dwellings, urged the preservation of the cliff houses, but visitors continued to carry away important artifacts. Due to its many advocates, Mesa Verde at last received federal protection in 1906.

PARK ACTIVITIES

In addition to tours of the cliff dwellings, the park offers a range of hiking and biking trails, drives with stunning overlooks, areas for birding and stargazing, and evening ranger programs. Mesa Top Loop Road winds past archaeological sites and Sun Point Overlook with its panoramic canyon views. Petroglyph Point Trail is known for its rock carvings. The Chapin Mesa Archeological Museum features exhibits on the ancient Native American culture. For overnights guests, Morefield Campsite provides tent, trailer, and RV facilities.

WILDLIFE AND PLANT LIFE

This landscape of deep canyons contains several habitats and is home to more than 1,000 animal and insect species, some found only in the park. The park hosts 74 species of mammals, 200 species of birds, 16 reptiles, 5 amphibians, 6 fish (4 native), and more than 1,000 species of insects and other invertebrates. Mammals include coyote, cougar, bobcat, black bear, mule deer, Rocky Mountain Elk, bat, long-tailed weasel, ermine, mink, skunk, gray and red fox, beaver, ringtail cat, prairie dog, and shrew. Avian life is represented by

THE PUEBLO

Pueblo is Spanish for "town," "village," or "people." At Mesa Verde, the term not only describes the multi-storied structures made of stone, adobe mud, or other local materials, but also the communities housed there. The pueblo dwellings usually surrounded an open plaza and were accessible via ladders raised or lowered by the inhabitants, protecting them from thieves, unwanted guests, and animal intruders. Larger pueblos might be occupied by hundreds or even thousands of people. On site are also numerous *kivas,* underground chambers used for religious rites based on kachina beliefs or for social or political gatherings. These sacred spaces became the "heart of the community," and were considered a bridge between the underworld and the living world.

numerous songbirds as well as raptors, owls, hummingbirds, woodpeckers, and game birds. There are 9 species of lizard and 7 snakes. Some insects recently discovered here are new to science or new to Colorado.

Plant ecosystems vary by elevation, typically increasing with altitude. From lowest to highest they are shrub-steppe, pinyon-juniper woodland, mountain shrub system, and Douglas fir/ponderosa pine woodland. Non-elevation dependent ecosystems include microclimates created by seep springs and riparian ecosystems along river banks. Water seeping through the permeable sandstone and limestone sustains plant life in the arid spaces. More than 640 species of trees and plants, among them many wildflowers, grow here. They include oak, Utah juniper, snowberry, skunkbush, yucca, cacti, and Oregon grape. Indicator species vulnerable to changing environmental conditions include Cliff Palace milkvetch, Mesa Verde wandering aletes, and Mesa Verde stickseed.

▲ **A curious coyote** peers out of the bushes in the parklands.

▼ **Cedar Tree Tower** was first discovered in 1888. It is one of several tower sites that have been discovered on the mesa tops of the park, most likely built during the Classic period (100 to 1300 CE).

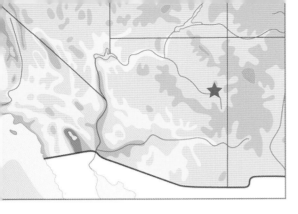

ARIZONA
PETRIFIED FOREST

The prehistoric past comes alive as visitors explore downed forests of fossil trees along with the exquisite Painted Desert.

LOCATION Navajo County and Apache County, AZ

CLOSEST CITY Holbrook, AZ

AREA 221,391 acres (895.94 km²)

ESTABLISHED December 8, 1906, as National Monument; December 9, 1962, as National Park

VISITORS 644,900+

ELEVATION 5,436 ft (1,657 m)

GEOLOGY Chinle, a variety of sedimentary rocks including beds of soft, fine-grained mudstone, siltstone, and claystone (mostly volcanic bentonite); sandstone, conglomerate, and limestone

WHAT TO LOOK FOR

The amazing park offers a wealth of gorgeous scenery and fun activities.

> Long Logs Trail

> Agate Bridge

> Blue Mesa Trail through the Painted Desert

> Newspaper Rock petroglyphs

> Painted Desert Inn Museum

DID YOU KNOW?

To counter the legend that those who take fossilized wood past park boundaries will be cursed with years of bad luck, hundreds of people have mailed back chunks of wood with apology letters. Park officials call the stack of returned rocks, the "conscience pile."

This northeastern Arizona park is known for its petrified trees, which lived—and died—in the Late Triassic Epoch, about 225 million years ago. Its boundaries extend into the Painted Desert, another exceptional natural landscape.

The Blue Mesa is famous for the stunning beauty of its striated landforms.

The park perches upon the Colorado Plateau, which was forced up thousands of feet by tectonic pressure and then subjected to erosive elements. That erosion has exposed most of the park's layers above the widespread and colorful Chinle Formation, for which the Painted Desert earned its name. Today the local topography combines semi-desert shrub steppe and richly hued badlands.

A SHORT HISTORY

This challenging landscape has been inhabited by indigenous peoples for more than 12,000 years, resulting in more than 1,200 archaeological sites within the park. Paleo-Indians were likely the first to arrive, leaving behind Clovis- and Folsom-type spear points. Around 8000 BCE nomadic groups established seasonal camps. The Basketmaker culture settled around 1000 BCE and thrived for many centuries, creating petroglyphs that chronicled their lives. Between 1250 and 1450 CE Ancestral Puebloan families gathered into large multi-quarter masonry structures known as pueblos, where several hundred people lived in close proximity.

Spanish explorers came through the region starting in the 16th century and named the Painted Desert in passing. When military expeditions inspected the land in the 1850s, after the Southwest became part of the United States, some members wrote about the fossil trees. As tourism began to increase during the 19th century, locals grew

▶ **The bright greens** and yellows of a collared lizard warming itself on a piece of petrified wood contrasts with the earth tones of the fossil.

The Teepees are a badland formation in the Painted Desert. This intriguing desert environment features petrified wood seen almost everywhere.

▲ **A road through the Petrified Forest** reveals an amazing landscape. The park has one main road with an entrance station at either end.

concerned that many petrified trees were being carried from the site for commercial use. In 1906 the Antiquities Act created the Petrified Forest National Monument.

PARK ACTIVITIES

Unlike many national parks, Petrified Forest welcomes leashed pets like cats and dogs, as well as horses for trail riding. Visitors may enjoy hiking to various landmarks, backpacking to campsites, birding, guided tours, and ranger talks. The maintained trails are either paved or graveled and are geared to hikers of all ages and abilities.

The Painted Desert Visitor Center offers historic architecture, an orientation film, a bookstore, gift shop, food, and gas. Painted Desert Inn National Historic Landmark, a former adobe trading post, now serves as a museum. Kachina Point, behind the museum, overlooks the red portion of the Painted Desert. At Puerco Pueblo, visitors can view Ancestral Puebloan homes and petroglyphs along a short looping trail. Another overlook furnishes views of

Newspaper Rock, home to more than 650 petroglyphs, some dating back 2,000 years. Blue Mesa, the otherworldly blue-purple-gray part of the Painted Desert, can be reached by hiking or driving.

THE MAIN ATTRACTION

Naturally, the park's top attractions are the many examples of petrified wood found throughout the grounds. These formed from tall conifers, tree ferns, and ginkgoes that lived over 200 million years ago and were felled by great floods, then buried under layers of mud or volcanic ash. Petrification occurred when minerals crystallized within the wood's cellular structure. Details of their ringed interiors and rough bark were often preserved.

Rainbow Forest Museum features exhibits on petrified wood, fossils, and prehistoric animals, while Giant Logs Trail is known for massive, colorful petrified trunks. Agate Bridge is an astonishing 110-foot petrified log that spans a gully. Jasper Forest offers a panoramic view of an area with

a high concentration of petrified wood. Meanwhile, the logs in Crystal Forest glimmer with quartz crystals. Long Logs Trail showcases some of the longest and most colorful specimens and is home to a partially restored pueblo, Agate House, built of petrified wood.

WILDLIFE AND PLANT LIFE

The park's larger residents include coyote, pronghorn, occasional mule deer, bobcat, and golden eagle. Smaller inhabitants include fox, Gunnison's prairie dog, western pipistrelle and pallid bats, deer mice, and jack rabbit. There are 16 kinds of lizards and snakes found here, and seven amphibians. More than 200 species of birds have been sighted here. Frequent fliers include common ravens, western meadowlarks, and Anna's hummingbirds. The grasslands support raptors, songbirds, and groundbirds, while riparian corridors along the Puerco River are home to warblers, vireos, avocets, and killdeer. Developed spots offer western tanagers, hermit warblers, and house finches; shorebirds and eastern vagrants also sometimes appear in the park.

In spite of its eroded badlands, the park's main habitat is semi-desert shrub steppes. This protected environment fosters some of the healthiest grassland in northeastern Arizona—and more than 450 species of plants. Furthermore, the rim of the Painted Desert with its rich volcanic soils is peppered with shrubs, small trees, grasses, and herbs. There are more than 100 species of grass, many of them native—bunchgrass, blue grama, sideoats grama, bearded sprangletop, and bush muhly—along with rushes and sedge. There are flowers like evening primrose, mariposa lily, and blue flax; shrubs such as sagebrush, saltbush, and rabbitbush; and trees that include willow, cottonwood, and the invasive Eurasian tamarisk.

▶ **A rusted 1932 Studebaker** marks where famed trans-American highway Route 66 once cut through the park.

FOSSILS

With its multilayered geology, the park contains more than 250 documented fossil sites. In addition to fossil plants, like lycophytes, ferns, cycads, conifers, and ginkgoes, there are vertebrate animal fossils that include the giant crocodile-like phytosaur, the large salamander-like Koskinonodon, and some early dinosaurs. Invertebrate fossils include freshwater snails and clams.

▲ **The variegated colors** and intricate patterns of petrified wood are a result of the fossilization process, with the wood's mineral composition reacting in different ways. Pure quartz is white, while manganese oxides form shades of blue, purple, black, and brown, and iron oxides render tones of yellow, red, and brown.

◀ **It might appear** as if the logs and trees scattered throughout the landscape had been felled by human hands, but quartz is extremely brittle, and, over time, the uplifting of the Colorado Plateau has fractured them.

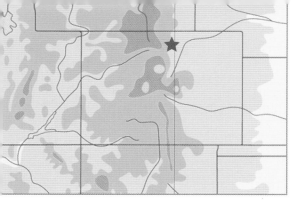

COLORADO
ROCKY MOUNTAIN

From snow-covered peaks to subalpine lakes to grassy meadows, this park's landscape is a study in extremes.

LOCATION Larimer, Grand, and Boulder counties, CO

CLOSEST CITY Estes Park and Grand Lake, CO

AREA 265,461 acres (1,074.28 km²)

ESTABLISHED January 26, 1915

VISITORS 3,305,000+

ELEVATION 14,259 feet (4,346 m) at Longs Peak

GEOLOGY Metamorphic core under sedimentary argillite with limestone and dolomite deposits

WHAT TO LOOK FOR

Explore the diverse landscapes of this park, which teem with fascinating wildlife.

> Trail Ridge Road, highest continuous paved road in the United States

> Flattop Mountain Tundra hike to Continental Divide

> Longs Peak

> Bear Lake

> Big Meadows

This national park, one of the country's highest, celebrates the natural wonders of the elegant, majestic Rocky Mountains. Located 55 miles north of Denver in northwestern Colorado, the site is bisected by the Continental Divide and surrounded by national forest land on all sides. The headwaters of the mighty Colorado River are located in its northwestern region.

The Rockies were created between 80 to 55 million years ago, as intense tectonic action under the American plate formed the broad belt of mountains that run down western North America. Their impressive height and sharp, craggy peaks indicate their relative youth, especially when compared to the rounded contours of the far older Appalachians in the East.

REGIONAL DIVISIONS

The park is divided into five regions. Region 1, west of the Continental Divide, is known for Big Meadows, Long Meadows, and the Kawuneeche Valley, open spaces that are great for picnics and birding in warm weather, snow-shoeing and cross-country skiing in winter. Lulu City, an abandoned silver mine is found there, as well as mountain passes that cross the Divide.

Region 2, the alpine region, has tundra trails at 12,000 feet and contains Mount Ida, with amazing views of the Divide. Forest Canyon Pass lies near the top of the Old Ute Trail that once linked villages.

Region 3, the wilderness area in the north, is home to the low, forested Mummy Range and waterfalls, lakes, ponds, dense woodlands, and meadows.

Region 4, the heart of the park, offers easy road and trail access, including the Flattop Mountain tundra hike to the top of Hallet Peak, an easy route to the Continental Divide.

Region 5 encompasses the backcountry and several waterfalls and features Longs Peak, rising more than 14,000 feet. Bear Lake, with its rocky shoreline, sprawls at its base.

◄ **Beaver Meadows Visitor Center.** Opened in 1967 and designed by Taliesin Associated Architects—Frank Lloyd Wright's architecture firm—it is one of the park's seven visitor centers.

▲ **A curious bull moose** pauses in his chomping of leaves to eye the photographer.

Snow-dusted peaks of the Front Range of the Rockies rise above the panoramic landscape. Rocky Mountain National Park is one of the highest in the park system, and it also one of the most popular parks in the country.

▲ **Longs Peak** viewed from Trail Ridge Road. This prominent mountain is the northernmost fourteener—a mountain peak with an elevation of at least 14,000 feet—and the highest point in the park and in Boulder County.

A SHORT HISTORY

More than 10,000 years ago, Paleo-Indians often traveled along what is now Trail Ridge Road to hunt mammoth and forage for food. Ute and Arapaho peoples subsequently hunted and camped in the area. In 1820, an expedition led by Stephen H. Long approached the Rockies via the Platte River. Kentuckian Joel Estes was the first settler; he moved into a hunting cabin with his family.

Homesteaders began arriving in earnest in the mid-1800s, displacing the Native Americans, most of whom had left the area voluntarily by 1860. Settlements like Lulu City, Dutchtown, and Gaskill in the Never Summer Mountains were established in the 1870s by prospectors searching for gold and silver. After the boom ended in 1883, most miners deserted their claims. The railroad reached Lyons, Colorado, in 1881, opening up the region to more travelers.

The 1920s saw an increase in lodge construction, including the Bear Lake Trail School, and the expansion of park roads. As with many pristine wilderness areas, a number of people were involved with preserving its beauty and cultural heritage. Those active in creating the national park included Enos Mills from the Estes Park area, James Grafton Rogers of Denver, and J. Horace McFarland of Pennsylvania.

ACTIVITIES AND AMENITIES

Popular pastimes include driving to spectacular overlooks, hiking more than 500 miles of trails, camping, canoeing, kayaking, fly fishing, birding, and horse riding. Mountain weather is very changeable, so visitors should always carry a warm, waterproof windbreaker or jacket. Campgrounds include Aspenglen, for tents and RVs; Glacier Basin; Longs Peak; Timber

▲ **A regal elk.** Some of the largest animals of the park, elk are common sights, especially during the autumn rut and the spring calving seasons.

Creek; and Moraine Park, the only site open for winter camping. There are five visitor centers: park headquarters are located at Beaver Meadows, a national historic landmark designed by the Frank Lloyd

Wright School of Architecture; the Alpine Visitor Center sits at the highest elevation of all National Park Service sites.

WILDLIFE AND PLANT LIFE

Animal inhabitants include black bear, coyote, cougar, bobcat, moose, elk, mule deer, bighorn sheep, yellow-bellied marmot, pika, beaver, and snowshoe hare. Birds are represented by 270 species, including both residents and migrants. Some park favorites are the three-toed woodpecker, white-tailed ptarmigan, dusky grouse, pine grosbeak, western tanager, red crossbill, Townsend's solitaire, great horned owl, red-tailed hawk, and wild turkey, along with many species of songbird and aquatic bird, and several hummingbirds.

  Different plant communities characterize each zone of a mountain—foothill, montane, subalpine, and alpine—and each zone may contain several types of plant communities. Thus, with its varied range of habitats, Rocky Mountain National Park supports more than 5,000 plant species.

PIKAS IN PERIL?

The rounded, furry pika *(Ochotona princeps)*, a relative of the rabbit, is an indicator species for the potential effects of climate change. Pikas are abundant in Rocky Mountain National Park, but there are concerns that their sensitivity to summer heat—and a lack of snowfall for insulation in winter—may affect their numbers. As a result, they are being monitored to detect changes in their locations in the park.

▼ **A tiny pika** nestles on a rock. Sometimes called a coney or rock rabbit, this rabbit relative is a denizen of the park's tundras.

▼ **Mount Hallet** casts its reflection in Sprague Lake, one of the 156 lakes found in the park.

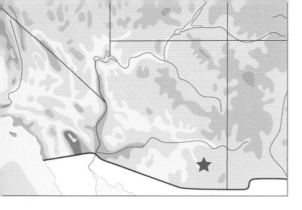

ARIZONA
SAGUARO

Tucson is the proud home of the giant saguaro, America's largest cactus and an enduring symbol of the American West.

LOCATION Pima County, AZ

CLOSEST CITY Tucson and Pima, AZ

AREA 91,716 acres (371.16 km²)

ESTABLISHED March 1, 1933, as National Monument; October 14, 1994, as National Park

VISITORS 957,400+

ELEVATION 8,664 feet (2,641 m) at Mica Mountain

GEOLOGY Horquilla limestone, Pinal schist, Catalina gneiss, and Escabrosa limestone

WHAT TO LOOK FOR

The stunning variety of cactus species is the main draw of the park, but a visit here is so much more.

> More than a million saguaro cacti located in the park

> Cactus Forest Loop in Rincon Mountain District

> Signal Hill Trail

> Petroglyphs in Tucson Mountain District

The towering Saguaro cactus grows only in a few regions of the Southwest. Saguaro National Park was established to protect these living treasures from land developers, cattle ranchers, invasive plants, and wildfires.

Located in southeastern Arizona, the park encompasses two districts on either side of Tucson—the eastern Rincon Mountain District (RMD) and western Tucson Mountain District (TMD). Both sectors work to preserve the Sonoran Desert, its habitats, its fauna and flora, and especially its precious cacti. The Rincons are significantly higher and wetter than the volcanic Tucsons. Part of the Madrean Sky Islands that lie between the Rocky Mountains and the Mexican Sierra Madre Oriental, the Rincons support many plants and animals not found in the TMD.

A SHORT HISTORY

The archaeological sites at the park trace back more than 8,000 years, covering both prehistoric and historic settlements. Artifact scatters have been found in Archaic sites, 3500 to 1450 BCE, and Hohokam sites, 500 to 1450 CE, which also include petroglyphs. These artifacts and remains represent farms, villages, campsites, and quarries. Historic sites include ranches, mines, and lime kilns.

The Hohokam people were followed by the Sobaipuri, Tohono O'odham, and Apache tribes. The inevitable Spanish explorers passed through in the 1540s; in 1692 Spanish priests set up a mission. Settlers did not really arrive until the mid-19th century, with Arizona statehood and the passing of the Homestead Act of 1862. After the close of the Apache wars—and the surrender of Geronimo—railroads opened the region. Communities sprang up, mines were excavated, cattle ranches were established; the latter two continuing well into the 20th century. In the 1920s, the University of Arizona and Professor Homer L. Shantz attempted to establish a sanctuary for the saguaro. In 1933, President Hoover used the Antiquities Act to create Saguaro National Monument in the Rincon Mountains. Among the park's notable rustic structures are ramadas, picnic tables, and restrooms built by the Civilian Conservation Corps between 1933 and 1941. Intended to conform to their natural surroundings, they consist mainly of quarried stone and other native materials.

◀ **Petroglyphs on Signal Hill** with the Tucson Mountains in the background. The petroglyphs were most likely created by the Hohokam People between 700 and 1,300 years ago.

Cacti line a narrow path along the slopes of Saguaro National Park. Desert hikers should remain vigilant to avoid extreme heat, dehydration, flash floods, cactus spines, snakes, cougars, black bears, and Africanized bees.

THE SAGUARO STORY

The saguaro cactus itself grows extremely slowly—the first arm does not even appear until the cactus is between 50 and 70 years old. They are considered mature at about 125 years and may live to 200 or older. Some specimens can attain 60 feet in height, weigh more than two tons, and hold up to 200 gallons of water. As a keystone species, they offer food or shelter to more than a hundred plants, birds, insects, and mammals. The park estimates their population at more than 1.8 million, along with another 24 cactus species—among them fishhook barrel, staghorn cholla, pinkflower hedgehog, Engelmann prickly pear, teddybear cholla, and jumping cholla.

▲ **A peregrine falcon** keeps a vigilant watch over the landscape of the park.

▼ **A Gila woodpecker** nibbles on a cactus. This common Sonoran Desert woodpecker makes nest cavities in the sides of saguaros, which provides them with safety from predators and refuge from extreme temperatures.

▲ **The park is the home** of a variety of desert vegetation, notably the giant organ pipe cactus.

◄ **The tall column** of a giant saguaro towers over other cacti and vegetation.

ACTIVITIES

Park visitors enjoy sightseeing along its paved roads and hiking its 165 miles of trails. Both districts allow bicycling and horseback riding on selected roads and trails. Both also host a visitor center. There are no campgrounds or lodgings in the park, but Rincon offers wilderness camping with a permit. A wide selection of lodgings is available in Tucson.

Rincon Mountain features the 8.3-mile Cactus Forest Loop Drive, which provides some trail access. Angling across the Rincon Mountain District from southwest to northeast is the Arizona Trail, an 800-mile national scenic trail that crosses the state from Mexico to Utah.

Tucson Mountain has 12 miles of paved roads and 8.5 miles of unpaved roads, including the 5-mile Bajada Loop Drive. Bicycling is allowed on paved roads, Bajada Loop Drive, Golden Gate Road, and the Belmont multi-use trail. The Signal Hill Trail leads to a site with dozens of petroglyphs, the 800-year-old rock art of the ancient Hohokam people. The Arizona-Sonora Desert Museum lies south of the TMD and combines aspects of a botanical garden, zoo, and natural history museum of the region.

WILDLIFE AND PLANT LIFE

Unlike the Great Basin, Mojave, and Chihuahuan deserts in the Southwest, with their hot dry summers and cold dry winters, the Sonoran Desert experiences more subtropic warmth and two wet seasons. The Rincon district in the east has pine-covered summits rising above the cactus forest, while the western Tucson district offers typical low desert views of the more arid mountains.

Because the Sonora rarely freezes, it supports a wider range of life than other American deserts. There are at least 30 mammal species in the park—like cougar, coyote, bobcat, white-tailed deer, mule deer, javelina, gray fox, ring-tailed cat, white-nosed coati, ground squirrel, and kangaroo rat. The endangered lesser long-nosed bat alternates between the park and Mexico. Bird sightings include wren, great horned owl, raven, kestrel, turkey vulture, roadrunner, woodpecker, hawk, quail, and hummingbird, along with the rare vermilion flycatcher and whiskered screech owl, and the threatened Mexican spotted owl. There are 37 reptiles including desert tortoise, mud turtle, diamondback rattlesnake, Gila monster, short-horned lizard, and spiny lizard, and three amphibians—lowland leopard frog, canyon tree frog, and the burrowing Couch's spadefoot toad.

Although urban sprawl, pollution, and habitat restrictions stress these park animals, their chief threat is the automobile. More than 50,000 vertebrates die in the park each year after being struck by cars.

A least 390 species of vascular plants grow here and 200 species of fungi. Plant types vary based on elevation—desert scrub with saltbush and brittlebrush at lower elevations; desert grasslands a bit higher up; and as altitude increases, oak woodland, pine-oak woodland, and finally mixed conifer forest, with Douglas fir, ponderosa pine, white fir, Gambel oak, and many understory plants. Invasive buffelgrass from Africa and Asia was imported as forage and to control erosion, but it fills the spaces between native plants and becomes a fire hazard.

NEW MEXICO
WHITE SANDS

Wave-like dunes of gleaming gypsum create a endless mineral landscape unlike any other.

LOCATION Otero County and Doña Ana County, NM

CLOSEST CITY Alamogordo, NM

AREA 145,762 acres (589.88 km²)

ESTABLISHED January 18, 1933, as National Monument; December 20, 2019, as National Park

VISITORS 600,000+

ELEVATION 3887 to 4116 feet (1185 to 1266m)

GEOLOGY White gypsum sand dunes

Located in the Tularosa Basin within the Chihuahuan Desert east of the Rio Grande, this National Park is famous for its sparkling white gypsum sand dunes. The dunefield is the largest of its type in the world—with a depth of 30 feet, dunes up to 60 feet in height, and containing 4.5 billion short tons of gypsum crystals. (Gypsum is a soft, while sulfate mineral that is used in fertilizer and to make plaster.)

WHAT TO LOOK FOR

White Sands features several different types of sand dunes

> Dome dunes, which are found around the southwest margins of the field

> Transverse and barchan dunes, located in the center of the field

> Parabolic dunes, found along the northern, southern, and northeastern margins of the field

The pristine sands of White Sands National Park. During the Permian Period, this region was covered with shallow seas that left behind gypsum (calcium sulfate). Tectonic action then raised the seabed to become part of the San Andres and Sacramento Mountains. Over time, rain dissolved the soluble gypsum and carried it down to the Tularosa Basin.

DID YOU KNOW?

This park has the distinction of being completely surrounded by the White Sands Missile Range, a military testing area for the US Army.

"THE DESERT COULD NOT BE CLAIMED OR OWNED—IT WAS A PIECE OF CLOTH CARRIED BY WINDS, NEVER HELD DOWN BY STONES, AND GIVEN A HUNDRED SHIFTING NAMES."

— Michael Ondaatje

HISTORY OF THE PARKLANDS

Around 12,000 years ago this region consisted of lakes, streams, grasslands, and Ice Age mammals. Today, a fossil trackway with footprints of both early humans and giant sloths indicate that these large land mammals were hunted by us during the Last Glacial Period. Around 1200 BCE, the Jornada Mogollon people settled the basin, leaving behind puddled adobe and pottery sherds. About 1300 CE, the area was inhabited by Apaches. In later centuries, the lack of a reliable water supply kept many European settlers away. Eventually salt from the salinas was harvested as public property. In the early 1900s prospectors for gold, oil, and coal, as well as gypsum, overran the Basin. But during the 1920s, Alamagordo businessman Tom Charles pointed out the economic benefits of preserving the white sands. In 1933, President Hoover declared White Sands a national monument.

WILDLIFE & PLANT LIFE

The plants that grow at the edges of the dunes help to stabilize them while providing food and shelter to the animal inhabitants. Among the tough, desert-dwelling flora are succulents like cane cholla and soaptree yucca and grasses like alkalai sacaton and Indian rice grass, along with Rio Grande cottonwood, skunkbush sumac, hoary rosemary mint, purple sand verbena, Mormon tea, and claret cup cactus, with its notably sweet fruit. Wildlife includes 50 mammals, 250 bird species, 30 reptiles, seven amphibians, and even one species of fish. Forty moths are endemic to the park, along with the Apache pocket mouse, the bleached earless lizard, and two camel crickets.

▶ **The soaptree yucca** is one of the succulents found at the edges of the park's expanse of white dunes.

▼ **The bleached earless lizard** evolved within a short time span to gain the white coloration necessary for survival in gypsum dunes.

▲ **Completed in 1938** as one of the WPA's projects, the picturesque visitor center, comfort station, three ranger residences, and maintenance buildings are made of terra cotta-colored adobe bricks.

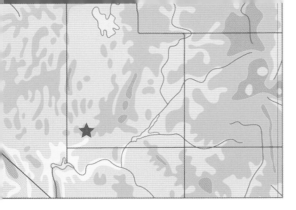

UTAH
ZION

The awe-inspiring pink, red, and cream sandstone peaks of Utah's first national park form nature's own monumental rock garden.

LOCATION Washington, Kane, and Iron counties, UT

CLOSEST CITY Springdale, Orderville, and Cedar City, UT

AREA 146,597 acres (593.26 km²)

ESTABLISHED July 31, 1909, as Mukuntuweap National Monument; November 19, 1919, as Zion National Park

VISITORS 3,590,000+

ELEVATION 8,726 feet (2,660 m) at Horse Ranch Mountain

GEOLOGY Sedimentary rock layers

Considering Zion's spectacular vistas and colossal rock formations—which include colorful sandstone mountains, canyons, buttes, mesas, rivers, slot canyons, and natural arches—it is no surprise that more than three million eager visitors make their way to this remote site each year. Located in southwestern Utah, the park is best known for Zion Canyon, which is 15 miles long and up to 2,640 feet deep. The northern sector of the park, the Kolob Canyons, was once itself a national historic monument.

Arising from a landscape that was at times under water or arid desert, the parklands' impressive peaks took 150 million years to form. Beginning 13 million years ago, tectonic events caused the Colorado Plateau to lift from 4,000 to 6,000 feet, subjecting surface areas to increased erosion.

EARLY CULTURES

The first human inhabitants settled here around 8,000 years ago, among them Paleo-Indian groups. The Basketmaker Ancient Puebloans dwelled here around 300 CE, followed by the westernmost Ancestral Puebloan group, once called the Virgin Anasazi, and the Parowan Fremont Culture around 500. By the late 1200s they were replaced by the Parrusits and several other Southern Paiute tribes.

Mormon homesteaders arrived in 1858 and had established farming communities by the 1860s. The canyon was originally known by its Indian name, Mukuntuweap, and in 1909 President Taft made it a national monument under that name. In 1918, the park was expanded by National Park Service director Horace Albright, and the name was changed to Zion National Monument. The change was partly because certain agency people in Washington believed Indian or Spanish names kept visitors from their parks. Zion was far more acceptable to them and was, furthermore, a term applied by the Mormons to the "pure in heart." In 1919, Woodrow Wilson designated Zion as a national park.

◀ **A persistent pinyon pine** grows atop a sandstone formation.

WHAT TO LOOK FOR

One of America's premier parks, Zion offers so much.

> Zion and Kolob Canyons
> Scenic hiking trails and overlooks
> Emerald Pools
> Virgin River

ACTIVITIES AND ATTRACTIONS

Popular activities include hiking, biking, swimming, backpacking, guided horseback tours, boating on the Virgin River, camping, stargazing, and climbing. Canyoneering and overnight bivouacs both require a permit. The park offers trails suitable for hikers of all aptitudes. They include the popular Narrows, the level Riverside Walk, and Angel's Landing Trail, where the upper reaches are challenging, but the view is breathtaking. Many of the massive rock formations have grand names like Court of the Patriarchs, the Altar of Sacrifice, the Temple, Tower of the Virgin, the Spearhead, Lady Mountain, and the Great White Throne. There are three visitor centers within the park—Springdale, Zion Canyon, and Kolob Canyons. For history buffs, the Zion Human History Museum, just north of the south entrance, showcases how people have left their mark on the area.

WILDLIFE AND PLANT LIFE

This park marks the convergence of the Great Basin, the Mojave Desert, and the Colorado Plateau. This composite, along with the diverse topography of the canyons and mesalands, offers plants and animals a mix of desert, riparian, woodland, and coniferous forest habitats. The park supports 79 mammals, 289 birds, 28 reptiles, 6 amphibians, and 7 fish species. Wildlife sightings include mule deer, coyote, cougar, fox, ringtail cat, porcupine, bobcat, bat, bighorn sheep, and rock squirrel.

Where there are desert conditions—on canyon bottoms and rocky ledges away from perennial streams—plants include sagebrush, prickly pear cactus, rabbitbrush, sacred datura, Utah penstemon, golden aster, and Indian paintbrush. Milkvetch and prince's plume grow in selenium rich pockets.

▲ **Bighorn sheep** are able to navigate the precipitous cliffs of Zion.

The Watchman rises high over the Zion landscape as rays of the setting sun illuminate the red cliffs that surround the Virgin River.

RANGER NATURALIST SERVICE

FIELD TRIPS • CAMPFIRE PROGRAMS
NATURAL HISTORY TALKS & EXHIBITS
GENERAL INFORMATION

ZION
NATIONAL PARK
U.S. DEPARTMENT
OF THE INTERIOR
NATIONAL PARK
SERVICE

Towers of the Virgin. These famous formations each bear a fanciful name. From left to right are the Sundial, the Witch Head, Broken Tooth, Rotten Tooth, and the Altar of Sacrifice.

▲ **Kanarra Creek Canyon Trail** offers an entertaining water hike that challenges park-goers to wade through streams and navigate around two waterfalls that block upstream travel through the narrow slot.

THE NINE FORMATIONS

There are nine known exposed geological formations in Zion National Park. Each shows the accumulation of 150 million years of Mesozoic-aged sedimentation as the area was at various times under water; a vast desert; and a dry near-shore environment. The formations are part of a super-sequence of rock units called the Grand Staircase.

· The Dakota Formation—cliffs found on Ranch Horse Mountain—features conglomerate and sandstone made by stream deposits.

· The Carmel Formation—cliffs at Mount Carmel Junction—is composed of limestone, sandstone, and gypsum formed by shallow seas and coastal desert.

· The Temple Cap Formation—cliffs at the West Temple—is sandstone and a layer of mudstone formed by coastal sand dunes and tidal flats.

· Navajo Sandstone—steep cliffs in Zion Canyon—is sandstone formed by sand dunes.

· The Kayenta Formation—rocky slopes found throughout the canyon—is sandstone and siltstone formed by streams.

· The Moenave Formation—slopes and ledges found in the lower red cliffs seen from the Human History Museum—is sandstone and siltstone created by streams and ponds.

· The Chinle Formation—purplish slopes above Rockville—is composed of shale, loose clay and conglomerate created by stream deposits.

· The Moenkopi Formation—chocolate cliffs with white bands found from Virgin to Rockville—is made of shale, siltstone, sandstone, mudstone, and limestone deposited by a shallow sea.

· Kaibab Limestone—a formation in the Hurricane Cliffs near Kolob Canyons—was formed by a shallow sea and contains the abundant fossils of Permian invertebrates and vertebrates.

▼ **The soaring peaks** of Mount Spry and the East Temple are extraordinary in any season.

▲ **The summit of Angels Landing** allows visitors to take in breathtaking views over the canyons of Zion. The hike to this scenic spot is so popular that it is now only available through a lottery system. It is also a trail for the experienced, considerate hiker who subscribes to a "leave no trace" ethic. The cairns stacked here may be decorative, but stacking rocks is illegal and ruins the view for other hikers.

▲ **A California condor.** These curious birds are attracted to human activity and are frequently spotted in Zion perched on or soaring above Angels Landing. Zion serves as a home base for this endangered species, and the park also acts as a refuge for other endangered and threatened wildlife species.

PARKS OF THE WEST

To many travelers the concept of the American West conjures certain images—parched deserts; distant horizons with abrupt, jutting peaks; towering buttes, and mesas; endless prairies; pristine streams and lakes; and dense, forbidding forests. Many of these visual expectations are certainly met for those who visit these national parks, but there is much more to take away than a series of pretty photos. The key purpose of most Western landscapes seems to be the need to awe, to inspire, to enthrall—larger-than-life mountains, roaring white-capped rivers, massive sculpted red monuments . . . and above them all the bluest, widest expanse of sky anyone has ever seen. No wonder they call this Big Sky Country.

Meanwhile, the coastal regions have a cachet all their own. California, with its mild, welcoming climate, surfing beaches, ocher mountains, and winding scenic drives, leaves visitors wondering why everyone hasn't relocated to this "golden" state. The Pacific Northwest—Oregon and Washington—combines rugged mountain terrain and rocky, picturesque shorelines with a charming, slightly offbeat culture.

The many parks of Alaska, last of the Wild Frontiers, await the adventurous souls who seek the serenity and solitude of true wilderness, while demanding the adrenaline rush of whitewater transit, challenging trails, and the most thrilling scenery nature has ever conjured.

◄ Lassen Volcanic National Park, California

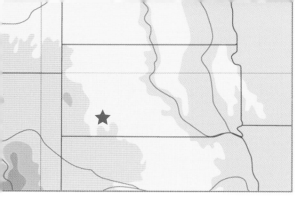

SOUTH DAKOTA
BADLANDS

In spite of resembling an alien landscape, with its eroded buttes and pinnacles and protruding fossils, the parkland is considered sacred ground by the Lakota people.

LOCATION Pennington County and Jackson County, SD

CLOSEST CITY Rapid City, SD

AREA 242,756 acres (982.40 km²)

ESTABLISHED January 29, 1939, as National Monument; November 10, 1978 as National Park

VISITORS 916,900+

ELEVATION 3,340 feet (1,020 m) at Red Shirt Table

GEOLOGY Volcanic and sedimentary rock

WHAT TO LOOK FOR

With its desolate landscaspe, this park may seem an intimidating place, but visitors here have much to appreciate.

> Badlands Loop Road and other scenic drives

> Sheep Mountain Table via dirt road

> Notch Trail, Medicine Root Trail, Fossil Exhibit Trail, and Cliff Shelf Nature Trail

> Yellow Mounds

> Conata Basin

▲ **Bighorn sheep** are common in Badlands.

This aptly named geologic phenomenon is located in western South Dakota, east of the Black Hills. When first beheld, these lands really do look "bad": forboding, forbidding, as if they would be difficult to navigate and almost impossible to cross.

Yet there is also beauty here, albeit stark and rugged, in the buttes, saw-toothed divides, gullies, and eroded mounds with their stratified colors of tan, pink, purple, gray, and gold. And even a short hike among the tortuous towers and ridges, which jut above a level green prairie, will quickly validate anyone's enthusiasm for this park.

HISTORY LESSONS

The park's unique, fossil-rich formations were created by wind- and weather-based erosion on the relatively soft volcanic and sedimentary rock. Even a strong rainstorm can alter the topography . . . providing a steady source of fresh fossils as outer rock is washed away. According to the park rangers, the many layers of the formations are like "pages of time," representing the passing of millions of years, from when the park formed the muddy bottom of a sea. Eons later, volcanic ash covered the area, burying many prehistoric animals that would later be dug up as treasured fossils—including saber-tooth tiger, camel, rhinoceros, and early horse.

The earliest inhabitants, Paleo-Indians, arrived 11,000 years ago to hunt and set up camps along streambanks. They were followed by the Arikira people, who are today incorporated with the Mandan and Hidatso in the Three Affiliated Tribes. One hundred and fifty years ago, the Great Sioux nation displaced other bands from the badlands. The Lakota still consider the region around Stronghold Table a sacred ceremonial site. Although the National Park Service manages the whole park, the South Unit is co-managed with the tribe.

Yet things between the Indians and the government were rarely that chummy. When the government set aside the 1868 treaty that exempted the Black Hills from white settlement—gold had been discovered there and prospectors were flooding in—the Indians were sent elsewhere. In protest, the displaced, starving Lakota performed the ghost dance there, summoning their dead and the souls of the vanished buffalo. Fearing it was fomenting rebellion, the government forbid the ritual. This led to the Wounded Knee Massacre, where more than 300 Indians were killed by the U.S. Army. The ghost

DID YOU KNOW?

Two Indian-themed movies, *Thunderheart* with Val Kilmer (1992) and *Dances with Wolves* with Kevin Costner (1990), were both partially filmed in Badlands.

"[THE BADLANDS] LOOK A BIT LIKE THE INSIDE OF A CAVE THAT HAS BEEN TURNED INSIDE OUT AND WARMED BY THE SUN."

— Stefanie Payne, *A Year in the National Parks*

▲ **American bison** still roam the prairieland of this national park.

Despite the harsh terrain, there is beauty in the eroded landscape of the Badlands. The erosion rate on the park's vulnerable sedimentary and volcanic rock is an astonishing one inch per year.

▲ **A ranch horse** grazes in the prairie grass. Visitors may bring their own mounts to journey along the park's trails.

dance was revived in the 1960s by the Red Power movement to restore Indian rights. In 1980, the U.S. Supreme Court awarded millions in damages to the Sioux for the broken treaty, but the tribe refused to accept the money, calling for the return of their land.

▲ **Door Trail** is an accessible quarter-mile boardwalk that leads park-goers through a break in the Badlands Wall known as "the Door" and to a magnificent view of the sun-bleached Badlands.

ACTIVITIES AND AMENITIES

There are two visitor centers that offer geological maps and other helpful information, as well as exhibits on the history of the Lakota and the many fossil sites throughout the park. Favorite activities include hiking, backpacking, camping, bicycling, birding, stargazing, and ranger talks. Visitors can bring in leashed pets and even transport their own horses to the trailheads. The scenic drives showcase different areas of the park; the popular Badlands Loop that gives an overview of the park, Sage Creek Road in the North Unit is known for wildlife viewing, and the South Unit offers amazing views.

WILDLIFE AND PLANT LIFE

The Badlands Wilderness area protects more than 64,000 acres; it is also home to the black-footed ferret, one of the most endangered animals in America. Considered extinct in the wild, captive-raised ferrets were reintroduced here starting in 1996 and continue to reproduce.

The grassy prairie that surrounds the rock formations supports bison, mule deer, bighorn sheep, pronghorn, coyote, swift fox, prairie dog, and at least nine species of bats. More than 200 bird species—both eastern and western migrants—have been reported here. There are raptors like the golden eagle, numerous songbirds like the meadowlark,

and unusual species like the black-billed magpie. Flat, moist areas called slumps offer birds the cover of junipers and shrubs and provide many great sightings. There are also nine species of reptiles—including bull snakes, rattlesnakes, and painted turtles, and six types of amphibians, including large tiger salamanders.

The mixed-grass prairie—a transition between eastern tall-grass prairie and western short-grass prairie—supports a wider range of plants than other prairies. There are more than 400 species of grasses, trees, shrubs, flowers, and succulents found here, including western wheatgrass, blue grama, buffalo grass, cordgrass, big bluestem, sunflower, milkweed, purple coneflower, sego lily, starvation cactus, yucca, woolly verbena, globe mallow, juniper, and cottonwood.

▶ **A prairie dog** peeks out of its Badlands burrow.

Tall summer grasses add color to the arid Badlands landscape, contrasting with the rugged terrain marked by dramatic rock formations, tall peaks, deep canyons, and steep cliffs.

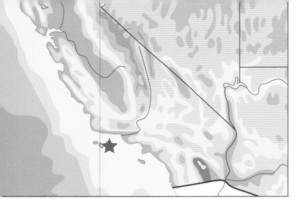

CALIFORNIA
CHANNEL ISLANDS

Sea and sand combine with rugged cliffs—and a history going back 37,000 years—in these island gems off the California coast.

LOCATION Santa Barbara County and Venture County, CA

CLOSEST CITY Santa Barbara, CA

AREA 249,561 acres (1,009.94 km²)

ESTABLISHED March 5, 1980

VISITORS 366,200+

ELEVATION 2,450 feet (750 m) at Devils Peak on Santa Cruz

GEOLOGY Sedimentary rock reworked from mainland sediment, volcanic deposits, and shells and skeletons of marine organisms

WHAT TO LOOK FOR

Each island has something to offter, but some highlights are worth noting.

> Scorpion Anchorage on Santa Cruz

> Seal and sea lion rookeries on San Miguel

> Caliche Forest on San Miguel

> Boat tours of the marine sanctuary and sea caves

DID YOU KNOW?

The Channel Islands are also an international biosphere preserve and a national marine sanctuary—meaning the underwater habitats that extend for a mile around each island are protected.

Like a lost world from a Stephen Spielberg adventure movie, these five islands capture the rugged landscapes, untamed wilderness, and oceanic character of a version of California long since vanished on the mainland. Marine mammals large and small and other forms of sea life teem in these churning waters. This is not a beach blanket vacation spot, but rather a more primitive venue . . . one that stirs the visitor's spirits and ignites their imagination.

An hour from the freeways of Southern California, the Channels offer exploration and education along with recreation. Altogether there are eight Channel Islands, but only five make up the park. Each island is distinct in topography and character.

Anacapa, a jutting volcanic island, is known for the fantasical Arch Rock standing offshore and a historic lighthouse.

Santa Cruz, the largest island of the park's islands, is full of natural diversity and split by a vast fault line.

Santa Rosa, with a landscape that transitions from mountains to marshland, is known for its rare Torrey pines, scenic canyons, and the remains of former ranches.

San Miguel, farthest out in the Pacific, is a windy wilderness, where seals and sea

Seabirds nest on Arch Rock. The constant pounding of waves has eroded the volcanic island of Anacapa, creating towering sea cliffs, sea caves, and natural bridges, such as this 40-foot-high arch, which has become a symbol of Channel Islands National Park.

lions breed in great numbers in beachside rookeries, and rolling dunes lead to the eerie Caliche Forest, the upright, fossilized remains of ancient trees.

Diminutive Santa Barbara, lying to the south of her siblings, is a mesa bookended by two peaks, with cliffs that drop straight down to the sea and beaches where seabirds nest.

ANCIENT ORIGINS

Based on radiocarbon dating of a fire area on Santa Rosa Island, the first human habitation is believed to go back 37,000 years. A burned mammoth bone dates from 30,000 years ago. Around 11,000 BCE, the Chumash people began settling coastal southern California and the Channels. The Chumash had evolved a relatively developed society, traveling the waters between the islands and the mainland in plank canoes, trading with each other, and devising a system of currency using shell beads. Their culture lasted thousands of years.

After the Spanish arrived in 1542, led by Juan Rodriguez Cabrillo—who died on San Miguel—many Chumash were struck down

► **A sea lion** on San Miguel Island peeks its head over a rock. Visitors here have the chance to view a wide variety of marine mammals.

by measles and smallpox, diseases for which they had no defenses. By the early 1800s the remaining Chumash had been forced to give up their culture and live in Christian missions on the mainland. (Today, they no longer speak their own language since Ineseño, the last speaker, died in 1965.) Meanwhile, fisherman, otter hunters, and sheep and cattle ranchers began frequenting the Channels. In 1938, Santa Barbara and Anacapa became national monuments, and in 1980, all five Channel Islands were combined to form the current national park.

ACTIVITIES AND AMENITIES

The main visitor center is located in Ventura Harbor on the California coast and offers exhibits on the five islands, plus a free film about their history. Smaller visitor centers are found on Santa Barbara, Anacapa, and at Scorpion Ranch on Santa Cruz. Scorpion Anchorage is the park's most visited area for day-trippers and campers. Park activities include hiking, backpacking, camping, kayaking (especially through the many sea caves), birding, whale and dolphin watching, swimming, snorkeling, scuba diving, and spearfishing. Autumn is the ideal time for visiting, as well as diving—offering sunny days with little wind and clear water. There is a ferry service from the mainland, with availability based on ocean conditions.

WILDLIFE AND PLANT LIFE

In spite of the islands' rocky terrain, more than 2,000 species of plants and animals are found here. The three mammals native to the island are the deer mouse, spotted skunk, and Channel Islands fox, which is also endemic, along with the island scrub jay and the island fence lizard. Other animals found here include Townsend's big-eared bat, island night lizard, island gopher snake, western pond turtle, barn owl, horned lark, meadowlark, American kestrel, and California brown pelican. Marine animals range from the massive blue whale to tiny sea creatures like krill and zooplankton. Visitors often spot pods of common, Risso's, and bottlenose dolphin, as well as humpback and fin whale, orca, and many species of seal and sea lion.

There are roughly 570 native plants on the island; solely endemic plants include

the Torrey Pine and island paintbrush. The vegetative communities here are classified as coastal dune, coastal bluff, coastal sage scrub, grasslands, chaparral, island oak woodlands, mixed hardwood woodlands, pine stands, and riparian areas. The most widespread communities are grasslands and coastal sage scrub.

► **Anacapa Island Lighthouse** stands on the highest point of East Anacapa Island. Anacapa is actually a chain of three small islands—East, Middle, and West—linked together by reefs that are visible only at low tide.

▼ **Potato Harbor, Santa Cruz Island.** Often called the park's prettiest harbor, visitors can get a great view of it from the Potato Harbor Trail that winds above the soaring cliffs.

◄ **The eerie Caliche Forest** on San Miguel is an ancient stand of fossilized vegetation composed of roots and trunks of plants, possibly including pines and cypresses.

▼ **A rare, wild island fox** searching for food on Santa Rosa Island. The island fox is found only on these islands and nowhere else in the world.

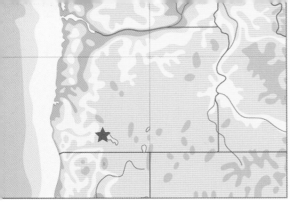

OREGON
CRATER LAKE

This rain-fed remnant of a massive volcanic eruption was once a sacred spot to Native Americans and now creates a dazzling vista for visitors.

LOCATION Klamath County, OR

CLOSEST CITY Klamath Falls, OR

AREA 183,224 acres (741.48 km²)

ESTABLISHED May 22, 1902

VISITORS 720,600+

ELEVATION 8,929 feet (2,722 m) at Mount Scott

GEOLOGY Volcanic and sedimentary rock

WHAT TO LOOK FOR

The pristine lake forms the centerpiece of this park, but a visit to this park offers a variety of views and activities.

> Rim Drive

> Garfield Peak, Watchman, and Cleetwood Cove trails

> Pinnacles

> Castle Crest Wildflower Garden

▲ **A Sierra red fox** gazes warily at the photographer as it makes its way through the park's snowy evergreen forest. This slender, bushy-tailed fox is one of the rarest mammals in the United States, and with its population threatened since the 1970s, it is now listed as an endangered species.

Chances are most Americans have seen pictures of Crater Lake. The deep blue lake—surrounded by wilderness and with a small volcanic island rising from its depths—has long been a favored subject for photographers and painters. Located in south-central Oregon, Crater Lake National Park is part of the Cascade Mountain Range that extends from British Columbia to northern California. The park's centerpiece is a stunning blue lake that formed in the caldera (basin) when Mount Mazama, a 12,000-foot stratovolcano, erupted, and then collapsed approximately 7,700 years ago.

It is the deepest lake in the United States at 1,943 feet, but its waters are not spring- or stream-fed; they come directly from snow or rain. Because no silt or mineral deposits are carried to the lake, it is one of the cleanest and clearest in the country. Two million gallons of water seep out of the lake every day, yet scientists have no idea where all that water goes. There are designated swim areas, but the water is typically quite cold.

THE LOST SYMBOL

Mount Mazama was a sacred symbol to the Makalak (now Klamath) people living in its vicinity when the massive eruption occurred more than seven millennia ago. Their legends say this was a fierce battle between the sky spirit and mountain spirit. When the battle ended—and the volcano collapsed—the people mourned the loss of their symbol. After the lake formed they named it Giiwas, and the region around it again became a revered place to pray, mourn, hunt, forage, and seek enlightenment. The first non-Native American to view Crater Lake was John Hillman, a young man who in 1853 financed a group of prospectors looking for the legendary "Lost Cabin" gold mine. In 1862 an article was published about the lake by another prospector, Chauncey Nye, but

visitors remained scarce. In 1870, Kansan William Gladstone Steel became intrigued after reading about the lake in the newspaper wrapping his lunch. After finally arriving at its shores in 1885, he was so affected by its beauty he began a 17-year crusade to have Crater Lake designated a national park.

PARK ACTIVITIES

Visitors enjoy hiking, cycling, swimming, stargazing, and birding. For anglers, the lake is home to Kokamee salmon and rainbow trout. The popular 33-mile Rim Drive circles the caldera and offers more than 30 scenic pullouts. The 30-plus trails are geared for hikers of every level. A portion of the Pacific Crest Trail, stretching from Mexico to Canada, runs through the park. Steel Visitor Center is ranger headquarters and open year-round. Rim Visitor Center, with its prominent views of the lake, is only open in summer. Notable park landmarks include the Pumice Desert, the Pinnacles, Mount Scott, Union Peak, and Crater Peak. Wizard Island, which rises more than 750 feet and is the remains of a volcanic cinder cone, is the largest island in the lake. In summer, visitors can take a boat to explore the island and climb to the summit. Phantom Ship Island is made of 400,000-year-old, erosion-resistant lava, the oldest rock found in the caldera. Crater Lake is one of the snowiest placed in America with an annual average snowfall of 43 feet. That doesn't stop the park from offering winter sports; visitors can enjoy snowshoeing with a park ranger, cross-country skiing, sledding, and snowmobiling.

Wizard Island in the west end of Crater Lake is a volcanic cinder cone that formed after the violent eruption 7,700 years ago of Mount Mazama, a large complex volcano. The lake itself partly fills the deep caldera created by the collapse of the volcano.

DID YOU KNOW?

The summer fire season at Crater Lake can scorch thousands of acres, but this natural occurrence has positive impacts on the ecosystem. Many plants have adapted to survive the fires and thrive afterward due to restored nutrients in the soil.

▲ **A golden-mantled ground squirrel** stops to munch on an offering of sunflower seeds on a hill overlooking the lake.

▼ **Crater Lake Lodge,** perched on a mountainside overlooking the lake, offers welcome warmth during the cold of winter.

▲ **A narrow passage** leads through the verdant evergreen forest that surrounds the lake.

◀ **Rocking chairs** sit ready at Crater Lake Lodge for visitors to enjoy the stunning lake views from the terrace.

"TO SAY THAT THIS WONDERFUL LAKE IS GRAND, BEYOND DESCRIPTION, IS TO GIVE AN IDEA OF ITS MAGNIFICENCE. EVERYONE GAZES AT IT IN ALMOST TEARFUL ASTONISHMENT."

— *Captain Franklin B. Sprague, U.S. Army, Fort Klamath, 1865*

WILDLIFE AND PLANT LIFE

The lake is surrounded by dense forests that abound with wildlife. Mammals residing in this rich habitat include Canadian lynx, bobcat, black bear, coyote, beaver, pronghorn, elk, deer, muskrat, fox, chipmunk, snowshoe hare, porcupine, marten, pika, and badger. Birds found in the park include ravens, Canada jays, bald eagles, American dippers, peregrine falcons, spotted owls, Clark's nutcrackers, Canada geese, and hummingbirds. Reptiles are represented by the alligator lizard, sagebrush lizard, short-horned lizard, western skink, garter snake, pine snake, racer, and Western pond turtle. Amphibious species include four frogs, one toad, and six species of salamanders. The Mazama newt is endemic to the park but threatened by non-native crayfish.

The park is home to some notable old-growth forest ecosystems; it is divided into four forest zones, each named for its predominant tree species— ponderosa pine forest, lodgepole pine forest, mountain hemlocks zone, and whitebark pines zone. As with most mountainous areas, species vary based on elevation and amount of precipitation. And although there are many shrubs, grasses, and sedges found here, wildflowers, which grow in a range of habitats, are the most diverse group of plants at Crater Lake.

▶ **Crater Lake** is a pristine blue viewed from an overlook along the Cleetwood Cove Trail. This is a short but steep switchback route that leads down to the lake's chilly waters.

CALIFORNIA AND NEVADA
DEATH VALLEY

Death Valley is replete with scenic wonders, historic sites, and abundant plant and animal life.

LOCATION Mono County, CA, Nye, Mineral, and Esmeralda counties, NV

CLOSEST CITY Lone Pine, CA; Beatty, NV

AREA 3,373,063 acres (13,650.30 km²)

ESTABLISHED February 11, 1933, as National Monument; October 31, 1994, as National Park

VISITORS 1,678,600+

ELEVATION 11,049 feet (3,368 m) at Telescope Peak

GEOLOGY Graben (depressed crust) with ancient metamorphic, volcanic, and sedimentary rock

WHAT TO LOOK FOR

Perhaps best known as the place with the lowest altitude in North America, this seemingly desolate region has much to offer visitors.

> Titus Canyon's ghost town, petroglyphs, and rare plants

> Badwater Basin salt flats for night viewing

> Trails to Telescope Peak, Zabriskie Point, Golden Canyon, and Mosaic Canyon

> Darwin Falls oasis

Death Valley, which straddles eastern California and western Nevada, is the largest national park in the lower 48 states, as well as the lowest (at 282 feet below sea level), hottest, and driest overall. Yet it boasts mountains that exceed 11,000 feet, complete with snowy summits. There are also earthen-hued badlands formations, miles of sand dunes, mining craggy canyons. The site is located within the Mojave Desert and borders the Great Basin Desert. Within its boundaries lie more than three million acres of designated wilderness.

HISTORY OF THE REGION

Despite the valley's inhospitable climate, it was a camping stop for Paleo-Indians some 9,000 years ago and settled by the Timbisha Shoshone Tribe around 1000 CE. The region got its name in 1849, when prospectors seeking a shortcut to the California goldfields took a nonexistent southern route through this extremely hot and dry region. After months of hardship, half the group made it back to civilization. Those remaining sent two men to walk 300 miles and return with horses, but while they waited, one of them died. When that second group finally departed, one man looked back and called out, "Goodbye, Death Valley." The name stuck. Gold and silver boom towns arose in the late 1800s, but mining borax ore, hauled out by famous 20-mule teams, was the only profitable industry. Tourism increased in the 1920s, after resorts were built at Stovepipe Wells and Furnace Creek, and before long Death Valley became the subject of books, movies, radio programs, and even a TV series.

PARK ACTIVITIES

Activities include hiking, cycling, stargazing, backcountry driving, and ranger-guided tours. The park offers a variety of camping options, from primitive to full hook-up. Pets are welcome, if park rules are followed. The main visitor center is at the oasis-like Furnace Creek, with many park attractions nearby, and another is at Scotty's Castle.

WILDLIFE AND PLANT LIFE

The park supports 400 animal species. Mammals include coyote, bobcat, desert bighorn sheep, nine bat species, gophers, kangaroo rat, cottontail, kit fox, badger, ringtail, and an occasional mountain lion.

◄ **Teakettle Junction,** where the dirt road from Ubehebe Crater meets roads to Racetrack Playa and Hunter Mountain, is marked with a sign upon which it has become a tradition for visitors to attach teakettles with messages written on them.

DID YOU KNOW?

Parts of the original *Star Wars* were filmed in Death Valley, and visitors can take self-guided tours of these famed spots.

There are desert tarantula here, one of 50 species found in the Southwest. Another nearby resident is the tiny, protected Devil's Hole pupfish, which lives in a 90-degree spring in a limestone cave. Birders might sight roadrunner, pied-bill grebe, cinnamon teal, American coot, prairie falcon, American kestrel, and Gambel's quail, as well as songbirds, owls, woodpeckers, ravens, and waders.

More than 1,000 species of plants manage to sustain themselves in Death Valley. Not even cacti grow in the valley's blazing hot low areas, but in the hills there are barrel cactus, cholla, beavertail, and cottontop. The olive-green creosote bush, the most drought-tolerant plant in North America, also is found here.

▶ **An old steam tractor** on display at Furnace Creek. Furnace Creek was formerly the center of Death Valley mining, with plants like the Harmony Borax Works beginning to process ore in the 1880s.

"THE DESERT DOESN'T CARE WHO YOU ARE, AND NEITHER DOES ANYONE OR ANYTHING WHO LIVES IN IT."

— *Author Deanne Stillman*

Hikers stand in awe of the stunning landscape at Zabriskie Point. At the edge of California's Black Mountains, it is one of the park's most popular areas and allows visitors to take in vistas of the undulating terra cotta–colored landscape of gullies and mud hills.

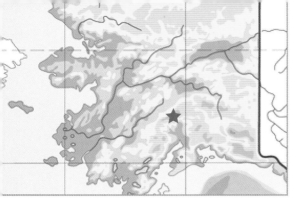

ALASKA
DENALI

Who can resist the lure of Denali—a sprawling national park where the Northern Lights dance in neon waves over the tallest mountain on the continent?

LOCATION Denali and Matanuska-Susitna boroughs, AK

CLOSEST CITY Healy, AK

AREA 4,740,911 acres (19,185.79 km²); preserve, 1,304,242 acres (5,278.08 km²)

ESTABLISHED February 26, 1917

VISITORS 594,600+

ELEVATION 20,310 feet (6,190 m) at Denali Peak

GEOLOGY Metamorphic and igneous rock surrounded by ancient sedimentary rock

WHAT TO LOOK FOR

Set off on an adventure that that allows you to explore the Alaskan frontier..

> Park Road scenic drive

> Polychrome Overlook

> Triple Lakes Trail

> Savage River area
  by car or bus

> Sled dog kennels

Once called Mount McKinley, but known as Denali to the native Alaskans, this loftiest North American mountain is the showpiece of the national park and preserve that bears its name. This park is famed for its ability to deliver a true wilderness experience, and in aid of this, there is only one road entering and leaving the park. Also, many areas are accessible only on foot or by air.

Located in the center of the Alaska Range, the park's acreage is greater than that of New Hampshire. More than two million of those acres are designated as a protected wilderness area. There are more than 400 glaciers in the park, the longest being Kahiltna. To the north lies the valleys of the McKinley, Toklat, and Foraker Rivers and the Kantishna and Wyoming Hills.

EARLY HISTORY

Hundreds of millions of years ago Alaska began to form when the precursor to the Pacific tectonic plate moved slowly north, carrying fragments of the Earth's crust. These fragments fastened onto the edge of the North American plate as the Pacific plate was thrust under it. It was from these amalgamated crustal pieces from the Pacific and other plates, known as accreted terranes, that Alaska was born. As the Pacific plate continued to be subducted under these terranes, enormous forces wrinkled and buckled them, eventually creating the Alaska Range.

Human hunting encampments in the region go back more than 11,000 years. Within the park are 84 archeological sites, relatively few due to the high elevation and harsh winters there. The oldest site, at Teklanika River, dates to roughly 7130 BCE. The Athabaskan settlements are from 1,500 to 1,000 years ago, although some researchers believe they were here thousands of years earlier. In the past 500 years, the principle groups in the region have been the Koyukon, Tanana, and Dena'ina people.

◄ **A bull moose** with velvet still on its new antlers munches on fireweed in Denali National Park.

"THIS PLACE, THE LAND IS MORE ANCIENT AND PURE; IT'S LIKE A CONCENTRATED TONIC FOR THE SOUL. IF YOU TAKE TOO MUCH IT CAN INFECT YOU, AND IF YOU DON'T TAKE ENOUGH YOU HAVE MISSED IT COMPLETELY, AND YOUR EFFORTS WERE IN VAIN."

— Danielle Rohr, *Denali Skies*

▲ **An Alaskan brown bear** finds a rocky perch in the middle of a river.

A view over Horseshoe Lake.
The untamed Denali landscape, featuring high hills and deep river valleys, forms a rich tapestry of smoky blues and lush greens.

The snow-covered peaks of Denali pierce through the cloud cover over the Alaska Range. At a staggering 20,310 feet above sea level, this mountain, also known as Mount McKinley, is North America's highest and the third-most prominent and third-most isolated peak in the world, after Mount Everest in the Himalayas and Aconcagua in the Andes.

UNITED STATES OF AMERICA

DENALI
20,310 ft

ALASKA

DID YOU KNOW?

There is a reason Denali appears
to rise to breathless heights.
The mountain's vertical relief
(distance from base to peak)
of 18,000 feet is the highest of
any peak in the world.

◄ **A prop plane** lands at the foot of Denali. Access to parklands is limited, and visitors must rely on air transportation to reach some the more remote areas.

▼ **Denali's Princess Wilderness Lodge,** a very popular tourist attraction, offers for sale charming sculptures of grizzly bears.

Denali was the first national park created to protect wildlife, specifically the Dall sheep. The bill was passed in 1917 after active lobbying by conservationists. The boundaries were expanded in 1922, 1932, and 1947, when the hotel and railroad were included. The park was designated an international biosphere reserve in 1976, and the surrounding region became Denali National Monument as proclaimed by President Carter in 1978.

Even before the creation of the park, however, there was local resentment over the naming of the mountain, which had been intended to honor newly elected President William McKinley. The native Koyukon called the peak Denali, or "Tall One." When the Denali National Monument was combined with Mount McKinley National Park in 1980, Alaska named the combined unit Denali National Park and Preserve. But it was not until 2015 that President Barack Obama gave federal recognition to the more traditional name.

PARK ACTIVITIES

Denali offers plenty of hiking trails, plus scenic drives and overlooks. Many visitors enjoy the popular bus tours. Recreational opportunities include cycling, birding, boating, swimming, rafting, and fishing. Winter activities include cross-country skiing, snowmobiling, and dog sledding, which is also how the rangers patrol in deep snow. The Denali Visitor Center and park headquarters are located just inside the entrance. Next door is the Morino Grill, the only sit-down restaurant in the park. Eielson Visitor Center, four hours into the park, offers daily ranger-led programs in summer and views of Denali. There are four camping areas in the interior: Sanctuary River, Teklanika River, Igloo Creek, and Wonder Lake, as well as a few privately owned lodges. Nearby Healy also has many accommodations and amenities.

WILDLIFE AND PLANT LIFE

The "big five" mammals that visitors hope to glimpse here are wolf, grizzly bear (brown bear), moose, caribou, and Dall sheep—Dall and bighorn are the only two species of North American wild sheep. Other park residents include black bear, coyote, hoary marmot, pika, snowshoe hare, and beaver, along with the more elusive red and Arctic fox, marten, Canadian lynx, and wolverine. Birders should keep an eye out for "bucket list" sightings, such as golden eagle, gyrfalcon, ptarmigan, and tundra swan, as well as many migratory visitors that spend spring and summer here. The park's sole amphibian, the wood frog, is found in the lakes along with trout, salmon, and Arctic grayling.

▲ **Northern lights** appear in cloudless, starry night sky over one of Denali's lodges.

▲ **An Alaskan huskie** enjoys a snooze at the sled dog kennel. This kennel is one of the most friendly places in the park, giving visitors a chance to meet some of the 30 dogs who live and work in Denali.

◀ **Dall sheep** relax on the one of the park's shrubby slopes.

At the lowest elevations, the landscape is a mix of forest, deciduous taiga—boreal forest with pine, spruce, and larch; tundra—treeless uplands—at middle elevations; and glaciers, snow, and bare rock at the highest elevations. There are more than 1,500 plant species represented here.

Numerous wildflowers in shades of purple, lavender, white, and yellow carpet the mountain meadows, while only a handful of trees can survive the frigid subarctic climate. More diversity is found, however, in shrubs, grasses, and sedges, ferns, mosses, liverworts, and lichens.

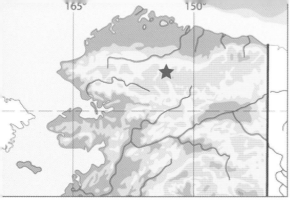

ALASKA
GATES OF THE ARCTIC

The ultimate destination for wilderness lovers, this vast park is located entirely above the Arctic Circle.

LOCATION Yukon-Koyukuk Census Area, AK

CLOSEST CITY Bettles, AK

AREA 8,472,506 acres (34,287.02 km²)

ESTABLISHED December 1, 1978, as National Monument; December 2, 1980, as National Park and Preserve

VISITORS 2,870+

ELEVATION 8,276 feet (2,523 m) at Mount Igikpak

GEOLOGY Igneous rock—granite and schist; marine sedimentary rock

WHAT TO LOOK FOR

For those up to a wilderness challenge, this park offers unapparelled adventure.

> The "Gates" of the Arctic—Mount Boreal and Frigid Crags

> Six Wild and Scenic Rivers: John, Alatna, Kobuk, North Fork of the Koyukuk, Noatak, and Tinaguk

> Ancient seabed formations

▲ **Hikers make their way** through the challenging terrain of the Itkillik River drainage, in a place known as Thunder Valley, a remote part of the Brooks Range surrounded by pinnacles of twisted sedimentary rock.

Gates of the Arctic National Park and Preserve straddles the Arctic Divide in America's northernmost mountain chain, the Brooks Range. The second-largest national park after Wrangell-St. Elias, it lies entirely north of the Arctic Circle.

The park is not near any main roads, and its interior is a labyrinth of glaciated valleys and craggy mountains ringed with boreal forest or treeless slopes of Arctic tundra north of the divide. Imagine a park the size of Switzerland that offers no facilities, visitor centers, or campgrounds, where visitors must hike in—and out. This is probably as wild as it gets within the National Park Service.

PARK HISTORY

Nomadic peoples have inhabited the Brooks Range for as long as 12,500 years, hunting caribou and other wildlife. The earliest Inupiat people appeared about 1200 CE and spread to the Brooks Range from the coast, becoming the Nunamiut. Today, the park region is home to 10 Alaska Native villages, but all have fewer than 400 residents.
  The park gained its name in 1929, when conservationist Robert Marshall discovered an unobstructed path north to the Arctic coast of Alaska while on the North Fork of the Koyukuk River. Upon seeing Mount Boreal and Frigid Crags flanking the river, Marshall named the portal the "Gates of the Arctic." The area was first protected as a U.S. National Monument in 1978.

PARK ACTIVITIES

A lack of amenities does not signal a lack of opportunities to explore or engage with the environment. Experienced backcountry travelers arrive for float trips, backpacking treks, and to set up base camps for day hiking and fishing. A few outfitters also offer guided rafting or hiking trips or dog mushing and cross-country skiing in winter. Floatable rivers include the John, the North Fork of the Koyukuk, the Tinayguk, the Alatna, and the Middle Fork of the Koyukuk River. Rafters and canoers enjoy the challenging headwaters of the Noatak and Kobuk Rivers. Whatever a visitor's goal, any activities here require careful planning and advance reservations. Most visitors fly into gateway communities like Bettles, Anaktuvuk Pass, and Coldfoot. Although the park lacks a visitor center, the Arctic Interagency Visitor Center in Coldfoot provides information. The Anaktuvuk Pass Ranger Station is seasonal, but the Bettles Ranger Station and Visitor Center is open all year.

DID YOU KNOW?

The only road that runs near Gates of the Arctic is Dalton Highway, which was made famous by the knuckle-biting TV series *Ice Road Truckers.*

A silty stream flows through the summertime landscape of this least-visited national park.

WILDLIFE AND PLANT LIFE

The park supports brown bear, wolf, lynx, Dall sheep, muskox, moose, wolverine, and wood frog. Bird sightings include arctic tern, bald eagle, golden eagle, peregrine falcon, osprey, great horned owl, and northern hawk owl. Anglers can fish for grayling and Arctic char in pristine streams and for lake trout in deeper lakes. Many hiking trails were made by half a million Western Arctic caribou, the largest herd in Alaska.

The park's boreal forest is characterized by black and white spruce mixed with poplar. Northward, the spine of the Brooks Range has been described as "Arctic desert."

▶ **An aerial view** of some of the lands of Gates of the Arctic can only hint at the size of this vast park.

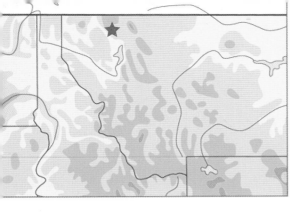

MONTANA
GLACIER

This hikers' heaven checks all the scenic boxes: wilderness trails, woodlands, lakes, waterfalls, rugged Rockies, and ice age glaciers.

LOCATION Flathead County and Glacier County, MT

CLOSEST CITY Columbia Falls, MT

AREA 1,013,322 acres (4,100.77 km²)

ESTABLISHED May 11, 1910

VISITORS 3,000,000+

ELEVATION 10,466 feet (3,190 m) at Mount Cleveland

GEOLOGY Late Precambrian fine-grained sedimentary rock

WHAT TO LOOK FOR

Hiking this park gives visitors endless opportunities to take in nature at its best.

> Going to-the-Sun Road—only open in summer

> Grinnell Glacier Trail

> Wild Goose Island View for photo ops

> St. Mary Falls, one of the park's 200 waterfalls

For visitors seeking a true wilderness experience in a challenging mountain setting, Glacier may be the best bet in the "lower 48." Located along Montana's border with Canada and home to the Lewiston and Lewis and Clark ranges, the park is named for the many glaciers that were once found here, which now number 26. Not only a UNESCO World Heritage Site, the park is also part of Waterton-Glacier International Peace Park, which was designated a United Nations Biosphere Reserve and is the first International Dark Sky transboundary park.

HISTORY AND MAJESTY

These mountains have stirred humans with their rugged beauty for many thousands of years. The earliest inhabitants were Native North Americans who arrived some 10,000 years ago. The forebears of current tribes included the Flathead, Kootenai, Shoshone and Cheyenne. The Blackfeet lived on the plains, as well as on the eastern slopes of the parkland and considered the mountains to be the "backbone of the world." Their reservation borders the eastern park today, while the Flathead Reservation is located to the south and west.

The famed Lewis and Clark expedition came close to what is now parklands while exploring the Marias River in 1806. In 1885 anthropologist George Bird Grinnell was guided through the area by explorer James Willard Schultz and was so impressed, he spent 20 years trying to establish the national park. In 1891, the Great Northern Railway crossed the Continental Divide just south of the parkland and helped popularize the region for nature lovers. The railroad also lobbied for protection for the glorious glacier vistas. It was they who constructed many Swiss-style hotels and chalets in the park to encourage tourism.

EXPLORE THE PARKLAND

Glacier is known for its extensive trails, more than 700 miles of them, including a section of the Continental Divide Trail that runs from Mexico to Canada. Sometimes called the "hiker's national park," Glacier offers options for hikers of all levels, as well as boardwalks for those who need wheelchair access.

There are five trail map areas—Lake McDonald includes the main entrance and shady, lower-altitude trails; the Many Glacier area in the northeast offers flat or strenuous trails with great views; North Fork, in the northwest, has numerous finger lakes accessed on rough gravel roads; Goat Haunt can only be reached via trail or through Canada; St. Mary runs along the Sun Road and features waterfalls and trails to high mountain passes; and Two Medicine in the southeast was a railhead and popular destination when the park opened, yet it is now the least crowded area.

◄ **Children have fun** balancing on a fallen tree in Avalanche Lake during a summertime park visit.

The brilliant blooms of wildflowers cover the slopes above Bullhead Lake. Rising above the lake is Mount Grinnell, located in the heart of the park, which is named after George Bird Grinnell, who tirelessly pushed to make the region a national park.

DID YOU KNOW?

Glacier is often called the "Crown of the Continent," a fitting name bestowed by early advocate George Bird Grinnell.

Guided horseback tours and glacier boat tours are also available. Other activities include swimming, biking, boating, fishing, and backpacking. At night there is stargazing, evening ranger talks, and entertainment at some hotels. Accommodations range from historic grand hotels to classic motor lodges to cabins to warm weather campsites. Handy park shuttles are free to hikers on certain trails and the quaint red buses travel between points in the park and to the train station.

There were once 150 glaciers in the park, but due to the effects of climate change, that number is now reduced to a mere 25. Due to their desire to view the dwindling glaciers, tourists began arriving in record numbers, causing crowding on the park roads, in the parking areas, and even on the trails.

WILDLIFE AND PLANT LIFE

This large, preserved ecosystem is primarily untouched wilderness. This means nearly all the flora and fauna European explorers found here are still present in the modern park. The lush, secluded forestland supports mountain goat—the park's symbol, black bear, grizzly bear, cougar, coyote, bobcat, Canadian lynx, bighorn sheep, mule deer, moose, and wolverine. Because some of the larger animals may pose a threat to humans, visitors should read all safety postings throughout the park. Even small mammals can be risky if people try to hand feed them. Birdlife includes many species of woodpecker

A Mountain goat takes advantage of one of the park's boardwalks to peer over its railing to Hidden Lake. The mountain goat is the official symbol of Glacier National Park.

◄ **Tiny Wild Goose Island,** dwarfed by the surrounding mountains, sits in the upper end of St. Mary Lake. Located on the east side of the park, Going-to-the-Sun Road parallels the lake along its north shore. The opening scene in the 1980 Stanley Kubrick film *The Shining* was shot at St. Mary Lake.

and owl, sandhill crane, swift, grouse, hummingbird, waders, shorebirds, ducks, cormorant, gyrfalcon, and bald eagle. Supporting more than 1,100 species of plants, the park terrain alters with increased altitude from grassland to aspen parkland, montane forest, subalpine, and finally alpine tundra. Visitors may discover a range of trees, shrubs, grasses, wildflowers, and fungi, including hair grass, rye grass, maidenhair fern, sword fern, fairy slippers, Oregon bitterroot, great horsetail, trillium, bog orchid, great sundew, Indian pipe, redcedar, ponderosa pine, Douglas fir, and paper birch.

► **The Triple Falls** in the Hanging Garden below Reynolds Creek are reached from the Hanging Garden Trail. The trail name comes from the alpine meadows that surrounds this picturesque route.

▼ **The historic Many Glacier Lodge,** built in 1914, draws visitors to its secluded, idyliic setting on the shoreline of Swiftcurrent Lake nestled at the base of Mount Grinnell inside Glacier National Park.

MORE TO EXPLORE
NATIONAL PRESERVES

National preserves are similar to national parks in that they protect areas with resources, but within them certain natural resource-extractive activities may be allowed. These activities can include hunting, grazing, logging, and mining. The stipulation is that the natural values of the resources must be preserved. Each preserve permits varying activities based on the enabling legislation determined for each site.

There are 21 national preserves located in 11 states that comprise more than 24,651,566 acres. Alaska, home to 10 preserves, including Noatak, the largest, makes up 86 percent of that vast acreage. All permit hunting, except for Tallgrass Prairie in Kansas. The preserves are overseen by the Park Service as part of the National Park System, but they differ from national parks in that management can be delegated to their home state.

The first preserves were Big Thicket in Texas and Big Cypress in Florida, both established in 1974. Big Thicket was at risk from logging interests, while the latter was on the verge of becoming an airport—plans got as far as one runway being laid. Congressional deliberation resulted in a new designation: a national preserve that bought out private landowners to conserve "the natural, scenic, hydrologic, floral and faunal, and recreational values" of these units.

▲ *Big Cypress National Preserve is dominated by wet cypress forest, such as the trees growing in the Sweetwater Slough on Loop Road.*

▲ *A hiker pauses to watch the sunset over the eerie landscape of Crater of the Moon. Local legend attributes the name to its resemblance to the lunar surface. This resemblance prompted the Apollo 14 crew to visit in 1969 to study the volcanic geology and to explore the harsh environment.*

▲ *Cinder cones stand along the North Crater Flow Trail in Craters of the Moon National Monument.*

◀ Craters of the Moon National Monument and Preserve

Location Central Idaho
Established 2002
Area 410,733 acres (1,662.2 km²)

This unique preserve includes most of the lava fields in Idaho's Great Rift, which erupted 15,000 to 20,000 years ago. The volcanic features include lava tubes and fissures, cinder cones, and spatter cones. The ancient basaltic flows are now home to wildflowers, shrubs, limber pines, and Rocky Mountain junipers.

◄ Big Cypress National Preserve

Location South Florida

Established 1974

Area 720,564 acres (2,916.0 km²)

One of the first two national preserves, Big Cypress adjoins Everglades National Park in southern Florida. It supports mangroves and cypress trees, alligators and Florida panthers. Activities include hiking, cycling, canoeing, kayaking, airboating, and swamp buggies.

▲ *An American alligator swims through the waters of Big Cyprus.*

◄ *Opened in 1924 to serve as a train station, Kelso Depot was renovated and reopened in 2005 as the visitor center for Mojave National Preserve.*

▶ *Banshee Canyon in Mojave National Preserve is a short slot canyon formed from the erosion of volcanic tuffs.*

▼ *The Mojave's Kelso Dunes is the preserve's top hiking destination. This sand dune field is famous as one of the only ones in the world that "booms." Millions of cascading sand particles blowing when the wind is just right produce the deep rumbling sounds.*

▶ Mojave National Preserve

Location Southeaster California

Established 1994

Area 1,547,955 acres (6,264.4 km²)

San Bernardino County's Mojave Desert has a warm but temperate climate, which sustains creosote bush, cholla cacti, and a forest of Joshua trees. Amongst its many features, visitors enjoy the booming sands of the Kelso Dunes and the Cima volcanic field, with its cinder cones and lava flows, as well as abandoned homesteads in the ghost town of Kelso, where the defunct 1923 Spanish "California mission"–style railroad depot serves as the visitor center. The historic Mojave Road, suitable for four-wheel drive vehicles, is a great way to see the preserve.

◄ Tallgrass Prairie National Preserve

Location Kansas
Established 1996
Area 10,882 acres (44.0 km²)

The largest expanse of tallgrass prairie left in the world, the preserve plays a crucial role in preserving this once ubiqutous American lanscape. Sadly, nearly all of the tallgrass prairie in the Midwest has been replaced by farmland, but this former ranch in the Flint Hills area maintains its diverse plant and animal life. Controlled burns and re-introduced bison help to keep the ecosystem fertile.

◄ A herd of bison graze in the wide open range of the Tallgrass Prairie National Preserve.

► Timucuan Ecological and Historic Preserve

Location Northeastern Florida
Established 1988
Area 46,262 acres (187.2 km²)

These wetlands, located at the mouth of the Nassau and St. Johns rivers in Jacksonville, Florida, contain salt marshes, tropical hardwood hammocks, and coastal dunes. Artifacts of the Timucua people dating back thousands of years have been excavated in the preserve. For hisotry lovers, the site also includes Kingsley Planation and Fort Caroline National Memorial.

▲ The historic slave quarters at the Kingsley Plantation, which was built in 1798 and is one of the last remaining plantation homes in Florida. Although the overseer's house is intact, vandalism over the years has left in ruins the 25 cabins that once housed 60 to 80 enslaved men, women, and children.

▲ A dogsled team competing in the Yukon Quest leaves Slaven's Roadhouse in the Yukon-Charley Rivers National Preserve.

▲ Yukon–Charley Rivers National Preserve

Location East-central Alaska
Established 1980
Area 2,526,512 acres (10,224.4 km²)

This large preserve includes the entire Charley River watershed and 131 miles of the Yukon River. It protects the habitats of Arctic wildlife such as caribou, salmon, and peregrine falcon. In summer, visitors float down the rivers to view remains of gold mines; in winter, dog sledders compete in the Yukon Quest.

▲ The western Brooks Range rings the pristine river basin at Noatak National Preserve. With no roads entering this wild and remote preserve, access is solely by air, boat, or snowmobile.

◄ Noatak National Preserve

Location Northwestern Alaska
Established 1980
Area 6,587,071 acres (26,656.9 km²)

Alaska's untouched Noatak River basin is found between the Baird and De Long Mountains in the Brooks Range, where the treeless upands of the tundra transition to the boreal, coniferous forests of the taiga. This isolated preserve is a major migration route for many thousands of caribou, Alaska moose, and brown bears.

▲ *The flats area of Big Thicket is a habitat for various hardwood tree species, such as basket oak, laurel oak, overcup oak, swamp post oak, and cedar elm. Dense stands of dwarf palmetto grow beneath the canopy, with resurrection fern drooping from the tree limbs.*

▶ *Arid sandyland habitat in the Big Thicket region shows Louisiana yucca growing among the sparse groundcover under longleaf pine trees.*

◀ Big Thicket National Preserve

Location Southeast Texas
Established 1974
Area 113,121 acres (457.8 km²)

Another of the first national preserves, Big Thicket is recognized as a biosphere reserve by UNESCO. Its relatively small area is home to a remarkably high diversity of plants and includes a variety of ecosystems: uplands, sandylands, savannas, slope forests, floodplain, baygalls, flats, cypress slough, mixed-grass prairies, and roadside and river edge systems. All these regions combined support more than 50 mammal species, 300 birds, 60 reptiles, 30 amphibians, and more than 90 fishes.

▼ Oregon Caves National Monument and Preserve

Location Southwestern Oregon
Established 2014
Area 4,070 acres (16.5 km²)

While the marble Oregon Caves wind underground for 15,000 feet, the preserve above them offers forests, meadows, streams, and mountains. Hiking trails include routes to Mount Elijah and the Bigelow Lakes, with their views of the Siskiyou Mountains.

▼ Bering Land Bridge National Preserve

Location Seward Peninsula, Alaska
Established 1980
Area 2,697,391 acres (10,916.0 km²)

This preserve sits on the pristine Seward Peninsula, what remains of the ice age Bering land bridge over which early peoples from Asia traveled to North America. The preserve's sites include Chukchi Sea coast, Imuruk Lake volcanic fields, and tundra wildlife, such as caribou, polar bear, walrus, muskox, and ribbon seal, along with 170 bird species.

▲ *The otherworldly landscape of Bering Strait Land Bridge features the granite Serpentine Tors, volcanic remnants formed deep belowground that, over time, have been exposed by erosion.*

◀ *The Chateau at Oregon Caves is listed as one of the National Park's Great Lodges and is a National Historic Landmark.*

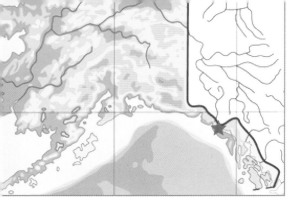

ALASKA
GLACIER BAY

Home to more than a thousand glaciers, this special park serves as a living laboratory.

LOCATION Hoonah-Angoon Census Area, Yakutat City and Borough, AK

CLOSEST CITY Juneau, AK

AREA 3,223,384 acres (13,044.57 km²)

ESTABLISHED February 25, 1925, as National Monument; December 2, 1980, as National Park and Preserve

VISITORS 597,900+

ELEVATION 15,300 feet (4,700 m) at Mount Fairweather

GEOLOGY Sedimentary rock, primarily limestone and argillite

Located between the Gulf of Alaska and Canada, Glacier Bay National Park and Preserve occupies the northernmost section of the southeast Alaska coastline. The globally significant site is a designated wilderness, a biosphere reserve, and a World Heritage Site. Its beauty is so compelling that cruise ships regularly stop here to treat passengers to the amazing views.

The park is named for its abundant tidewater and terrestrial glaciers, which number 1,045. Due to the effects of climate change, however, the Park Service reports, "In general, tidewater and terrestrial glaciers in the park have been thinning and slowly receding over the last several decades." A number are still advancing, including Johns Hopkins and the glaciers in Lituta Bay.

WHAT TO LOOK FOR

Visitors can explore numerous glaciers from the land or from a cruise ship.

> Tidewater glaciers
> Terrestrial glaciers
> The Wilderness Area

A humpback whale breaches the chilly waters of Glacier Bay.

HISTORY OF THE REGION

The earliest traces of human occupation in the region date to about 10,000 years ago. Evidence of human activity is scarce, however, due to glacial activity. Most archaeological evidence is from the last 200 years. The Haida, Eyak, and Tlingit all could have occupied the coast until more modern times, when the Tlingit came to dominate the area. Within the park and preserve are two significant Tlingit ancestral homelands. Although most Tlingit live across Icy Strait in the village of Hoonah, the bay remains their spiritual haven.

The first European to travel the Alaskan coast, Jean-Francois de Galaup, arrived in Glacier Bay in 1786 and made contact with the Tlingit. Russian fur traders and English explorers passed through during the following century, and in the 1890s, Americans in search of riches flocked north for the Klondike Gold Rush.

PARK ACTIVITIES

The park and preserve hosts many outdoor activities such as hiking, mountaineering, kayaking, rafting, and birding. Sport fishing lures anglers to try for deep-sea halibut and freshwater Dolly Varden and rainbow trout. Sport hunting and trapping are allowed only in the preserve. No roads lead to the park, which is most easily reached by air travel. During some summers there are ferries to the marina at Bartlett Cove. About 80 percent of visitors arrive on cruise ships. In-park accommodations are available at the Glacier Bay Lodge, which is located in Bartlett Cove, along with the visitor center, kayak rentals, and other amenities.

WILDLIFE AND PLANT LIFE

The park is home to brown and black bear, timber work, coyote, moose, Canadian lynx, black-tailed deer, Arctic and red fox, otter, mink, wolverine, marmot, Dall sheep, and mountain goat. Birds that breed here include bald eagle, golden eagle, woodpeckers, hummingbirds, raven, falcon, hawk, osprey, and 10 species of owl. Marine mammals include sea otter, harbor seal, Steller sea lion, Pacific white-sided dolphin, orca, minke whale, and humpback whale.

The terrain in the Lower Bay is mostly wet tundra along with Sitka spruce and western hemlock forests. The Upper bay features tidewater glaciers, where post-glacial meadows form on recently deglaciated land. The peaks here support alpine tundra, glaciers, and ice fields. On the shoreline flats, dense vegetation can make hiking difficult.

▼ **A tour in Tracy Arm** at Dawes Glacier allows kayakers to get a closer look at the astounding glacial landscape this Alaskan park has to offer its visitors.

DID YOU KNOW?

A glacier is defined as a persistent body of dense ice that is constantly moving under its own weight. A glacier forms where the accumulation of snow exceeds its ablation (erosive process) over many years, often centuries.

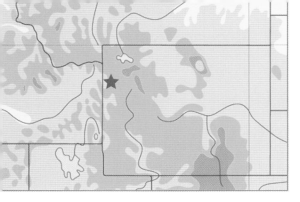

WYOMING

GRAND TETON

These youngest of the Rocky Mountains are more than equipped to challenge their siblings in terms of scenery, scope, and a big-time wow factor.

LOCATION Teton County, WY

CLOSEST CITY Jackson, WY

AREA 310,000 acres (1,300 km²)

ESTABLISHED March 15, 1943, as Jackson Hole National Monument; February 26, 1929, as Grand Teton National Park

VISITORS 3,289,600+

ELEVATION 13,770 feet (4,200 m) at Grand Teton Peak

GEOLOGY Metamorphic schist, gneiss, and amphibolite, with eroded sandstone

WHAT TO LOOK FOR

The park offers both amazing scenery and engaing history.

> Mormon Row and its historic barns

> Jenny Lake (parts are wheelchair accessible)

> Death Canyon Trail to Lake Phelps

> Hidden Falls, Inspiration Point, and Cascade Canyon

Visitors should not feel ashamed if they stand with mouth agape at the sight of these lofty mountains. Everyone from early Native Americans to French trappers to modern mountaineers has found them impressive and even daunting.

Located in northwestern Wyoming, Grand Teton is half an hour from Yellowstone National Park. They are both part of the Greater Yellowstone Ecosytems, one of the world's largest intact mid-latitude temperate systems. The terrain and features in each park are quite different, however, so they are both worth investigating. In fact, Grand Teton holds its own as one of the 10 most-visited national parks.

HISTORY OF THE TETONS

The youngest range in the Rockies, the Tetons began forming between six and nine million years ago; the range rises abruptly from the flatlands without any foothills. In addition to towering Grand Teton Peak, another nine peaks soar over 12,000 feet. Eight of them, located between Avalanche and Cascade Canyons, comprise the photogenic Cathedral Group. North of Cascade Canyon is imposing Mount Moran, at 12,605 feet. The park is also known for its many glacier-formed lakes and its complex geology—it contains some of the oldest rock found in any national park. Human occupation began roughly 11,000 years ago, when the nomadic hunter-gatherers called Paleo-Indians migrated here, seeking game in the warmer months. When easterners first came to the area in the early 19th century, it was eastern Shoshone Indians they encountered. The Lewis and Clark expedition had passed north of the site, but it was expedition member John Colter who was the first Caucasian to view the Tetons as he led fur trappers to explore the Yellowstone River in 1807. Fur trading companies competed for beaver pelts there, and the first homesteaders appeared in Jackson Hole in the 1880s. It was around this time that efforts began to protect the mountains; in 1929 Grand Teton National Park was born. Conservationists led by industrial tycoon John D. Rockefeller Jr. began purchasing land in Jackson Hole Valley to add to the existing national park. In 1943, despite opposition, the valley was proclaimed Jackson Hole National Monument. In 1950, most of the monument land became part of Grand Teton.

◀ **Hidden Falls,** located on Cascade Creek, drops approximately 100 feet near the eastern end of Cascade Canyon.

Mormon Row, formerly known as the town of Grovont, is home to the John Moulton Barn, one of the most-photographed structures in this historic district.

ACTIVITIES

The park offer numerous options in terms of trails, campsites, sightseeing, and even dining. Top activities include hiking, backpacking, camping, horse riding, swimming, fishing, and boating. There are hundreds of campsites, but backcountry campsites, accessible by foot or horseback, require permits. Boating is allowed, with motor craft permitted only on Jackson Lake and Jenny Lake. Anglers can fish all waterways with a Wyoming fishing license. In winter, the park is open for snowshoeing and cross-country skiing and limited snowmobiling on Jackson Lake.

Park landmarks include the four historic barns at Mormon Row in the Antelope Flats

▶ **An American bison** seems a fitting animal to be seen in this quintessentially western park.

area, shallow String Lake, the vista from Schwabacker Landing, Jenny Lake—offering boats that cross the lake for trail access—and the Snake River, a magnet for wildlife. The lively, artsy town of Jackson is also worth a visit.

The Craig Thomas Discovery and Visitor Center lies adjacent to the park headquarters at Moose, Wyoming. To the north is the seasonal Colter Bay Visitor Center and Indian Arts Museum. South of Moose is the Laurence S. Rockefeller Preserve Center. The seasonal Jenny Lake Visitor Center was constructed as an art studio in the 1920s for photographer Harrison Crandall. Overnight guests can choose from historic lodges, cabins, and hostel-style accommodations. Some lodges also provide restaurants and shops. The Triangle X Ranch is the last remaining dude ranch in the park.

WILDLIFE AND PLANT LIFE

The park mammals include black bear, grizzly bear, moose, otter, marmot, and pika; wildlife is best viewed at Blacktail Ponds, Mormon Row, Moose Bridge, Jenny Lake, and Oxbow Bend, among other spots. The park supports songbirds, waterfowl, waders, grebes, pheasants, and grouse and offers desired sightings of snow goose, sandhill crane, white-faced ibis, and both brown and white pelican.

The rugged mountain terrain is known for conifers like lodgepole, limber, and whitebark pine; Engelmann and blue spruce; and Douglas and subalpine fir. The higher alpine regions appear drab and forbidding, but there are many plants there that have adapted to the harsh climate.

▶ **A curious great gray owl** peers around the papery bark covering the trunk of an aspen.

"IT IS SAFE TO SAY THAT THE TETON RANGE IS AS BREATHTAKING AS ANY MOUNTAIN LANDSCAPE ONE COULD EVER SEE."

— Stefanie Payne, *A Year in the National Parks*

◀ **A carpet of cheerful wildflowers** borders Death Canyon Trail. Despite its the ominous-sounding name, the path offers visitors a hike through a dramatic canyon that leads to flowering meadows set beneath the rugged peaks of the upper canyon. Hikers do need to be aware that wildlife—such as bears—is commonly active in the area.

▲ **Autumn transforms aspen trees** into a golden sea beneath the Teton Range.

▶ **A fly fisher** tests out his luck in Jenny Lake.

BATTLE FOR THE SUMMIT

Starting in 1875, mountaineers and explorers began competing in the Tetons to see who would become the first to scale the premier peak. This might have been a moot effort, as Native American relics— including The Enclosure, an obviously human-made structure—were found about 530 feet below the summit of Grand Teton. The first non-Indian ascent of Grand Teton was made by William O. Owen, Frank Petersen, John Shive, and Franklin Spencer Spalding on August 11, 1898. By the mid-1930s, more than a dozen climbing routes had been established there.

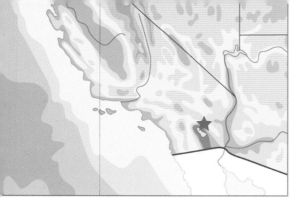

CALIFORNIA
JOSHUA TREE

Once a hippie haven, this desert park still exudes mystical vibes that beckon even jaded travelers to tune in.

LOCATION Riverside County and San Bernardino County, CA

CLOSEST CITY Twentynine Palms, CA

AREA 790,636 acres (3,199.6 km²)

ESTABLISHED August 10, 1936. as National Monument; October 31, 1994, as National Park

VISITORS 2,399,500+

ELEVATION 5,813 feet (1,772 m) at Quail Mountain

GEOLOGY Metamorphic rock—gneiss, quartz, and schist; igneous rock from magma intrusions

Located in southeastern California, Joshua Tree National Park lies east of San Bernardino and Los Angeles and north of Palm Springs. In area it is slightly larger than Rhode Island and includes more than 670 square miles of protected wilderness. The southwest portion of the park is traversed by the Little San Bernardino Mountains.

The park is named for the Joshua tree (*Yucca brevifolia*), which can grow to between 20 and 60 feet. With its knife-like leaves and sprawling, zig-zagging branches,

WHAT TO LOOK FOR

Hike among the desert plants, including the native Joshua trees, or scale water-sculpted rock formations.

> Hidden Valley Trail

> Lost Horse Mine

> Desert Queen Ranch and Mine

> Ryan Mountain

> Arch Rock

> Barker Dam Trail

> Keys View

The Milky Way forms in the night sky over Joshua Tree's Arch Rock.

it looks like something from a surrealist fantasy. In Spanish it is called *izote de desierto,* or "desert dagger."

TWO DESERTS, TWO HABITATS

The park encompasses sections of two deserts, the Mojave in the west and the Colorado in the east—each with an ecosystem determined by elevation. The cooler, higher Mojave is the preferred habitat for Joshua trees, which dominate the region and can occur in dense forests or as isolated specimens. Other flora includes California juniper, pinyon pine, desert scrub oak, Tucker's oak, chuckwalla cholla, and dollarjoint pricklypear. In the higher elevations are found Great Basin montane forest/southwest forest vegetation. The Mojave's bare-rock ocher hills are popular with rock climbers and scramblers, people who "walk" up steep terrain using their hands.

The Colorado Desert portion of the park, lower and drier, supports creosote bush scrub, ocotillo, desert saltbush, yucca, and cholla cactus. To the southeast lies the lower Coachella Valley, with its sandy soil grasslands and desert dunes.

PARK HISTORY

Humans have occupied these parklands for thousands of years. The earliest known inhabitants were members of the Pino Culture; based on their stone tools and spear points, they lived, hunted, and gathered seasonal plants here between 8,000 and 4,000 years ago. They were later followed by the Serrano, the Cahuilla, and the Chemehuevi peoples, among others. These hunter-gatherers lived in small villages near water sources or oases. A fourth group, the Mojaves used local resources while traveling between the Colorado River and the Pacific coast. Today, all four tribes are found in small numbers living near the park, and the descendants of the Chemehuevi maintain a reservation at Twentynine Palms.

In 1772, a group of Spaniards pursuing runaway natives being converted to Christianity were the first Europeans to view the parklands. Later American trappers and explorers traveled through the region on the

▶ **The mystical landscape** of the park is filled with hardy desert plants and trees scattered amid fascinating rock formations.

A big storm over Joshua Tree National Park leads to a breathtaking sunset of cloudy, steel gray skies.

DID YOU KNOW?

The only palm tree native to California, the California fan palm (*Washingtonia filifera*) occurs naturally in Joshua Tree. These palms grow at five oases, where water flows year-round and many types of wildlife abound.

▲ **The iconic Route 66** is lined with Joshua trees as it runs through the Mojave Desert. Just a short detour takes you to the park, which incorporates both the Mojave and the Colorado deserts.

◀ **A chuckwalla** basks on a rock. These desert lizards thrive in the hot and dry climate of Joshua Tree.

Mojave Trail. By 1870, settlers were grazing cattle on the region's tall grass, and a gang of rustlers even hid cattle in one of the canyons. Invasive dams and catchments were built to retain precious water. From the 1860s to the 1940s, the area supported 300 mine pits. Most were small, but the Lost Horse and the Desert Queen were both successful, the former producing $5 million in gold and silver.

Thanks to advocate and activist Minerva Hoyt, in 1936 President Franklin D. Roosevelt established a national monument here to protect the vulnerable ecosystems. During the mid-to-late 20th century, the serene, aesthetic desert landscape held great allure for hippies, artists, writers, and other outsiders, a fascination that continues today.

ACTIVITIES

Joshua Tree offers scenic trails for all levels, breathtaking desert overlooks and natural landmarks, and historic remnants of the area's colorful past. These attractions include Hidden Valley Trail, Barker Dam Trail (which has water!), Mastodon Peak Loop, Arch Rock, Cholla Cactus Garden, Ryan Mountain, Wall Street Mill, and Lost Horse Mine. Recommended activities include visiting Keys View at sunset, taking the Desert Queen Ranch tour, exploring the Desert Queen Mine, and following the Geology Tour Road for four-wheelers. There are also fanciful rock formations like Skull Rock, Heart Rock, Cap Rock, Cyclops, PeeWee, and Penguin Rock. Hikers should note that this is a desert park; they should always carry extra water and avoid long hikes during the summer months.

There are three visitor centers—Oasis, Cottonwood, and Joshua Tree—plus a wildlife center at Black Rock. All have exhibits and offer water and flush toilets. Two the park's nine established campgrounds, Cottonwood and Black Rock, also provide water and flush toilets.

PARK WILDLIFE

Most animals that thrive here have adapted to desert living. Park visitors are most likely to see birds, lizards, and ground squirrels, but larger animals include bighorn sheep, coyote, and bobcat. The threatened desert tortoise inhabits creosote bush lowlands, while California tree frogs seek permanent water sources. There are tarantulas and giant desert scorpions to keep things interesting. Meanwhile, yucca moths are responsible for pollinating the Joshua trees.

More than 250 bird species inhabit or visit the park. Resident birds include the greater roadrunner, golden eagle, cactus wren, northern mockingbird, LeConte's thrasher, and Gambel's quail. The park lies along the Pacific flyway, so many migrating species also make a quick, restorative stop here.

"IT'S THE JOSHUA TREE'S STRUGGLE THAT GIVES IT ITS BEAUTY."

— *Author Jeannette Walls*

▲ **A campground** places an RV at the perfect vantage point for campers to enjoy a sunset over the mountains.

◄ **A windswept pinyon pine** seems poised to catch a precariously balanced rock.

A weathered wooden cyanide tank and tack room are part of the remains of the Desert Queen Mine, which operated from 1895 to 1961.

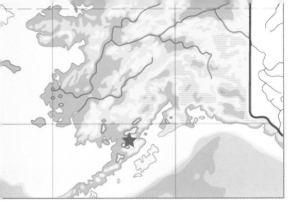

ALASKA

KATMAI

This volcanic park is bear country, especially around Brooks Falls, where visitors get a close-up view of brown bears fishing for salmon.

LOCATION Lake and Peninsula, Kodiak Island, Kenai Peninsula, and Bristol Bay boroughs, AK

CLOSEST CITY King Salmon, AK

AREA 4,093,077 acres (16,564.09 km²)

ESTABLISHED September 24, 1918, as National Monument; December 2, 1980, as National Park and Preserve

VISITORS 37,800+

ELEVATION 7,606 feet (2,318 m) at Mount Denison

GEOLOGY Volcanic and sedimentary rock with abundant marine fossils

WHAT TO LOOK FOR

The remote wilderness park is best known for its numerous volcanoes and wild brown bears.

> Valley of Ten Thousands Smokes

> Brooks River to view bear fishing

> Brooks Camp

▲ **Elevated boardwalks** guide Katmai hikers through the park, helping to ensure both visitor and employee safety by reducing the risk of human-bear conflicts.

Located in southwest Alaska—on the Alaska Peninsula northwest of Kodiak Island and southwest of Homer—Katmai is home to at least 24 volcanic mountains, all part of the Aleutian Range. The park was established in 1918 to protect the area of volcanic devastation called the Valley of Ten Thousands Smokes after the major eruption of Novarupta.

Katmai National Park and Preserve also conserves 9,000 years of human history and is an important habitat for sockeye salmon and for thousands of Alaska's magnificent brown bears. The park is somewhere between Connecticut and New Jersey in size, and the majority of land is a designated wilderness area.

EARLY HISTORY

The first inhabitants of the region likely arrived 9,000 years ago, with the oldest sites in Katmai belonging to the Paleoarctic tradition. Recovered artifacts are similar to those from early collections found in Asia, so it is surmised that these people originally crossed the land bridge to North America by foot or the widening Bering Strait by boat. Brooks Camp is an important archaeological site that dates back 4,500 years and is listed on the National Register of Historic Landmarks. Indigenous people with later historic ties to Katmai, mostly of Alutiiq descent, now live in Western Alaska. Many of these Katmai descendants are actively involved in subsistence activities (using park resources) and participate in park management. Others who settled or passed through the area during the 19th century include Euro-American trappers, Russian explorers, and American entrepreneurs.

RECREATION

The park is open year-round and offers activities like hiking, backpacking, camping, backcountry skiing, boat tours, bear tours, and sport fishing. King Salmon and Brooks Camp are the two seasonal visitor centers; Mt. Griggs Visitor Center is open during tours of the Valley of Ten Thousand Smokes. The park service mandates a bear safety orientation for visitors explaining regulations and providing instructions for handling bear encounters. Visitors may find closed gates on certain paths due to the presence of an active bear or even a sleeping bear on the trail—called a "bear jam"—and hikers must wait until the bear moves for the trail to reopen. At Brooks Falls, where the bears wade into the water to feed on salmon, three viewing platforms overlook the riverbanks. Brooks Lodge at Brook's Camp serves three buffet-style meals a day and invites visitors to relax around a circular

The rugged Katmai coastline. The 1989 *Exxon Valdez* oil spill into Prince William Sound created an ecological disaster as extensive contamination spread along the Katmai coastline. More than 8,000 birds alone died as a result.

fireplace. Float planes are available to carry visitors to Katmai from King Salmon and outlying towns.

WILDLIFE AND PLANT LIFE

Katmai is home to 29 mammal species, 137 bird species, 24 freshwater fish species, and four anadromous (migratory) fish species. The park protects the world's largest population of brown bears, around 2,000 in number. Currently brown bears (*Ursus arctos*) are thought to have two subspecies: grizzly bears and Kodiak bears.

Other examples of wildlife include timber wolf, coyote, lynx, wolverine, marten, beaver, Arctic and red fox, weasel, porcupine, moose, and caribou. Marine mammals include harbor seal, sea lion, sea otter, beluga whale, gray whale, and orca. Birders may spot diverse subjects like spruce grouse, bald eagle, raven, magpie, great horned owl, yellowlegs, godwits, swans, ducks, loons, grebes, and abundant passerines. The large sockeye salmon are the most critical fish in the park; during their spawning journeys through the local rivers, typically from June to October, they supply food for bears, bald eagles, and other carnivores.

There are a number of plant habitats found here: white spruce, birch, and/or balsam poplar forests; alder and willow thickets; and grasslands dominated by blue joint grass and blue grass. The park's rolling tundra supports succulents, while in the coastal forest Sitka spruce is the dominant coniferous tree. Native wildflowers include beachhead iris, nootka lupine, and woolly geranium.

▲ **Volcanic debris** lines the canyons of Katmai's Valley of Ten Thousand Smokes.

ERUPTION OF THE CENTURY

The unearthly landscape of the Valley of Ten Thousand Smokes is filled with layers of cooled ash flow from the massive 1912 eruption of Novarupta, the largest by volume in the 20th century. The vent volcano belched for more than 60 hours, producing a cloud of suffocating ash and gas that blackened the skies above the town of Kodiak. Residents sought shelter in the U.S. Coast Guard Cutter *Manning*, but they could not flee the island; the dense atmosphere made navigation impossible. The eruption also caused a withdrawal of magma beneath stratovolcano Mount Katmai, resulting in the summit's collapse. The lake that filled the caldera is now 800 feet deep. The Alaska Volcano Observatory monitors the Katmai Cluster, which includes the park's five active stratovolcanos: Mount Katmai, Trident Volcano, Mount Mageik, Mount Martin, and Mount Griggs.

DID YOU KNOW?

From June through October the park streams a bear cam on the web, which features bears fishing for salmon and interacting at Brooks Falls. Fat Bear Week, held from late September to early October, celebrates the successful salmon catches that ensure the survival of Katmai's bear population.

"FAT BEAR WEEK HIGHLIGHTS SOME OF THE RESOURCES AT STAKE. IT CAN BE A REMINDER THAT THE BEARS DEPEND ON A HEALTHY ECOSYSTEM AND THE WORLD'S GREATEST SALMON RUN."

— *Jim Adams, Alaska regional director of the National Parks Conservation Association*

▼ **A brown bear** faces off with a gull that waits for its leftovers during the annual summer sockeye salmon run in the Brooks River.

▲ **Bears flock** to the salmon-rich Brooks Falls to wait for a catch.

◄ **An Alaskan brown bear sow** and her cubs emerge from the forest to make their way to the banks of the Brooks River.

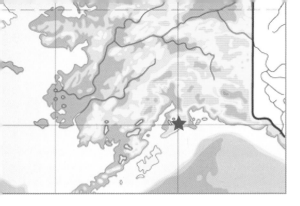

ALASKA
KENAI FJORDS

Jagged mountains meet coastal glaciers in this wilderness park, where whales and orcas rule the teal-blue waters.

LOCATION Kenai Peninsula Borough, AK

CLOSEST CITY Seward, AK

AREA 669,984 acres (2,711.33 km²)

ESTABLISHED December 1, 1978, as National Monument; December 2, 1980, as National Park

VISITORS 321,500+

ELEVATION 6,450 feet (1,970 m) at unnamed ridge

GEOLOGY Local igneous rock plus shoreline terranes from elsewhere

WHAT TO LOOK FOR

This icy park shows coastal Alaska at its best.

> Exit Glacier

> Harding Icefield

> Aialik Glacier

> Boat tours of the coast

▼ **An orca** breaches in Resurrection Bay. It is just one of the many marine species visitors might see on a trip to Kenai Fjords.

Kenai Fjords is located in south-central Alaska, on the southern tip of the Kenai Peninsula. It was in part established to maintain the Harding Icefield, its glaciers, and its coastal fjords and islands. The park combines breathtaking mountain scenery with a plenitude of wildlife, while boat excursions along the coast offer thrilling marine life encounters.

HISTORY OF THE REGION

The park's mountains lost altitude as the Pacific tectonic plate subducted beneath the North American Plate. This also resulted in a variety of terranes, or crust fragments, "suturing" to coastal areas, creating a mixture of rocks from other places, along with the local igneous rocks. The park is 51 percent glacial ice, and Harding Icefield receives 60 feet of snow annually.

According to archeologists, the park's earliest human visitors came only to hunt and forage. Their sites were likely coastal and probably inundated by rising waters. Other documented sites date between 1200 and 1920, some doubtless inhabited by the local Alutiiq (Sugpiaq) people. During the early 20th century, 11 gold mines were excavated in the parklands around Nuka Bay.

Kenai is the only Alaska national park that did not originally allow subsistence use by Native Americans (allowing access to renewable resources like food, shelter, fuel, and materials for handicrafts), but native village corporations still have interests in private holdings within the park and have established subsistence rights on those properties.

ACTIVITIES AND AMENITIES

Park activities include hiking, camping, salmon fishing, kayaking, and canoeing. Exit Glacier, which offers a nature center, is the only park area reachable by road. Hiking trails and boat tours give access to other sites. The visitor center in Seward makes a great first stop. Here lies the start of the Glacier View Loop Trail, a short, paved trail that is handicapped accessible. This links with the more difficult Glacier Overland Trail. Finally, there is the strenuous Harding Icefield Trail. But by far the best way to see the park is aboard a modern excursion ship that explores Kenai's inlets and bays. Aialik Cape is especially beautiful with its craggy cliffs and tall, tree-covered rock islands. Seward is a destination for cruise ships, as well as home to the coastal tour companies.

The park has two restaurants, casual Rafters and the more formal Rod and Reel, along with on-site lodging at Kenai Fjords Glacier Lodge. There are campsites and cabins in the park and other campgrounds, lodges, and hotels in Seward.

WILDLIFE AND PLANT LIFE

Park wildlife includes brown bear, moose, mountain goat, sea otter, and puffin. The coastal tours showcase harbor seals and endangered Steller sea lions basking on the rocks, while humpback whales, fin whales, Dall's porpoises, and orcas sound just beyond the boats.

Glacial retreat shaped the park's vegetation—newly exposed surfaces were stony, lacking in soil. Lichens and mosses broke down rock into soil, while Sitka alder enriched the soil. Willows were followed by black cottonwoods, and then Sitka spruce. Mature forests now support spruce and mountain hemlock, towering over wild berries and lady fern. Deciduous forests grow in sections where glaciers recently spread, and richer soils support grasses. Above the treeline grow alpine dwarf shrubs, which can be damaged by foot traffic.

▶ **A popular destination** for boat day trips, Aialik Glacier drains from the Harding Icefield into Aialik Bay.

DID YOU KNOW?

In 1978, President Jimmy Carter invoked the Antiquities Act to protect 17 untouched areas of Alaska. One of the national monuments he created was Kenai Fjords.

Cove of the Spires is one of the uniquely beautiful sites visitors can admire during boat tours of Kenai Fjords.

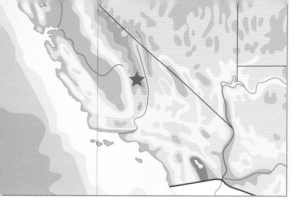

CALIFORNIA
KINGS CANYON

Home to the world's largest grove of sequoia trees and the deepest canyon in America, this park offers landmarks on a grand scale.

LOCATION Fresno County and Tulare County, CA

CLOSEST CITY Fresno, CA

AREA 461,901 acres (1,869.25 km²)

ESTABLISHED October 1, 1890, as General Grant National Park; March 4, 1940, as Kings Canyon National Park

VISITORS 415,000+

ELEVATION 14,242 feet (4,341 m) at North Palisade

GEOLOGY Igneous intrusive rock

WHAT TO LOOK FOR

Above or below ground, scenic wonders await park visitors.

> Grant Grove and General Grant Tree

> Glen Grove and giant redwoods

> Boyden Cavern

> Zumwalt Meadow

Kings Canyon National Park is home to the deepest canyon in the United States, at more than a mile and a half below sea level, and features the largest remaining grove of sequoia trees in the world. Also known for its dramatic, glacier-carved valleys and eroded rock formations, the park inspired naturalist John Muir to call it "a rival to Yosemite." Although it sits adjacent to Sequoia National Park, Kings Canyon was established 50 years later, in 1940.

PARK HISTORY

The region is the homeland of the of the Mono (Monache), Yokuts, Tübatulabal, Paiute, and Western Shoshone people. Archaeological artifacts represent both prehistoric and historic sites and include pictographs and grinding holes. In the late 19th century, naturalist and author John Muir, called the "Father of Our National Parks," lobbied for conservation of pristine wilderness areas and helped establish Yosemite and Sequoia and Kings Canyon as national parks.

THING TO DO

Park activities include hiking, backpacking, camping, and canoeing. Sledding, show-shoeing, and cross-country skiing are popular during the winter months. Visitors can also check out the year-round visitor center in Grant Grove Village or explore the Giant Forest Museum.

The park is divided into two scenic areas: Grant Grove, near the entrance, and Cedar Grove, on the canyon floor. Among Grant Grove's towering sequoias is General Grant, the second-largest tree in the world. (The top honor goes to the General Sherman Tree, located in nearby Sequoia National Park.) A short paved loop trail showcases other landmarks—Gamlin Cabin, Fallen Monarch, and Centennial Stump. Grant Grove Stables, located near the park gates, offers guided horseback tours.

Cedar Grove is home to Redwood Canyon, one of the largest sequoia groves in the park. The spectacular glaciated valley offers miles of hiking trails, horseback riding, and camping—for the perfect "old West" wilderness experience. Beneath the parkland lies Boyden

◄ **Lively golden-mantled ground squirrels** scurry through the park's grounds and trees.

DID YOU KNOW?

Every December, the Park Service hosts the "Trek to the Tree," a celebration at the Nation's Christmas Tree, the 2,000-year-old General Grant Tree, which also serves as a "living shrine" to American soldiers.

▲ **General Grant,** at 267.4 feet tall, is the world's second-largest giant sequoia. This ancient tree is about 1,650 years old and can boast of having the third-largest footprint of any living giant sequoia, measuring 107.6 feet in circumference at ground level.

Cavern, a high marble cave with massive stalagmites, stalactites, flowstones, and more, that offers 50-minute walking tours.

WILDLIFE AND PLANT LIFE

Animal inhabitants include black bear, mule deer, cougar, pika, and 17 species of bats, while there are more than 200 species of birds, including the California quail and the rare northern pygmy owl. The 21 species of reptiles include 1 pond turtle, 14 species of snakes and 6 lizards.

The park supports more than 1,200 plant species, 20 percent of all plant species in the state. Vegetation communities are based on elevation: the dry Sierra foothill zone consists of oak, sycamore, willow At middle elevations live montane mixed conifers: ponderosa pine, incense cedar, white fir, sugar pine, and giant sequoias. At the subalpine line are red fir, lodgepole pine, whitebark pine, mountain hemlock, and foxtail pine.

▶ **The Painted Lady** rises above Upper Rae Lake. The Rae Lakes Loop is one of several popular backpacking treks in the park.

The Sphinx, one of the most-photographed sites in the park, is seen at center from a view of Kings Canyon looking south from Paradise Valley. In 1976, UNESCO designated Kings Canyon as part of the Sequoia–Kings Canyon Biosphere Reserve.

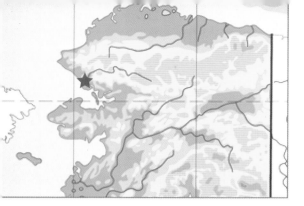

ALASKA

KOBUK VALLEY

Remote and inaccessible, this Alaskan national park awaits the true adventurer, the visitor who craves the ultimate primal wilderness experience.

LOCATION Northwest Arctic Borough, AK

CLOSEST CITY Kotzebue, AK

AREA 1,750,716 acres (7,084.90 km²)

ESTABLISHED December 1, 1978, as National Monument; December 2, 1980 as National Park

VISITORS 14,900+

ELEVATION 4,760 feet (1,450 m) at Mount Angayukaqsraq

GEOLOGY Sedimentary rock: shale, sandstone, graywacke, conglomerate, and siltstone

WHAT TO LOOK FOR

Visitors can follow game trails to many of this remote park's worthwhile sights.

> Kobuk River

> Onion Portage area

> Great Kobuk Sand Dunes

> Iñupiat villages

> Caribou herds

Located in northwest Alaska, 25 miles north of the Arctic Circle, Kobuk is the heart of a vast ecosystem between Selawik National Wildlife Refuge and Noatak National Preserve. Here, a wide river winds through a broad, wetlands valley, with mountain peaks rising on either side. During the winter, if solar activity is high, the Aurora Borealis often shimmers above the park.

Below the river lie three sets of sand dunes, Great Kobuk, Little Kobuk, and Hunt River, the remnants of dunes that once covered more than 200,000 acres, created by the rise and retreat of glaciers. In the park's southern sector lies the Kobuk Valley Wilderness.

There are no roads leading to the park, which can be reached by foot, dogsled, snowmobile, or air taxi. Although it is approximately the size of Delaware, the park contains no designated roads or trails. Not surprisingly, Kobuk Valley is one of the least visited national parks, but for an experienced backcountry hiker it can offer a worthwhile, even unforgettable, encounter with nature.

PAST HISTORY

Around 12,500 years ago, the people of the Paleoarctic tradition arrived here. They were followed by the people of the Archaic tradition, then by the Arctic small tool tradition. The Onion Portage archaeological district, a national historic landmark, has documented nine cultural complexes that existed from 6000 BCE to 1700 CE. By the 19th century, two Iñupiat societies, the Iñupiat and the Kuuvaum Kangianirmiut, occupied the area. A short-lived gold rush, or "stampede," in 1899 brought prospectors who set up 32 camps and reportedly made contact with the native peoples. The Iñupiat's descendants still use the park and live in the villages of Kiana, Ambler, Kobuk, and

Shungnak. They have subsistence hunting and fishing rights, and the twice-yearly crossing of massive caribou herds at the Kobuk River ensures their survival. Nearly 81,000 acres of the park are owned by native corporations and the state of Alaska.

ACTIVITIES AND RANGER SUPPORT

In summer, camping, hiking, backpacking, "flightseeing," photography, and fishing are popular. For those with Arctic winter survival skills, snowmobiling, skiing, and dog-sledding are also possible. The Northwest Arctic Heritage Center is in Kotzebue, 100 miles west on the Bering Sea coast, but there are seasonal ranger stations on the Kobuk River at Kallarichuk in the west and at Onion Portage in the east.

WILDLIFE AND PLANT LIFE

The wildlife is typical of arctic and subarctic fauna—wolf, red fox, black and brown bear, caribou, moose, beaver, river otter, marten, mink, wolverine, and Canadian lynx. The park supports 162 bird species, while migratory birds alight here from all seven continents. Sightings include tundra swan, Arctic tern, northern goshawk, and harlequin duck. The streams run with Chinook, pink, chum, and sockeye salmon.

The park lies in a transition zone between boreal forest and tundra. Due to its Arctic location, the ground is permanently frozen below much of the park. This "permafrost" prevents drainage and causes many wet areas in the summer. To live here, plants must survive fierce winds, sub-zero winters, thin soil, and a short growing season. Spruce, willow, and birch are found along streams, while an endemic plant, a flowering herb called Kobuk locoweed, grows on the sand dunes.

▲ **The historic Giddings cabin** and elevated cache was built by famed archeologist J. Louis Giddings, who studied the Arctic region before the establishment of the national park. The Onion Portage area is a National Historic Landmark.

The Great Kobuk Sand Dunes look barren, but plants like grasses, rye, and the rare Kobuk locoweed, thrive along the edges and slopes, and animals like bears, wolves, moose, and foxes leave tracks in the massive mounds of soft golden sand.

DID YOU KNOW?

NASA has funded studies of the Great Kobuk Sand Dunes, the largest active Arctic dune field in North America, using them as analogs for Martian polar dunes.

"ONLY THE WIND KNOWS THE WAY OF THE CARIBOU."

— *Eskimo proverb*

▲ **A herd of caribou swimming the Kobuk River.** Twice a year, caribou make this migration from riverbank to riverbank—north in the spring and then south in the autumn—enabled by their big hooves that act as paddles and their hollow hair that aids in buoyancy.

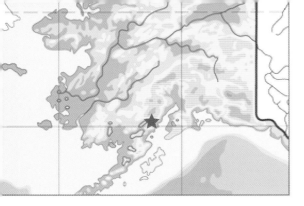

ALASKA
LAKE CLARK

This hidden gem is a wilderness getaway that combines an active volcano with a memorable coastline, brown bear viewings, and marine mammal sightings.

LOCATION Lake and Peninsula, Kenai Peninsula, and Matanuska-Susitna boroughs, and Bethel Census Area, AK

CLOSEST CITY Anchorage, AK

AREA 4,030,015 acres (16,308.89 km²)

ESTABLISHED December 1, 1978, as National Monument; December 2, 1980, as National Park and Preserve

VISITORS 14,400+

ELEVATION 10,457 feet (3,187 m) at Redoubt Volcano

GEOLOGY Volcanic rock

One of America's most isolated national parks, Lake Clark is also one that deserves to be explored. Located in southwest Alaska, the park protects rainforests along Cook Inlet, alpine tundra, glaciers, glacial lakes, major salmon-bearing rivers, and two volcanoes, Mount Redoubt and Mount Iliamna. Salt marshes wend through the coastal flats, where wildlife shows itself in relief, making population tallies of brown bear and other animals relatively simple for rangers.

WHAT TO LOOK FOR

Here, scenic wonders and fascinating wildlife vie for the attention of visitors.

> Redoubt Volcano
> Cook Inlet and salt marshes
> Kijik Village archaeological site

A float plane lies berthed on Crescent Lake. This inland lake is popular with grayling fishermen and provides excellent bear viewing in the summer months.

Lake Clark National Park and Preserve is truly remote—it has no roads leading to it and can only be reached by boat or small plane. The Jay S. Hammond Wilderness takes up 2,619,550 acres—excluding preserve lands and the Cook Inlet coast—and is named for a former Alaskan governor.

EARLY HISTORY

The earliest human presence here was at Bristol Bay, settled by people of the Paleoarctic culture who lived between 10,000 and 7,500 years ago. They were followed by the northern Archaic tradition, who left behind two sites at the park.

▼ **Autumn colors** are reflected in Lake Clark. Along with several lakes, the park is home to three National Wild and Scenic Rivers: the Chikkadrotna, the Mulchatna, and the Tlikakila.

The northern Athabaskan Dena'ina, who currently dwell in the area, lived in Kijik Village, the park's primary archaeological site, until the early 20th century.

British explorer Captain James Cook surveyed the inlet that bears his name in 1778. Russian traders established themselves in the region decades later, and by the 1890s American traders had arrived. Over time, the indigenous population was reduced by imported diseases. In the early 20th century the parkland supported a few isolated settlers, including Richard Proenneke, who shot films of a rugged life spent hunting and salvaging meat from hunters' kills. This footage was made into a popular documentary, *One Man's Wilderness: An Alaskan Odyssey*. His cabin is now owned by the Park Service.

PARK ACTIVITIES

Recreational options include hiking, rafting, backpacking, camping, kayaking, fishing, boating, and birding. The visitor center at St. Alsworth is seasonal, although the park is open all year. Redoubt, Lake Clark's active volcano and a favorite landmark, began its most recent active phase on December 14, 1989, with ash eruptions that curbed air traffic. The peak stayed quiet until March and April 2009, when it erupted with pyroclastic flows that melted ice, creating lahars—violent mudflows—on the Drift River.

WILDLIFE AND PLANT LIFE

The saltmarshes found along the Cook Inlet represent one of the most productive ecosystems here, accounting for less than 1 percent of the park, but providing sustenance in early summer for brown and black bears. Other wildlife includes Dall sheep, moose, caribou, timber wolf, coyote, marten, Arctic and red fox, wolverine, river otter, beaver, Canadian lynx, bald eagle, and golden eagle. The coastal waters are home to sea lion, harbor seal, beluga whale, and porpoise, while the Kvichak River is the world's most productive watershed for sockeye salmon. Their offspring account for 33 percent of the species caught in the United States and 16 percent of world production.

◄ **Coastal brown bear cubs** stage a mock fight.

▼ **Fumarole on Mount Redoubt.** A day before the eruption of March 3, 2009, the volcano showed steam venting and the summit glacier melting and breaking in an "ice piston" feature.

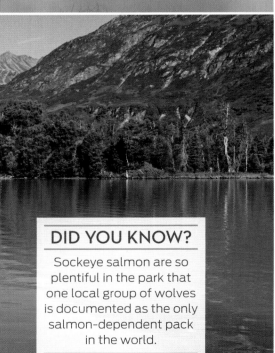

DID YOU KNOW?

Sockeye salmon are so plentiful in the park that one local group of wolves is documented as the only salmon-dependent pack in the world.

CALIFORNIA

LASSEN VOLCANIC

Mark up your volcano bingo card! This starkly beautiful park offers a rare combination of all four volcano types—plug dome, shield, cinder cone, and stratovolcano.

LOCATION Shasta, Lassen, Plumas, and Tehama counties, CA

CLOSEST CITY Redding and Susanville, CA

AREA 106,452 acres (430.80 km²)

ESTABLISHED May 6, 1907, as Cinder Cone and Lassen Peak National Monuments; August 9, 1916, as Lassen Volcanic National Park

VISITORS 499,400+

ELEVATION 10,457 feet (3,187 m) at Lassen Peak

GEOLOGY Volcanic rock

WHAT TO LOOK FOR

Visitors can explore the many volcanic "hot spots" around the park.

> Mount Lassen

> 30-mile scenic highway

> Cinder Cone and the Fantastic Lava Beds

> Bumpass Hell and Sulphur Works hydrothermal areas

This geologically unique park is located in northeastern California, at the northern end of the Sacramento Valley. It is home to Lassen Peak, the largest plug dome volcano in the world and the southernmost volcano in the Cascade Range.

EARLY HISTORY

This region has been volcanically active for at least three millions years. Lassen Peak rises near the remains of Mount Tehama (Brokeoff Mountain), a stratovolcano, or composite volcano, that once rose a thousand feet higher than Lassen. After a series of eruptions, it either collapsed into itself or was eroded by acidic vapors. There is also Cinder Cone (northeast of Lassen) and four shield volcanoes: Mount Harkness (southwest corner), Red Mountain (south-central boundary), Prospect Peak (northeast corner), and Raker Peak (north of Lassen). Each of these is topped with a cinder cone volcano.

The Atsugewi people have lived in the shadow of Lassen Peak for many generations. They even believed that the peak, full of fire and water, would one day blow itself apart. Incoming settlers used the peak as a landmark leading to the fertile Sacramento Valley. One of their guides was Danish blacksmith Peter Lassen, for whom the volcano was named. In spite of sporadic activity from Cinder Cone in the mid-1800s, geologists calculated the last major eruption occurred 200 years earlier. Still, after the eruption of Mount St. Helen, they began monitoring the park's volcanoes more closely.

ACTIVITIES

Park visitors enjoy hiking on 150 miles of trails, camping, backpacking, boating, and fishing. There are also hydrothermal features like boiling mudpots, steaming ground, and roaring fumaroles. A full-service visitor center near is located near the southwest entrance.

WILDLIFE AND PLANT LIFE

Lassen Volcanic National Park is home to approximately 300 species of vertebrates—57 mammals, 6 reptiles, 6 amphibians, and 9 fish. Mammals include black bear, coyote, cougar, Sierra Nevada red fox, river otter, weasel, mink, marten, fisher, badger, mule deer, squirrel, and pika. At least 216 bird species have been sighted in the park, and 96 are known to breed there.

The park's array of flora is found in three ecological zones. The mixed conifer zone (below 6,500 feet) contains ponderosa and Jeffrey pine, sugar pine, and

DID YOU KNOW?

In 2021 the extensive Feather River Canyon Dixie Fire entered the park and burned 73,240 acres of parkland, but most of Lassen Volcanic is expected to be open for the 2022 season.

THE PLUG DOME

A lava dome or plug dome is a circular, mound-shaped protrusion at the summit of a volcano. It is caused by the slow extrusion of viscous lava, typically from the central vent. About 6 percent of eruptions on earth result in lava domes.

white fir, along with manzanita, gooseberry, ceanothus, iris, spotted coralroot, violets, and lupine. The red fir forest (up to 8,500 feet) contains red fir, western white pine, mountain hemlock, and lodgepole pine, as well as satin lupine, woolly mule's ear, and pinemat manzanita. The subalpine zone reaches to the treeline (10,000 feet) and includes rugged whitebark pine, mountain hemlock, rock spirea, lupine, Indian paintbrush, and penstemon.

◄ **The Loomis Seismograph Station,** built in 1927 of local volcanic rock, now serves as a museum and visitor center. In 1975, it was listed on the National Register of Historic Places.

▶ **Bumpass Hell** may be the most spectacular geothermal area in the park, with hot springs and fumaroles that attest to its former volcanic activity. A boardwalk leads through its stunning scenery.

A view from Cinder Cone reveals a landscape of colorful dunes and fantastic lava beds.

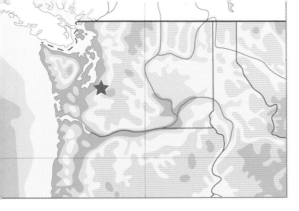

WASHINGTON
MOUNT RAINIER

Revered and majestic—and often clouded in mist—Rainier is an active volcano and the highest point in the lofty Cascade Range.

LOCATION Pierce County and Lewis County, WA

CLOSEST CITY Tacoma, WA

AREA 236,381 acres (956.60 km²)

ESTABLISHED March 2, 1899

VISITORS 1,518,400+

ELEVATION 14,411 feet (4,392 m) at Mount Rainier

GEOLOGY Volcanic rock

WHAT TO LOOK FOR

This park offers majestic mountain views and hikes through a stunning landscape.

> Wonderland Trail

> Paradise area

> Longmire area

> Carbon and Emmons glaciers

> "IN THE DEEP FORESTS OF MOUNT RAINIER, THE SUN DOESN'T RISE, IT LEAKS IN THIN BANDS THROUGH THE TREES."

— Bruce Barcott
The Measure of a Mountain: Beauty and Terror on Mount Rainier

Mount Rainier, snow-capped above and ringed with ancient forests below, is perhaps the most iconic emblem of Washington State. The park that surrounds it was the fifth national park to be established and the first created from a previous national forest. Its purpose is to protect and preserve unimpaired the stately presence of Mount Rainier "along with its natural and cultural resources, values, and dynamic processes."

The highest point in the Cascade Range, Mount Rainier is an active stratovolcano, the most glaciated mountain in the contiguous United States, and the source of five major rivers. In excess of 25 glaciers have formed on its flanks, and the clouds that collect there often drop record amounts of rain and snow. The park offers scenic valleys and waterfalls, vivid subalpine meadows, and 91,000 acres of old-growth forest. Nearly the entire park is preserved as a wilderness area, which abuts the Tatoosh, Clearwater, Glacier View, and William O. Douglas Wildernesses. Mount Rainier has also received National Historic Landmark status.

Mount Rainier looms over the clear blue Eunice Lake, as seen from Tolmie Peak.

▶ **Wildflowers in bloom** add color to the park's foggy landscape on a spring morning.

REGIONAL HISTORY

Humans have utilized the parkland, likely for seasonal hunting, for many millennia. A projectile point found along Beach Lake Trail that dates back 5,800 to 4,000 years is the earliest evidence of human presence in the parkland. Meanwhile, a 1963 Washington State University archaeological study concluded that prehistorical peoples used the area extensively between 8,000 and 4,500 years ago. A rock shelter discovered near Fryingpan Creek contained early hunting artifacts whose age indicates the site was used by Columbia Plateau tribes from 1,000 to 300 years ago. It is speculated that the parkland was divided

▶ **The open entrance gate** invites visitors to explore the park's snowy winter landscape.

▲ **An aerial view of lofty Mount Rainier** shows clouds floating beneath the peaks of this large, active stratovolcano. Mount Rainier is the most glaciated peak in the contiguous United States, spawning five major rivers.

among five tribes—the Nisqually, Puyallup, Muckleshoot, Yakama, and Taidnapam (Upper Cowlitz).

ACTIVITIES AND AMENITIES
Favorite park activities include hiking, cycling, camping, backpacking, non-motorized boating, and fishing. Rainier is a popular peak for mountaineers; roughly 10,000 climbers attempt the summit each year, with 50 percent succeeding. Areas to explore include Wonderland Trail, which circles the mountain and passes glaciers and snowfields; Carbon Glacier, the largest glacier by volume in the lower 48 states; and Emmons Glacier, the largest by area.

The Paradise area, 5,400 feet up the south slope of Mount Rainier, is the most popular park destination. Located near the subalpine valley of the Paradise River, it is home to the historic 1916 Paradise Inn, the 1920 Paradise Guide House, and the 1966 Henry M. Jackson Visitor Center, which was renovated in 2008.

Longmire Visitor Center is found in the Nisqually River valley between the

Ramparts Ridge and the Tatoosh Range. Surrounded by old-growth Douglas fir, western redcedar, and western hemlock, it is home to the Longmire Museum, the Wilderness Information Center, and the National Park Inn, the only park lodging open all year. Nearby is Cougar Rock Campground and a trailhead for the Wonderland Trail. Sunrise Visitor Center is located in the northeastern park; there are miles of trails here, such as Mount Fremont, Burroughs Mountain, and Sourdough Ridge. Ohanapecosh to the southeast has a seasonal campground with 188 individual sites and 2 group sites, a visitor center, and a ranger station. The Ohanapecosh Hot Springs, Grove of the Patriarchs, and Silver Falls are all located in this area.

WILDLIFE AND PLANT LIFE

Mammals that inhabit the park include cougar, black bear, coyote, bobcat, red fox, marten, elk, mountain goat, snowshoe hare, hoary marmot, and pika. Common bird sightings include thrush, chickadee, kinglet, willow flycatcher, Clark's nutcracker, Canada jay, Steller's jay, grosbeak, finch, spotted owl, northern goshawk, bald eagle, golden eagle, peregrine falcon, ptarmigan, harlequin duck, and grouse. Fish are plentiful, including migratory fish like Chinook, pink, and coho salmon. Anglers can try their luck against bull, cutthroat, and rainbow trout, mountain whitefish, and sculpins.

Known for its exuberant wildflower displays, the park also supports diverse vegetation in its three zones. The extensive forest zone contains Pacific silver fir, Alaska yellow cedar, western white pine, and noble fir, while higher elevation forests are characterized by subalpine fir, mountain hemlock, and Alaskan yellow cedar, with whitebark pine and Englemann spruce in drier sites. Forests range from young woodlands to old-growth stands. The subalpine zone consists of scattered tree clumps and lush meadows. The alpine zone is divided into four broad vegetation types: fell fields, talus slopes, snow beds, and heather communities.

▶ **A young hoary marmot** grooms its mother while she suns herself on a rock.

▶ **Starting from just outside** the Paradise area, a short hike along a flowered-lined trail leads to Myrtle Falls. A footbridge over the Edith Creek Basin affords visitors a great view in any direction.

▼ **Riotous autumn colors** surround a trail through the Paradise area of the park.

DID YOU KNOW?

In 1792 Captain George Vancouver sailed into Puget Sound and named the mountain for his friend Peter Rainier, a Royal Navy officer. Native American tribes called the mountain *Tacoma* or *Tahoma*, "the source of nourishment from many streams."

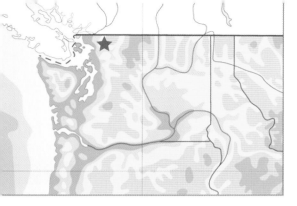

WASHINGTON
NORTH CASCADES

If wilderness hiking is on your agenda, this richly forested glacial park has much to offer in scenery, history, and wildlife.

LOCATION Whatcom, Skagit, and Chelan counties, WA

CLOSEST CITY Sedro-Woolley, WA

AREA 504,654 acres (2,042.26 km²)

ESTABLISHED October 2, 1968

VISITORS 30,000+

ELEVATION 9,206 feet (2,806 m) at Goode Mountain

GEOLOGY Mesozoic crystalline and metamorphic rocks

North Cascades is the largest of the three parks that make up the North Cascades National Parks Complex. Its expansive glacial system boasts the most glaciers of any U.S. park outside Alaska, 321 in number, and a third of all the glaciers in the lower 48 states.

This pristine site features rugged mountain peaks, the headwaters of numerous waterways, and expansive forests with the highest degree of plant biodiversity of any American national park. Considered a backpacker's

WHAT TO LOOK FOR

Glaciers, alpine blue lakes, and forested trails combine with brisk mountain air in the Northwest park.

> Diablo Lake
> Ross Lake and Dam
> Thunder Lake
> Cascade Pass Trail
> Goode Mountain
> Mount Shuksan

Washington Pass along the North Cascades Highway during the autumn season. Larch trees and snow on the hills signal the approach of winter in the North Cascade Mountain Range.

DID YOU KNOW?

In summer, Diablo Lake turns an opaque turquoise—the result of suspended fine rock particles refracting sunlight. Called glacial flour, these particles are eroded from the surrounding mountains and carried into the water through glacial streams.

paradise, it is almost entirely a protected wilderness area, with few structures, roads, or other improvements.

NATIVE PEOPLES

This area was first settled from 10,000 to 8,000 years ago, at the end of the last glacial period, when Paleo-Indians advanced from Puget Sound to interior regions as the ice withdrew. Artifacts like prehistoric chert microblades have been excavated at Cascade Pass, and another 260 prehistoric sites have been identified in the park as well. By the time European explorers arrived, the parklands were inhabited by the Skagit tribe, numbering roughly 1,000. To the north and east, the Nlaka'pamux ("Thompson Indians"), Chelan, Okanogan, and Wenatchi (Wenatchee) tribes lived in the eastern regions of the mountains.

The fur trade brought British and American trappers to the region, and after the 49th parallel was established as the border between the United States and Canada, surveyors came to chart routes for roads and railways. Logging and mining occurred on a limited scale, but the building of several hydroelectric dams on the Skagit River in the 1920s, had a decided impact. In 1968, after environmentalists lobbied to protect this vulnerable Eden, the park was established.

ACTIVITIES

Visitors enjoy hiking, backpacking, cycling, horseback riding, swimming, boating, canoeing, kayaking, and fishing. In order to protect wilderness areas, guests wishing to drive to a campground must do so in the adjacent national forests or national recreation areas. Camping inside the park requires entering on foot, on horseback, or by boat, and stays are regulated to ensure the wilderness is not overexploited. Mountaineering is popular here, but only unobtrusive clean climbing is allowed. The park remains open all year, but the main operating season is May to September. The North Cascades Visitor Center in Newhalem and the Golden West Visitor Center in Stehekin are both seasonal.

WILDLIFE AND PLANT LIFE

Local wildlife includes apex predators like black bear, cougar, bald eagle, bobcat, and lynx, along with wolverine, river otter, mountain goat, elk, deer, Douglas squirrels, martens, Townsend chipmunks, red tree voles, and bushytail wood rats. There are also at least 12 species of bats.

The park contains more than 1,630 vascular plants and spans the Cascade Crest from the wet rainforests of the west side to the dry ponderosa pine terrain of the east. Ecoregions based on altitude are the lowland forest, an often dense combination of western redcedar, western hemlock, Sitka spruce, Alaska cedar, and Douglas, grand, and silver fir; the highland forest, where Pacific silver fir mixes with Alaskan cedar, mountain hemlock, and subalpine fir; and the subalpine/alpine zone, dominated by mountain hemlock. Meadows feature a mix of heathers, mountain huckleberry, and sedges.

▼ **A backpacker** pauses to admire the stunning view of frozen Thorton Lake and Trappers Peak.

▲ **Rustic holiday cabins** line Ross Lake, affording visitors amazing views of the lake and mountains.

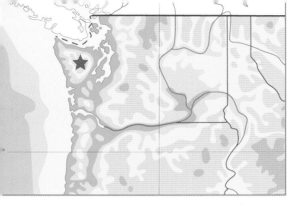

WASHINGTON
OLYMPIC

Washington's untamed seacoast borders this vast wilderness where a rainforest rises up to meet the mountains.

LOCATION Jefferson, Clallam, Mason, and Grays Harbor counties, WA

CLOSEST CITY Port Angeles, WA

AREA 922,650 acres (3,733.8 km²)

ESTABLISHED March 2, 1909, as Mount Olympus National Monument; June 29, 1938, as Olympic National Park

VISITORS 2,499,000+

ELEVATION 7,962 feet (2,427 m) at Mount Olympus

GEOLOGY basalts, sedimentary rock, and metamorphic rock

WHAT TO LOOK FOR

Multiple ecosystems beckon explorers in this Northwest treasure.

> Hoh, Queets, and
   Quinault rainforests
> Hurricane Ridge overlook
> Sea coast and marine wildlife
> Wilderness Information Center

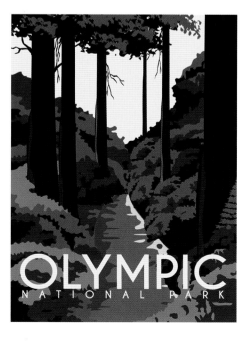

This popular national park is located on the Olympic Peninsula in northwestern Washington State. The park is divided into four topographic regions: the 70 miles of shoreline, the glacier-capped Olympic Mountains, the temperate rainforest in the west, and the drier forests to the east.

Originally protected by Theodore Roosevelt as Mount Olympus National Monument, the site received national park status under Franklin D. Roosevelt in 1938. It was later designated a UNESCO International Biosphere Reserve and in 1981 became a World Heritage Site. In 1988, nearly 95 percent of the park was further protected as the Olympic Wilderness, renamed Daniel J. Evans Wilderness in 2017 for the former governor and conservationist.

EARLY INHABITANTS

The first people to camp on the peninsula—based on a mastodon skull with an embedded projectile—were Paleo-Indian hunters who arrived around 13,500 years ago. By 1300 BCE, Makah people were living in Neah Bay, and 300 years ago Ozette villagers carved the petroglyphs on Wedding Rocks near Cape Alava. In the late 1700s, smallpox carried by European settlers killed nearly 30 percent of the Northwest native population.
 Nine tribes lived on the Peninsula—the Hoh, Skokomish, Squaxin Island, Lower Elwha Klallam, Jamestown S'Klallam, Port Gamble S'Klallam, Quinault, Quileute, and Makah. They shared many aspects of trade and religion and customs such as reverence for elders. Many of their cultural sites have been identified in the parklands and important artifacts recovered. Today, indigenous communities live at the mouths of two rivers—the Hoh River is home to the Hoh people, and the town of La Push, at the mouth of the Quileute River, is home to the Quileute people.
 When commercial interests first encroached on the peninsula in the late 1800s, their goal was harvesting resources such as fish, game, and, especially, timber. The locals began to grow alarmed about logging after seeing clearcut hillsides denuded of trees. From this community concern the movement to preserve the peninsula took shape. President Theodore Roosevelt created the national monument in large part to protect the calving grounds and summer range of the Roosevelt elk, which had been named for him.

ACTIVITIES AND SIGHTS

Favorite activities include sightseeing, hiking, fishing, backpacking, photography, swimming, bicycling, and kite flying. There are no roads in the interior, but a network of hiking trails leads to a variety of destinations, landmarks, and views.

· The Main Visitor Center and Wilderness Information Center are recommended first stops for visitors. Here visitors find a hands-on Discovery Room for kids, an orientation film, a bookstore, and two trailheads just outside.

· Hoh Rainforest, with an annual rainfall of more than 140 inches, is a lush, green Eden, where mosses and ferns appear to cover every surface.

▶ **Low tide at Shi-Shi Beach** brings colorful sea stars and green sea anemone to the rocky tidepools.

The Hall of Mosses Trail circles an older section the Hoh Rainforest above the river. In this unique section of the park, mosses drape the boughs of hemlock, spruce and fir that can stand more than 200 feet high.

▲ **Sol Duc Waterfall,** called the most beautiful falls in the park. Trails through the Sol Duc Valley feature views of imposing towering trees, impressively cascading waterways, clear alpine lakes, and snowcapped mountain peaks, along with plenty of opportunities to see wildlife.

► **Wind-sheared trees** top the sea stacks standing in the waters off Rialto Beach. The park's 73-mile long wilderness coastline features several of these fascinating formations, which are home to nesting seabird colonies.

- Hurricane Ridge is an easily accessed mountain clearing with stunning views.
- Kalaloch and Ruby Beaches offer views of offshore islands called sea stacks and marine animal sightings. Mora and Rialto Beaches, likewise, provide dramatic scenery along with seals, sea lions, otters, whales, seabirds, and eagles.
- Staircase Rapids Loop Trail travels beside the Skokomish River and beneath a canopy of Douglas firs.

WILDLIFE AND PLANT LIFE

Animal inhabitants include Roosevelt elk, black bear, cougar, coyote, Canadian lynx, red fox, beaver, weasel, fisher, marten, black-tailed deer, snowshoe hare, and six species of bats. (The non-native mountain goats are being moved from the park.) Avian sightings include numerous song birds, shore birds, and waterfowl, as well as bald eagle, spotted owl, and northern pygmy owl. There are also three species of snake and one species of lizard. Because the park is on a peninsula and cut off from the south by mountains, there are several endemic species, including the Olympic marmot, Piper's bellflower, and Flett's violet. The iconic Roosevelt elk is found only on the coastline of the Pacific Northwest. The best places to spot wildlife include Elwha Valley, Hoh Rainforest, Hurricane Ridge, Kalaloch and Ruby Beach, Lake Crescent, and Quinault Rainforest.

More than 1,450 types of vascular plants are found here, nearly as many as in all the British Isles. The park contains three distinct ecosystems. The subalpine forests and wildflower meadows of the glaciated mountains include Indian paintbrush and shooting star along with lush grasses for elk to graze on. In the temperate rainforest, plant life is understandably profuse—mosses, spike mosses, ferns, and lichens lend the landscape a jungle-like feel. The shoreline's coastal forest occasionally gives way to prairie wetlands with wild cranberry, crowberry, bog laurel, Labrador-tea, sundew, and sphagnum. The dominant trees throughout the park are Sitka spruce, western hemlock, western redcedar, and Douglas fir along with several deciduous species.

"BETWEEN EVERY TWO PINE TREES THERE IS A DOOR LEADING TO A NEW WAY OF LIFE."

— John Muir, naturalist and author

A black-tailed deer peeks around a stand of trees on Sunrise Point Trail. At just over 5 miles long, this wildflower-lined route provides an easy hike with 1,000 feet of elevation that gives spectacular views of Mount Angeles and the Hurricane Ridge.

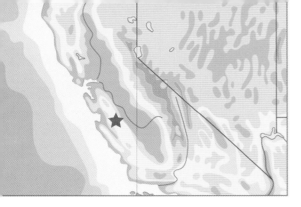

CALIFORNIA
PINNACLES

Discover the soaring, eroded segments of a volcano that now lie 200 miles from the site of the original eruption.

LOCATION San Benito County and Monterey County, CA

CLOSEST CITY Soledad, CA

AREA 26,606 acres (107.67 km²)

ESTABLISHED January 16, 1908, as National Monument; January 10, 2013, as National Park

VISITORS 222,100+

ELEVATION 3,304 feet (1,007 m) at North Chalone Peak

GEOLOGY Volcanic igneous rock

WHAT TO LOOK FOR

Shaded trails lead to hidden caves and craggy volcanic remnants.

> High Peaks area

> Bear Gulch Cave and Reservoir

> Balconies Cave

> Condor Gulch Trail to overlook

▲ **The Bear Gulch Cave Trail** meanders through an open cave system created by large volcanic talus boulders at the cave's entrance.

Pinnacles is located in Central California, east of the Salinas Valley and two and a half hours south of San Francisco. It is named for the jagged volcanic rock formations that jut above the treeline like alien skyscrapers.

These eroded spires were the result of an eruption of the Neenach Volcano that occurred 23 million years ago near present-day Lancaster. A section of rock was split from the main volcano by the movement of the Pacific plate along the San Andreas fault, and it was shifted 195 miles to the northwest and deposited close to modern Soledad. As one of the country's newest national parks, Pinnacles might not have a high profile, but its many repeat visitors appreciate its dramatic scenery, rock and cave formations, and relaxed atmosphere.

HISTORY

Archeologists have found 13 Native American sites in the park, one possibly dating back 2,000 years. Artifacts include stone tools used by the Chalon and Mutsun groups of the Ohlone peoples. When the Spanish arrived in the 1700s, they brought novel diseases and cultural upheaval to Indian life. Many indigenous people died or were dispersed. It is thought that the last Chalon died in 1810. From that time until 1865, when homesteaders arrived, the Pinnacles region remained wild and uninhabited. People from surrounding communities eventually picnicked in the parklands, which they called the Palisades. In 1908, this unique landscape became Pinnacles National Monument under Theodore Roosevelt.

ACTIVITIES AND AMENITIES

Hiking, camping, swimming, stargazing, and rock climbing are popular activities. High Peaks Trail offers incredible panoramas of the park's upper elevations. Bear Gulch Cave Trail leads to the cave and then scenic Bear Gulch Reservoir. Balconies Cave Trail runs through several caves and winds upward to an alternate view of the Pinnacles. The park's caverns are not volcanic tubes, but rather talus caves, which are natural holes in the ground created by rock fall-ins. Visitors may take self-guided tours through the caves—which have stairs and walkways with handrails—but they must bring their own flashlights.

  Park facilities include East Pinnacles Bookstore, East Pinnacles Visitor Center, Bear Gulch Nature Center, and West Pinnacles Visitor Contact Station. There is one campground that is accessed from the park's east side.

DID YOU KNOW?

In 2003, Pinnacles joined the California Condor Recovery Program as a release and management site. The park co-manages all the wild condors in central California along with the Ventana Wildlife Society.

WILDLIFE AND PLANT LIFE

Endangered California condors are the most celebrated residents here, but there are also black-tailed deer, bobcat, gray fox, raccoon, jackrabbit, brush rabbit, ground squirrel, and 13 species of bat, as well as greater roadrunner, golden eagle, prairie falcon, peregrine falcon, a host of songbirds and waders, waterfowl, woodpeckers, and hummingbirds.

The park includes five plant communities. Chaparral vegetation include chamise, manzanita, holly-leaved cherry, mountain mahogany, and buck brush. Woodlands support blue oak, non-native grasses, native perennial and annual species, gray pine, California buckeye, and valley oak. Riparian areas along streams foster western sycamore, Fremont's cottonwood, California buckeye, oak, willow, and mule

▲ **The Balconies Cave Trail** leads visitors through chaparral strewn with enormous volcanic boulders.

► **A small dam** creates a reservoir on the Bear Gulch Creek in Pinnacles' arid volcanic landscape.

fat. Grassland plants include fiddleneck, lomatiums, non-native filaree, and brome. Rock and scree areas, with little to no soil, may have bitterroot and two-leaved onion.

The golden hour just after sunrise sheds warm natural light over the dramatic High Peaks area. Theodore Roosevelt declared this region a national monument early in the 20th century, but it was not until 2013 that President Barack Obama designated Pinnacles as America's 62nd park.

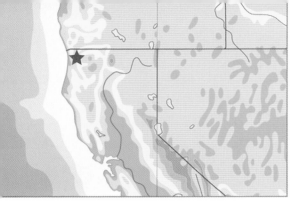

CALIFORNIA
REDWOOD

The towering groves of coast redwoods within the park will both awe and inspire visitors.

LOCATION Humboldt County and Del Norte County, CA

CLOSEST CITY Crescent City, CA

AREA 138,999 acres (562.51 km²)

ESTABLISHED October 2, 1968

VISITORS 405,700+

ELEVATION 3,170 feet (970 m) at Coyote Peak

GEOLOGY Marine sedimentary rocks of the Franciscan Assemblage, including sandstone, siltstone, shale, and chart; some metamorphic greenstone

WHAT TO LOOK FOR

Wander among the groves of giants or follow a woodland trail to the Pacific shore.

> Big Tree Wayside

> Newton B. Drury Scenic Parkway

> Howland Hill Road

> Stout Memorial Grove Trail

> Trillium Falls Trail

Redwoods National Park in northwest California is part of a complex that also includes three state parks, all of them cooperatively managed by the National Park Service and the California Department of Parks and Recreation. Extremely tall, with straight, upright trunks, coast redwoods (*Sequoia sempervirens*) are now considered national treasures, but for many decades they were simply a convenient source of lumber for the building trades.

In 1850, California's old-growth redwood forest covered more than 2,000,000 acres of the coast. By the time the national park was finally created, nearly 90 percent of the coast redwoods had been felled. Redwoods can reach heights of 360 feet and live between 400 and 700 years, though some are thought to be at least 2,000 years old. The four parks currently protect 45 percent of all remaining coast redwood old-growth forests, totaling at least 38,982 acres. These parks also preserve other indigenous plants, animals, grassland prairie, oak woodlands, Native American cultural resources, wild waterways, and 37 miles of undeveloped coastline.

HISTORY

Present-day tribes like the Yurok, Tolowa, Karok, Chilula, and Wiyot have deep historical ties to this region and its trees, and some indigenous groups still live in the park. Based on archaeological evidence, their forebears arrived in the parklands 3,000 years ago. As Minnie Reeves, a Chilula tribal elder and religious leader, explained in 1976, the Chilula are "people from within the redwood tree." For many tribes it was, as scholars noted, as though their lives and culture "were enmeshed in the character and fabric of the trees." The Yurok believed the trees were divine beings standing guard over sacred places.

In 1828 frontiersman and pioneer Jedediah Smith was likely the first Easterner to leave the coast and explore this inland region. The discovery of gold at Trinity River in 1850 brought miners into the area, resulting in conflicts with the native peoples; many were forcibly removed or massacred. Some disillusioned miners joined with loggers who were harvesting giant, old-growth redwoods to help develop booming cities like San Francisco. By 1910, extensive logging had conservationists scrambling

▲ **A whimsical signpost** directs visitors to the sights that they have come here to see.

"DESTROY THESE TREES AND YOU DESTROY THE CREATOR'S LOVE. AND IF YOU DESTROY THAT WHICH THE CREATOR LOVES SO MUCH, YOU WILL EVENTUALLY DESTROY MANKIND."

— *Minnie Reeves, Chilula tribal elder*

The Lady Bird Johnson Grove, named for first lady of the president who declared Redwood a national park, is an easy walk on a fern-studded pathway through the lush old-growth redwood landscape.

to preserve the remaining trees. The Save the Redwoods League, founded by the Boone and Crockett Club, managed to purchase several groves and forests, while three areas still sheltering redwoods became state parks—Prairie Creek Redwoods, Del Norte Coast Redwoods, and Jedediah Smith Redwoods. (Humboldt Redwoods State Park is not part of the same system.) But it was not until 1968 that Lyndon Johnson signed a bill creating the national park.

RECREATION AMONG THE TREES

Park activities include scenic drives and hiking and biking along dozens of trails within the park complex that total more than 100 miles. Recommended trails include Stout Memorial Grove in the north, which runs next to the Smith River, and the family-friendly Prairie Creek–Foothill Trail Loop and Lady Bird Johnson Grove. Tall Trees Grove Loop requires a drive

◄ **The jagged California coastline.** The Coastal Trail offers visitors 70 miles of hiking paths to explore the marine aspect of the park, including a chance to spy delicate tidepool creatures amid the sandy beaches.

▼ **Campers pitch their tents** beneath the shelter of sky-scraping ancient redwoods.

DID YOU KNOW?

The park is home to the tallest tree in the world, Hyperion, and 5 of the 10 tallest trees on earth— Hyperion, Helios, Icarus, Nugget, and Orion.

▲ **Prairie Creek Redwoods State Park** is part of the Redwood National Park complex that provides sanctuary for old-growth redwood forest. The Prairie Creek Trail leads through Fern Canyon, an amazing wonder that was used as a primeval backdrop in the movie *Jurassic Park II, The Lost World*.

and a hike—and a permit. Anglers can fish for salmon and trout in the Smith and Klamath rivers and surf-cast for smelt and surfperch along park beaches. For camping enthusiasts, there are four developed campgrounds and seven backcountry campsites. Leashed pets are allowed in designated areas.

WILDLIFE AND PLANT LIFE

The park ecosystem acts as a refuge for threatened species, such as the tidewater goby, Chinook salmon, northern spotted owl, and Steller sea lion. Other animals found here include black bear, bobcat, fisher, pine marten, raccoon, black-tailed deer, and Roosevelt elk, and smaller fry like banana slugs, Pacific giant salamanders, and red-bellied newts. Bird species include brown pelican, double-crested cormorant, sand-piper, merganser, osprey, and great blue heron. Tidal pools may contain anemones, sea stars, sea cucumbers, crabs, isopods, mussels, and snails. Visitors might also glimpse marine animals like harbor seal, elephant seal, sea lion, harbor porpoise, gray and humpback whale, and orca.

In addition to the redwoods, the forests contain Douglas fir, with an understory of Pacific poison oak, tanoak, madrone, California bay or laurel, and red alder, sword fern, and redwood sorrel rhododendron, huckleberry, salal, and azalea. The coastal areas support beach pea, beach strawberry, and sand verbena, along with hardy Sitka spruce, while the hills are covered in white alder. At higher elevations, the redwoods give way to mixed evergreens.

TUNNEL TREES

In the late 1800s and early 1900s, it became a fad to dig large tunnels through a number of California's big trees. Photos of tourists driving, cycling, or walking through the trees became part of the parks' advertising strategy. The burgeoning number of motorists were especially targeted with opportunities to take pictures in the drive-thru trees. However charming these images might be, tunneling inflicts severe damage on a tree's health and strength. With the welfare of the trees coming to the fore, the trend waned and is no longer practiced.

▲ **The Klamath Tour Thru Tree.** On the way to the Avenue of Giants and Redwood National Park, just off the stretch of U.S. Highway 101 known as the Redwood Highway, are three "drive-thru" trees. This newest one sits atop a hill near Redwood National Park, carved out in 1976 by craftspeople who kept the health of the tree in mind, avoiding critical areas of living wood.

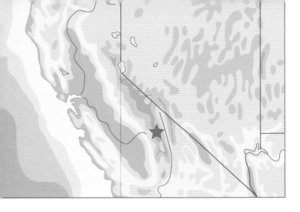

CALIFORNIA
SEQUOIA

Visitors to this park will be astonished by trees so massive that in previous centuries Easterners doubted their very existence.

LOCATION Tulare County, CA

CLOSEST CITY Visalia, CA

AREA 404,064 acres (1,635.19 km²)

ESTABLISHED September 25, 1890

VISITORS 1,229,600+

ELEVATION 14,505 feet (4,421 m) at Mount Whitney

GEOLOGY Intrusive igneous rock—granite, diorite, and monzonite—and metamorphic marble

WHAT TO LOOK FOR

Discover towering trees, marble caves, and stunning water features.

> General Sherman and the Giant Forest

> High Sierra Trail and Tokopah Falls Trail

> Crystal Cave

> Hospital Rock and pictographs

> Mount Whitney

▼ **A spot atop the summit** of Mount Whitney, the highest peak in the continental United States, which lies on the boundary of Sequoia National Park and Inyo National Forest, provides a sweeping panorama of the rugged Sierra Nevada landscape.

Located adjacent to Kings Canyon National Park in the southern Sierra Nevada, Sequoia was established 50 years before its sibling. It was the first national park created to protect a living organism, the sequoia tree. This is in contrast to Denali, which was the first created to protect an animal, the Dall sheep. Both Sequoia and Kings Canyon contain old-growth forests that resemble the California landscapes from before the arrival of European settlers.

One of the park's highlights is the sequoia called General Sherman, the largest tree by volume in the world. Measuring a whopping 52,500 cubic feet, its age is estimated at between 2,200 to 2,700 years. It grows in the Giant Forest, which is home to 5 of the 10 largest trees in the world. In addition to the remarkable trees, there are canyons carved by rivers and glaciers, numerous lakes and streams, rugged peaks, and a system of underground caverns.

PARK HISTORY

Early residents known as the "Monachee" (Western Mono) lived in the Foothills region of the parklands, perhaps as far back as 1350 CE. In summer they would travel the mountain passes to trade with tribes to the east. Their pictographs are found at several sites, including Potwisha and Hospital Rock, a substantial, pinkish quartzite rock near an area that was once home to a large Native American village. These people also left behind mortars used to grind acorns, a food staple.

When groups of settlers arrived, they already found these tribes decimated by smallpox. Hale Dixon Tharp, an early homesteader, actually built a cabin from a hollowed-out sequoia in the Giant Forest near Log Meadow. Conservationist John Muir often visited Tharp's cabin and called the meadow the "Gem of the Sierra." Tharp also appreciated the beauty around him and fought against logging in the region. Unfortunately, the timber trade continued, even though sequoia wood splintered easily. Once the park was established in 1890, most logging ceased.

ACTIVITIES

Park visitors enjoy hiking and camping . . . and gazing in wonder at the many supersized sequoias. Favorite trails include Sherman Tree Trail, a short, paved trail leading to the base of the General Sherman tree and a grove of giant sequoias, and High Sierra Trail, which crosses the Great Western Divide. The trail to beautiful Tokopah Falls starts in Lodgepole Campground. Tunnel Log, which measured 275 feet, fell across a roadway and now has a tunnel cut through it for vehicle traffic.

Crescent Meadow is a small, sequoia-rimmed sierran montane in the Giant Forest region. Moro Rock, a granite dome lies in the center of the park between Giant

DID YOU KNOW?

In its early days, the park was managed by U.S. army troops known as the Buffalo Soldiers, who were African-American men from the South. They completed park infrastructure projects as well as taking on park management duties.

General Sherman is not only the largest tree in the park, but also contains a greater volume of wood in its trunk than any other tree on Earth.

GENERAL SHERMAN

A curving road cuts through a mountainside leading into Sequoia National Park with wide vistas of the rugged Sierra Nevada range.

SEQUOIA VS. REDWOOD

These two trees might be closely related, but they exhibit many characteristics that distinguish them from each other.

- Sequoias grow singly or in scattered groups along the western slopes of the Sierra Nevada. Redwoods grow near the Pacific Ocean in a continuous belt along the northern California coast.

- Both trees grow from seeds, but redwoods can sprout from stumps, roots, and burls.

- Sequoia foliage is scaly, like a juniper; redwood foliage forms two-ranked needles, like hemlock.

- Sequoia trees are the largest in volume (their girthy trunks show little tapering); redwoods are the tallest trees, with slender trunks.

- Sequoia cones and seeds dwarf those of the redwood.

- Sequoia wood is coarser than redwood, with wide growth rings; both species are resistant to decay.

- Sequoia bark is a vivid reddish brown, while redwood bark is a dull cocoa brown.

◄ **Giant sequoias of the Giants Forest** line the Generals Highway. The forest connects to Sequoia National Park to the Kings Canyon General Grant Grove via this scenic route.

► **Tharp's Log** is a hollowed-out sequoia nestled along the Crescent Meadow Trail. Built as a cabin by rancher Hale Tharp, its guests have included famed naturalist John Muir. Today, hikers to the meadow can make a stop at this unique structure, which still contains an old bed, table, and bench.

Forest and Crescent Meadow. A 351-step stairway, built in the 1930s by the Civilian Conservation Corps, gives access to the summit. The stairway is listed on the National Register of Historic Places. The park also contains more than 270 known caves, including Lilburn Cave which is California's longest at nearly 17 miles. The only cave open to visitors is the marble karst Crystal Cave.

There are three campgrounds in the Foothills area—Potwisha, Buckeye Flat, and South Fork—and four at higher elevations—Atwell Mill, Cold Springs, Lodgepole, and Dorst Creek. Ash Mountain is the headquarters for Sequoia and Kings Canyon National Parks and also for the Sequoia Natural History Association.

WILDLIFE AND PLANT LIFE
Animals found here include coyote, black bear, bobcat, cougar, badger, wolverine, bighorn sheep, deer, fox, beaver, muskrat, and opossum, plus California quail, scrub jay, 11 species of woodpecker, and 3 types of owl, plus various species of turtle, snake, and frog.

More than 1,300 native plant species live in Sequoia and Kings Canyon National Parks.

◄ **A steep staircase** carved into Moro Rock leads to its summit, affording jaw-dropping views to the Sierra Nevadas and Mount Whitney.

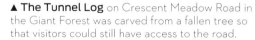

▲ **The Tunnel Log** on Crescent Meadow Road in the Giant Forest was carved from a fallen tree so that visitors could still have access to the road.

◄ **A distinctive spiderweb gate** guards the entry into Sequoia's Crystal Cave.

In the lower elevations, where summers are hot and dry, vegetation is largely chaparral, with blue oak woodlands, grasslands, California buckeye, and yucca. The low- to mid-mountain elevations contain mixed forests of ponderosa pine, incense cedar, white fir, sugar pine, and scattered groves of giant sequoia. The higher alpine zone features tundra with Jeffrey pine scattered on dry granitic slopes and stands of red fir and lodgepole pine. In warmer months, upland meadows ringed with quaking aspen are lush with wildflowers.

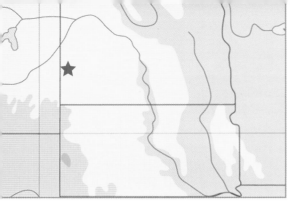

NORTH DAKOTA

THEODORE ROOSEVELT

These craggy, contorted badlands once gave comfort to a future president who would go on to preserve many of America's natural resources.

LOCATION Billings County and McKenzie County, ND

CLOSEST CITY Medora, ND

AREA 70,446 acres (285.08 km²)

ESTABLISHED April 25, 1947, as Theodore Roosevelt National Memorial Park; November 10, 1978, as Theodore Roosevelt National Park

VISITORS 749,300+

ELEVATION 5,013 feet (1,528 m) at Rankin Ridge

GEOLOGY Volcanic and sedimentary rock

▼ **Wild horses** graze the valleys of the park. These free-ranging feral horses are descendants of the small bands that eluded capture after the park was fenced and a 1954 roundup had removed 200 branded animals.

Located in northwest North Dakota, in the rugged badlands, the park is divided into three sections. The North Unit and South Unit lie 68 miles apart, with the Elkhorn Ranch Unit located in between them. The Little Missouri River winds through all three units and the Maah Daah Hey Trail connects them.

Nature and the outdoors were deeply important to President Roosevelt, the "wilderness warrior," and this park commemorates his efforts toward the conservation of America's natural resources.

A PLACE OF PERFECT FREEDOM

New York State politician Theodore Roosevelt first visited the North Dakota badlands to hunt bison in September 1883. He bagged his bison and quickly became enamored of the West's rugged lifestyle and its "perfect freedom."

WHAT TO LOOK FOR

This park combines magical scenery with American history.

> Scenic Loop Drive

> Painted Canyon Overlook

> Elkhorn Ranch site

> Maltese Cross Cabin

> Prairie Dog Town

DID YOU KNOW?

This is the only national park named in honor of a president or a single individual.

The rugged terrain of the Dakota badlands forms a colorful landscape of buttes, mesas, washes, and valleys carved out by the Little Missouri River.

▲ **The Maltese Cross Cabin,** constructed of ponderosa pine, was Theodore Roosevelt's first cabin in the Dakota Territory. He used it from 1883 to 1884 when it stood in its original site in the wooded bottomlands of the Little Missouri River. It now stands directly behind the Theodore Roosevelt National Park Interpretive Center and currently displays some of Roosevelt's belongings.

He decided to invest in the Maltese Cross Ranch, a cattle spread seven miles south of Medora. After the deaths of both his wife and mother on February 14, 1884, Roosevelt fled to his North Dakota ranch to grieve alone in his small cabin. Over that summer he started a second ranch called Elkhorn, 35 miles north of Medora, where he often went to unwind. His writing desk from the site is on display in the park.

ACTIVITIES

The park is popular for backcountry hiking and horseback riding. Both main units offer scenic drives, around 100 miles of foot and horse trails, and plenty of scenic vistas. There are three developed campgrounds: Juniper in the North Unit, and Cottonwood and Roundup Group Horse in the South Unit. A museum at the South Unit Visitor Center highlights Roosevelt's ranching days and also features his Maltese Cross Cabin. Elkhorn Ranch is located in a more remote area of the park, accessible by gravel roads. Here, the foundation of the ranch house and some outbuildings have been preserved. The Maah Daah Hey Trail is longest continuous single-track mountain biking trail in America. At the South Unit entrance lies the town of Medora, with its planked sidewalks and quaint shops, perfect for that "Old West" experience. From June to September the Burning Hills Amphitheater puts on the *Medora Musical,* tracing the history of the area with references to Teddy Roosevelt.

WILDLIFE AND PLANT LIFE

Grazing animals include bison, feral horses (mustangs), elk, bighorn sheep, white-tail and mule deer, pronghorn, and prairie dogs. The park also maintains a herd of historic long-horn cattle. Notably absent are large predators. Bison can be unpredictable, however, so visitors should view them from a distance. The park is surrounded by a 7-foot woven wire fence to keep bison in and commercial livestock out. Other park animals are able to circumvent the fence in specific locations. Resident birds include golden eagle, wild turkey, white-breasted nuthatch, and great-horned owl. Migratory birds that pass through the park include huge flocks of sandhill cranes.

The park's vegetation is surprisingly diverse. From sun-drenched buttes to cool north slopes, to flood plains and grasslands, more than 400 plant species are found here. The seasons effect startling changes on the landscape—in early summer, brown, dormant winter grass transforms into green meadows laced with hundreds of wildflowers.

SOUTH DAKOTA
WIND CAVE

Cave walls filled with lace-like calcite formations draw visitors to this underground marvel.

LOCATION Custer County, SD
CLOSEST CITY Hot Springs, SD
AREA 33,847 acres (136.97 km²)
ESTABLISHED January 9, 1903
VISITORS 448,400+
ELEVATION 5,013 feet (1,528 m), at Rankin Ridge
GEOLOGY Sedimentary rock

DID YOU KNOW?

In addition to boxwork, Wind Cave also displays cave popcorn, small nodes of calcite, aragonite, or gypsum that form clusters, and moonmilk, a creamy precipitate found inside many limestone caves.

Located in the Black Hills in western South Dakota, Wind Cave was inaugurated under Theodore Roosevelt, becoming the country's seventh national park and the park system's first official cave.

It is considered the densest cave system in the world, and at more than 150 miles in length it is the seventh longest. The boxwork formations for which it is famous are actually calcite fins that were thought to resemble mailbox slots at the post office.

A SHORT HISTORY
The Black Hills, the oldest mountain range in America, have been home to Native peoples for 10,000 years. The Arikara arrived around 1500 CE, followed by the Cheyenne, Crow, Kiowa, and Pawnee. In the 1700s the Lakota claimed the region for their own people. These mountains, which had been sacred to the Omaha, Cheyenne, Arapaho, Kiowa, and Kiowa-Apache tribes were also revered by the Lakota, who called them *Paha Sapa*, or "hills that are black."

The first reported discovery of the cave was in 1881 when two hunters, brothers Tom and Jesse Bingham, felt a large gust of wind blow out of a small round hole in some rocks. They realized a large cavern beneath them was "exhaling." Of course the Indian tribes that lived in the region knew about the cave. The Lakota spoke about the hole that "blew air," and believed their people—along with the bison—had emerged from the underworld through that opening. The first person to actually start exploring the cave—using a ball of string—was 17-year-old Alvin McDonald in 1890. He also conducted tours by candlelight.

ACTIVITIES AND AMENITIES
Visitors enjoy hiking the 30 miles of trails—including two pet-friendly trails, birding, photographing wildlife, camping, and, of course, taking ranger-

◄ **A boxwork geological formation** is typical of the cave's makeup. The cave maintains a steady, slightly cool temperature of 54 degrees F.

WHAT TO LOOK FOR

The park features two areas to discover, one above ground, one below.

> Wind Cave
> Herds of buffalo grazing on the grasslands
> Elk browsing at dusk

A cow and her calf settle into a grassy meadow. They are members of the park's free-roaming Plains bison herd, which now numbers about 250 to 400 individuals.

guided tours of the cave. The visitor center features exhibits on the geology and history of the cave, the area's natural history, and the work of the Civilian Conservation Corps in the park. Nearby Elk Mountain Campground has 75 sites for tents and RVs and is open year-round.

WILDLIFE AND PLANT LIFE

The parkland contains the largest remaining natural mixed-grass prairie in the United States. Vast herds of bison once roamed there, but by the early 1900s they were virtually extinct. So in 1913 the Bronx Zoo in New York City donated 14 of their own bison to the park; six more came from Yellowstone. From that stock a new herd arose, believed to be one of only seven free-roaming and genetically pure herds on public lands in North America.

The park supports two ecosystems—an open mixed-grass prairie and a ponderosa pine forest on rocky hillsides. The transitional area is called the ecotone. The prairie supports bison, pronghorn, black-footed ferret, coyote, and prairie dog, an important part of the food web. The forest offers shade and shelter to wildflowers, shrubs, and ferns, as well as animals such as mule deer, squirrel, and wild turkey. Elk

are found in the ecotone: they remain at the edge of the forest by day and venture onto the prairie at night to feed. Natural fires preserve the ecotone and keep the forest from encroaching on the prairie.

▼ **The mixed-grasses** growing on the parklands outside the cave are part of the largest tract of prairielands left on the North American continent.

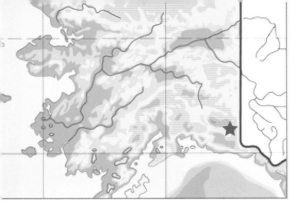

ALASKA
WRANGELL-ST. ELIAS

Soaring volcanic peaks and glacial ice fields lure wilderness lovers to this largest of national parks.

LOCATION Chugach Census Area, Copper River Census Area, Southeast Fairbanks Census Area, and Yakutat City and Borough, AK

CLOSEST CITY Copper Center, AK

AREA 13,175,799 acres (53,320.57 km²)

ESTABLISHED December 1, 1978, as National Monument; December 2, 1980, as National Park and Preserve

VISITORS 79,400+

ELEVATION 18,008 feet (5,489 m) at Mount St. Elias

GEOLOGY Some volcanic rock plus 7 "exotic" terranes formed elsewhere and grafted onto the continent's edge

DID YOU KNOW?

In 1912, Dora Keen, age 41, was the first to climb 16,390-foot Mount Blackburn, assisted by future husband, George Handy. Keen's was the first expedition to use dogs on a mountain, the first to succeed without Swiss guides, the first to camp in snow caves, and the first to make a prolonged night ascent.

Located in southeast Alaska, Wrangell–St. Elias National Park and Preserve was designated to protect the largest wilderness in the United States. This park is so immense, it could fit six Yellowstones inside its boundaries.

A FIERY HISTORY

The park's challenging terrain was sculpted by the indomitable forces of both volcanoes and glaciers. Mount Wrangell is a massive, active shield volcano, one of several in the Wrangell Mountains. Mount Churchill, in the St. Elias Range—the highest coastal range in the world, experienced a major eruption roughly 2,000 years ago. One quarter of U.S. glaciers are found in this park, including Malaspina, North America's largest piedmont glacier; Hubbard, Alaska's longest tidewater glacier; and Nabesna, the world's longest valley glacier.

Native Alaskan peoples, likely caribou hunters, first visited the region 8,000 years ago, and once the glaciers retreated, they established settlements. The Ahtna and Upper Tanana Athabascans resided in the interior of the park, while the Eyak and the Tlingit lived in villages along the Gulf of Alaska. In the early 1780s, Russian trappers

WHAT TO LOOK FOR

Two scenic roads allay the need for backcountry trekking.

> McCarthy Road and Nabesna Road

> Mount St. Elias, the second highest elevation in the U.S. and Canada

> Kennecott Mine and town of McCarthy

> Root Glacier Trail and Copper River

▼ **A Super Cub Piper** bush airplane flies campers to the snowy wilderness of Wrangell-St. Elias. The park, which is home to Bagley Icefield, comprises 60 percent of all permanently ice-covered terrain in Alaska.

seeking fur in the Copper River Basin were possibly the first non-natives in the parklands. The huge Copper River was full of salmon, but it also supplied Athabaskans with blue-green chunks of copper ore. The boomtown of Kennecott arose from 1903 to 1938 after a major copper deposit was discovered on Kennecott Mountain. The "ghost town" village and mine site are now a National Historic Landmark.

ACTIVITIES AND LANDMARKS

Visitors enjoy scenic drives, hiking, camping, guided tours, floating, boating, and sport fishing. Recommended trails include Root Glacier, Bonanza Mine, Goat Trail, all rated hard; Skookum Volcano, Crystalline Hills, and Caribou Creek, rated moderate, and West Kennecott Glacier and Boreal Forest Loop, rated easy. There are two roads in the park—42-mile Nebesma and 65-mile McCarthy—that cover a great deal of the park. Shuttles travel from quaint McCarthy to the mining center at Kennecott, where there is a lodge, a restaurant, and a visitor center.

WILDLIFE AND PLANT LIFE

Animal life abounds in this remote park, where humans are diminished to a flyspeck against the monumental backdrops. Mammals include moose, black and brown bear, coyote, fox, river otter, beaver, wolverine, marten, Canadian lynx, marmot, pika, and ground squirrel. The 95 species of birds include songbirds, hawks, gulls, waterfowl, waders, woodpeckers, and

gamebirds. The coastal waters are home to sea lions, harbor seals, sea otters, porpoises, and whales. Anglers may fish for Arctic grayling, trout (Dolly Varden, lake, cutthroat, steelhead, and rainbow), whitefish, salmon (sockeye, coho, and Chinook), and northern pike.

Vegetation ranges from lowland habitats that include alder, dwarf birch, crowberry, Labrador tea, shrub cinquefoil, willow, blueberry, and moss to wetlands that feature sedge, grasses, horsetail, spike rush, moss, bog rosemary, and sweetgale to uplands that support paper birch,

spruce forest, aspen woodland, grasses, sagebrush, juniper, and herbaceous perennials. The subalpine regions feature spruce forest, meadow, and tundra shrubs. Alpine habitats display heath, polar willow, mountain sorrel, spring beauty, and moss.

▼ **A National Historic Landmark,** Kennecott is widely regarded as the best remaining example of early-20th-century copper mining. Interpretive exhibits at the various structures include an extensive collection at the General Store and Post Office, where they also show essential bear safety videos.

▲ **Skookum Volcano Trail** leaves the Nabesna Road to lead visitors through a landscape of alpine plants and wildlife, but it is most appreciated for its picturesque volcanic terrain. This route travels through an extinct volcano system, with deeply eroded areas that expose dramatic rhyolite and dacite domes, andesite lava flows, vents, and many erosion-resistant dikes.

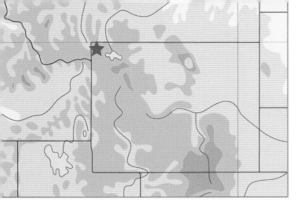

WYOMING, MONTANA, AND IDAHO
YELLOWSTONE

Arguably the best-known of the national parks, Yellowstone is replete with natural wonders—hydrothermal hot spots, epic scenery, and diverse wildlife.

LOCATION Park and Teton counties, WY; Gallatin and Park counties, MT; and Fremont County, ID

CLOSEST CITY West Yellowstone, MT

AREA 2,219,791 acres (8,983.18 km²)

ESTABLISHED March 1, 1872

VISITORS 3,806,300+

ELEVATION 11,358 feet (3,462 m) at Eagle Peak

GEOLOGY Metamorphic gneiss and schist; sedimentary sandstone, limestone, and shale; igneous rhyolite lava flows with obsidian

WHAT TO LOOK FOR

Park visitors run out of time before they run out of things to see.

> Old Faithful and other hydrothermal sites

> Grand Canyon of Yellowstone and Great Falls

> Grand Prismatic Trail, Mystic Falls Loop, Mammoth Terraces Loop, Avalanche Peak Trail

> Yellowstone Lake

Yellowstone has the honor of being the first national park ever established. Located in the northwestern corner of Wyoming and extending into Montana and Idaho, the park's landscape was born of fire, the result of a massive supervolcano eruption. To this day, the park's underground hydrothermal pressure is relieved via 500 geysers—the greatest number found anywhere. The park is named for the expanses of yellow rock revealed where the Yellowstone River eroded the surface of canyon walls.

HISTORY OF "COLTER'S HELL"

This section of the Rocky Mountains was once an ocean floor, thrust upward more than 8,000 feet and contorted by tectonic plate movements. Below the park and beneath Yellowstone Lake lies the Yellowstone Caldera, which is the largest supervolcano on the continent. Now considered dormant, it erupted several times in the past two million years, with one massive explosion as recent as 600,000 years ago.

Based on the finding of a prehistoric Clovis point, archeologists estimate that Paleo-Indians came here to hunt and fish at least 11,000 years ago. They used obsidian found in the park to make cutting tools and weapons, which they likely traded with tribes as far away as the Mississippi Valley.

When the Lewis and Clark Expedition entered this region in 1805, the explorers were met by Nez Perce, Crow, and Shoshone Indians, but they never investigated Yellowstone proper. When expedition member John Colter left the group, he crossed the parkland and witnessed at least one geothermal feature. He'd survived wounding in a battle with Crow and Blackfoot, so when he described a place of "fire and brimstone," many people attributed his vision to fever. This land of mystery became known as "Colter's Hell." Any further reports of geothermal oddities, like the tales of mountain man Jim Bridger, were held to be fanciful. But when U.S. Army surveyor Captain William F. Raynolds and his party entered the parklands in 1860, they viewed the wonders firsthand. In 1869 the Cook-Folson-Peterson Expedition followed the Yellowstone River to Yellowstone Lake, and their journals spurred subsequent exploration.

A Montana lawyer and writer, Cornelius Hedges, proposed in the early 1870s that the region called the Great Geyser Basin be protected. But it was Ferdinand V. Hayden, a geologist on the Raynolds expedition, who persuaded Congress to create the first national park in 1872, which President Grant then signed into law. After that, sadly, Native Americans who had seasonally hunted or foraged in the parkland were excluded from entry, and the government refused to recognize the claims of any tribe that had traditionally used Yellowstone.

By 1915, more than 1,000 automobiles per year were entering the park. In the 1930s, the Civilian Conservation Corps—the New Deal relief agency for young men—helped develop Yellowstone. They not only built most of the original visitor centers and roads, they were involved in reforestation, development of trails and campgrounds, and fire-fighting.

ACTIVITIES AND DESTINATIONS

Park activities include hiking, biking, and running on nearly a thousand miles of trails, camping, boating, and fishing. In winter there is cross-country skiing, snowshoeing, snowmobile rentals, ice fishing, and Snowcoach Tours. One of the park's must-see destinations is Old Faithful, the famous geyser that erupts every 50 to

◄ A fox takes a flying leap to hunt for a hidden mouse in Yellowstone's Hayden Valley on a snowy winter day.

Spray from its impact rises hundreds of feet above the Lower Falls of the Yellowstone River as it cuts its way through the Grand Canyon. Yellowstone set early standards for conservation of resources and was often labeled the park that "saved the vanishing West."

"YELLOWSTONE, OF ALL THE NATIONAL PARKS, IS THE WILDEST AND MOST UNIVERSAL IN ITS APPEAL.... DAILY NEW, ALWAYS STRANGE, EVER FULL OF CHANGE, IT IS NATURE'S WONDER PARK. IT IS THE MOST HUMAN AND THE MOST POPULAR OF ALL PARKS."

— *Yellowstone Park for Your Vacation* (circa 1920s)

127 minutes. Geysers occur when spring water is superheated by hot rocks deep underground until the pressure increases so much that water and steam rush to the surface and erupt into the air.

To help visitors navigate the sprawling park, it is divided into geographic sections. Each division has its own scenic drives, hydrothermal regions, natural wonders, and guest amenities, such as campgrounds, lodges, hotels, cabins, visitor centers, information centers, general stores, and museums.

- Yellowstone Grand Canyon and Canyon Village are home to Dunraven Pass, North Rim Drive, and South Rim Drive; Mud Volcano; several waterfalls; Hayden Valley and Mount Washburn; plus a campground, lodge, general store, and visitor education center.
- Old Faithful is an area known for many geothermal sites and views of the Continental Divide; there are two general stores, several lodges, and a visitor education center.
- Fishing Bridge, Lake Village, and Bridge Bay in the east offer Gull Point Drive and Lake Butte Scenic Drive; Mud Volcano and Steamboat Point; landmarks like Natural Bridge, Mary Bay, Sedge Bay, Storm Point, and Yellowstone Lake, and amenities like a marina, general store, visitor center, campground, and hotel and cabins.
- Madison and the western park offer Firehole Canyon Drive and Firehole Lake Drive; geysers and hot springs; waterfalls; Madison River and Purple Mountain; plus an information station and visitor information center.
- Mammoth Hot Springs and the north park are known for Blacktail Plateau and Upper Terrace Drives, Fort Yellowstone (now park headquarters), Apollinaris Spring, Obsidian Cliff, Bunsen Peak, Sheepeater Cliffs, and Swan Lake Flat. Guest services include Albright Visitor Center, Indian Creek and Mammoth Campground, a general store, and a hotel with cabins.
- Norris Geyser Basin is home to the Museum of the National Park Ranger; geothermal paintpots, basins, and geysers; Caldera Boundary and Gibbon Meadows; along with Norris Campground and Norris Geyser Basin Museum.

And don't overlook Tower-Roosevelt area in the northeast and West Thumb and Grant Village in the south. Both offer scenic landmarks, hydrothermal phenomenon, accommodations, and general stores.

◀ **Grand Prismatic Spring,** the premier attraction of the Midway Geyser Basin, is the park's largest hot spring. Its name comes from the rainbow of colors produced by the microbial mats around its edges interacting with the mineral-rich water.

▲ **The Mammoth Hot Springs** are a stunning complex of travertine terraces unique from other thermal areas elsewhere in the park, growing far more rapidly. Although these springs lie outside the caldera boundary, they are an expression of the deep volcanic forces at work in Yellowstone.

▶ **Old Faithful Inn,** a National Historic Landmark and the most sought-after lodging in the park, was built in 1903–1904 from local lodgepole pine and rhyolite stone and features a soaring gabled, cedar-shingled roof. Built in a style known as "National Park Service Rustic," it is possibly the largest log cabin structure in the world.

Old Faithful, the most famous symbol of just about any national park, is a highly predictable geothermal cone geyser. One of nearly 500 geysers in Yellowstone, it sends a jet of steam and boiling water to heights of 100 to 180 feet. Eruptions typically last between 1.5 to 5 minutes.

There are 12 campgrounds throughout the park with more than 2,000 sites that can be reserved in advance. Yellowstone National Park Lodges operates nine hotel- or cabin-style lodges that offer more than 2,000 rooms. All are open from late spring through fall, but only Old Faithful Snow Lodge and Mammoth Hot Springs Hotel remain open in the winter.

WILDLIFE AND PLANT LIFE

Yellowstone is proud of its bison herds. It is the only place in the country where *Bison bison* has lived continuously since prehistoric times. Yet due to lax stewardship and poaching, only 23 bison remained on park land in 1884, and every gray wolf, their ancestral adversary, was gone by 1926. The balance of nature, the normal cycles of prey and predator, had been destroyed by the hand of man. Today, the restored bison herd numbers nearly 5,000, and new generations of wolves (reintroduced from Canada in 1995) prey mainly on elk, whose carcasses provide food to other animals down the food chain. Early studies indicated that wolf recovery would likely lead to greater biodiversity throughout the park, although the ultimate effect of park wolves still being assessed.

Yellowstone supports 67 species of mammals, nearly 300 species of birds, 16 fish, five amphibians, and six reptiles. In addition to bison and wolves, mammals include grizzly bear, black bear, coyote, cougar, Canadian lynx, elk, moose, mule deer, white-tailed deer, pronghorn, bighorn sheep, non-native mountain goat, river otter, and wolverine. Birdlife includes many raptors, songbirds, shorebirds, and waterfowl. Lively cliff swallows in mud-daub colonies are a highly visible presence.

Vegetation communities in the park often overlap, with combinations of Rocky Mountain species, Great Plains flora from the east, and species from the western intermountain region. There are four basic habitats: upper- and lower-elevation forests; sagebrush-steppe; wetlands; and geothermal areas. Forests may be dominated by lodgepole pine; spruce and fir (older forests); whitebark pine (upper elevations); and Douglas fir (below 7,600 feet). Wetland plants include woody vegetation, forbs, rushes, and grasses. Streamsides support cottonwoods, willows, and deciduous shrubs. Meadows come alive with wildflowers during the warmer months.

▼ **A herd of bison** moves quickly along the Firehole River near the Midway Geyser Basin.

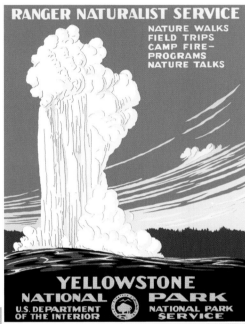

RANGER NATURALIST SERVICE

NATURE WALKS
FIELD TRIPS
CAMP FIRE—
PROGRAMS
NATURE TALKS

YELLOWSTONE
NATIONAL PARK
U.S. DEPARTMENT OF THE INTERIOR
NATIONAL PARK SERVICE

CALIFORNIA
YOSEMITE

One of America's most popular national parks, Yosemite combines unparalleled natural beauty with a rich history and cultural heritage.

LOCATION Tuolumne, Mariposa, Mono, and Madera counties, CA

CLOSEST CITY Mariposa, CA

AREA 759,620 acres (3,074,1 km²)

ESTABLISHED October 1, 1890

VISITORS 2,268,300+

ELEVATION 13,114 feet (3,997 m) at Mount Lyell

GEOLOGY Plutonic igneous rock—granite, granodiorite, tonalite, quartz monzonite, and quartz monzodiorite

WHAT TO LOOK FOR

The venerable park is home nature at its best..

> Ring Road and Tunnel View

> Tioga Road scenic highway

> Glacier Point, Washburn Point, and Valley View

> Waterfalls, including Yosemite, Bridalveil, Vernal, and Nevada

> Reconstructed Indian Village of Ahwahnee

This gem of a national park, situated on the western slopes of the Sierra Nevada, lies only 165 miles from San Francisco. Yet in many ways, it is worlds apart from bustling, distracting, everyday life. This park places a pinpoint focus on the glories of nature . . . and once here, few are able to resist the allure of these sublime outdoor spaces.

Most visitors are drawn first to Yosemite Valley. While only eight miles long and one mile wide, it offers a cornucopia of visual delights, among them several of the most photographed natural landmarks in the world. To the north lies the park's high country, with sites like Olmstead Point, Tenaya Lake, Tuolumne Meadow, and several alpine trails.

AN EVOLVING PROFILE

As the last Ice Age dwindled, receding glaciers scraped and contoured the valleys below the high peaks. Yosemite's dramatic landscapes and breathtaking vistas were the result of that process. Even though native people visited this region for 10,000 years, evidence indicates they only settled in Yosemite around 1000 BCE. Several tribes—including the Ahwahneechee, related to the Paiute and Mono—had villages scattered along Yosemite Valley, where they benefited from lush vegetation and plentiful wildlife. Archaeologists have documented at least 36 settlements on the valley floor.

When the California Gold Rush brought thousands of prospectors into their territory, the Ahwahneechee were forced onto a reservation, but then some were allowed to return home. In 1852, after the Indians killed eight miners, a bitter conflict with U.S. forces resulted in the death of the their chief and their absorption into the Paiute tribe.

Once commercial interests began viewing Yosemite as a source of revenue, a bill to protect the area—the Yosemite Grant—was signed by Abraham Lincoln in 1864. The novel concept of preserving a park for public use paved the way for the designation of Yellowstone as the first national park. Yosemite became the third such site, after Sequoia, and then followed by Mount Rainier and Crater Lake.

The classic Tunnel View, made famous by Ansel Adams, showcases the austere granite majesty of El Capitan, rounded Half Dome, and ethereal Bridalveil Fall and is easily the most photographed spot in the park.

DID YOU KNOW?

The park's early inhabitants, the Ahwahneechee, believed that inhaling the mist rising from Bridalveil Fall increased one's chances of finding a marriage partner.

ACTIVITIES, LANDMARKS, AND AMENITIES

Popular park activities include hiking on 800 miles of trails, cycling on 12-miles of bike paths, fishing, boating, camping, and guided tours. Climbers flock here to test themselves against El Capitan, a 3,000-foot monolith. Drivers entering the park from the western Ring Road, should consider a side trip to Tunnel View, an iconic overlook showcasing El Capitan and Bridalveil Fall, with Half Dome in the background. The Ring Road follows the Merced River, a national wild and scenic waterway, and is dotted with trailheads. Recommended trails include the Mist Trail, Yosemite Falls, Half Dome via John Muir,

▼ **A fearless hiker** stands atop an overhanging rock to enjoy the view towards famous Half Dome at Glacier Point overlook.

Mirror Lake, Sentinel Dome, Glacier Point, Clouds Rest, and Valley Loop to Mirror Lake.

The museum at Yosemite Village highlights the valley's indigenous residents, while the visitor center's exhibits cover ranchers, miners, and artists. There is also a gallery dedicated to photographer Ansel Adams, one of Yosemite's best interpreters.

Accommodations here require some forethought. The park's 13,000 campsites are all booked before high season, and tent cabins and lodge rooms also go quickly. The Park Service recommends reserving spots a year in advance.

WILDLIFE AND PLANT LIFE

Yosemite is home to more than 400 species of vertebrates, the result of diverse habitats being allowed to remain intact. Animal sightings include black bear, cougar,

▶ **The Bachelor and Three Graces,** giant sequoias in the Mariposa Grove, stand firmly rooted to the ground in a stand near a roadside.

gray wolf, bison, mule deer, elk, pronghorn, bighorn sheep, red fox, fisher, marmot, pika, California ground squirrel, and 17 species of bats. At least 262 bird species have been documented, along with many migrating species. The park even has its own subspecies of great gray owl, *Strix nebulosa Yosemitensis*. There are 12 species of amphibians and 22 reptiles. Native fish like California roach, Sacramento pikeminnow, hardhead, and riffle sculpin, inhabit lower elevations, while introduced species, mostly trout, are found throughout the park.

With altitudes that range from 2,000 to 13,123 feet, Yosemite is home to five major vegetation zones. The dry chaparral/oak

▲ **The Ahwahnee Hotel** sits in the majestic main valley inside Yosemite Park near the base of Half Dome and Glacier Point. This up-scale hotel, with its striking granite façade, was built in 1927 and is now listed as a National Historic Landmark.

A hike on the Half Dome Trail presents a panoramic vista of the autumn tones surrounding El Capitan and the Merced River.

"I KNEW MY DESTINY WHEN I FIRST EXPERIENCED YOSEMITE."

— *Photographer Ansel Adams*

A winter storm descends upon Yosemite Falls, the park's highest waterfall

▶ **A mountain lion** rests on a moss-covered rock to survey the park's springtime landscape. Visitors need to keep a respectful distance from all animals, even those that appear benign. More human injuries have resulted from encounters with "gentle" deer than any other creature in the park.

◀ **Yosemite Chapel** sits in an enchanted wintertime spot amid snow-dusted trees.

woodlands support chamise, ceanothus, manzanita, blue oak, interior live oak, and gray pine. With its Mediterranean climate, the lower montane forest features California black oak, ponderosa pine, incense-cedar, and white fir, plus Yosemite's giant sequoia groves; the cool, moist upper montane

forest shelters red fir, lodgepole pine, Jeffrey pine, western juniper, and many wildflowers. Subalpine regions, with long snowy winters, contain western white pine, mountain hemlock, lodgepole pine, and flowering meadows. The harsh alpine zone is rocky and treeless, with limited vegetation. Specialized, isolated plant communities that occupy the dry, cold plateaus of the Sierra Nevada are called sky islands and are studied by scientists.

► **Olmsted Point** is a famous vista that offers a view south into Tenaya Canyon, showing the northern side of Half Dome and Clouds Rest, and, to the east, a view of Tenaya Lake.

PARKS OF HAWAI'I AND OTHER U.S. ISLANDS

Leaving the mainland to explore the National Park system's island getaways leads travelers to some of the most captivating landscapes in the world. America's 50th state, the tropical Eden known as Hawai'i, is home to two national parks, both based around active volcanoes—Haleakalā on Maui and Kīlauea and Mauna Loa on the Big Island. Here, fascinating flora and fauna found nowhere else in the world make their home.

Another Pacific Ocean park lies in the U.S. territory of American Samoa, where stunning beaches are surrounded by forest lands that hold hidden wonders and are home to the endangered flying fox. Traveling south to the turquoise waters of the Caribbean, visitors can enjoy all that the U.S. Virgin Islands are famous for—fabulous coral reefs, white-sand beaches shaded by coconut palms, and a vibrant culture—while learning about the region's turbulent colonial history.

In these lovely island parks, a long hike through serene wilderness, a trek to the crater of an awe-inspiring volcano, a kayak trip to explore the coastline, a snorkeling adventure in pristine waters, or a tropical cocktail at a beachside bar are just a few of the delights that await the visitor.

◄ Hawai'i Volcanoes National Park, Hawai'i

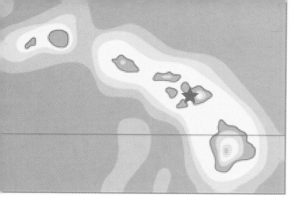

MAUI
HALEAKALĀ

Stark volcanic vistas and lush rainforest contrast in this sacred landscape that blends ancient and modern Hawai'ian culture.

LOCATION Maui County, HI

CLOSEST CITY Pukalani, HI

AREA 33,265 acres (134.62 km²)

ESTABLISHED August 1, 1916, as Hawai'i National Park (with Hawai'i Volcanoes); July 1, 1961, as Haleakalā National Park

VISITORS 1,044,000+

ELEVATION 10,023 feet (3,055 m) at Pui'u 'Ula'ula (Red Hill).

GEOLOGY Volcanic rock

WHAT TO LOOK FOR

Explore this park on foot to fully appreciate these stunning and uniquely Hawai'ian lands.

> Summit District

> Sliding Sands Loop

> Hosmer Grove

> Kīpahulu District

> Pīpīwai Trail

> Kūloa Point Trail

> Makahiku and Waimoku Falls

> Hale Hālāwai

No one who has visited this special place can feel unmoved by the grandeur of its landscape and the vibrant culture that venerates the bond between the land and its people. Haleakalā National Park has taken as its mission the preservation of this land and the protection of its endangered species, some of which exist nowhere else in the world.

THE PARKLANDS HISTORY

The first humans to colonize the Hawai'ian Islands were the Polynesians, somewhere in the first century CE to 800 CE, and they began using land at the Haleakalā Crater around 660 to 1030 and what is now the parklands by 1164 to 1384. In 1778, explorer Caption James Cook led the expedition that resulted in the first European contact with Hawai'ians. By the early 19th century, American missionaries and whalers had arrived on Maui, and it was three missionaries who left the first written record of an ascent to the summit of Haleakalā. With sugar production from sugarcane beginning in 1881, a diverse range of immigrants began arriving in the area. The 1880s also saw the establishment of the Haleakalā Ranch, and cattle began grazing on the slopes of Haleakalā and were pastured in Haleakalā Crater until 1922. Ranching was also established in Kipahulu after sugar production ended in the mid-1920s.

In 1898, the United States annexed the Republic of Hawai'i as a territory. The park's history began in 1916, when the U.S. Congress established Hawai'i National Park, which included the Haleakalā unit on Maui and Hawai'i Volcanoes on the Big Island. During the 1930s, the parklands were developed: a road to the summit was built and the Civilian Conservation Corps was enlisted to construct the Haleakalā Visitor Center, as well as backcountry cabins. The World War II years saw the closure of the park from 1941 to 1943, with U.S. Army occupation

of Haleakalā. Postwar building included park headquarters and the observatory at Red Hill, and in 1952 the park expanded to include the Kīpahulu Valley. In 1961, two years after Hawai'i became the 50th state, Hawai'i National Park was separated into two distinct parks re-designated as Haleakalā National Park and Hawai'i Volcanoes National Park. In 1974, the National Register of Historic Places listed the Crater Historic District in its rolls. Since then, park expansion has seen the Ka'apahu lands added in 1999 and the Nu'u lands in 2008.

HIKING THE PARK

On foot is the best way to experience all that Haleakalā has to offer. By law, to protect fragile Hawai'ian ecosystems, hikers must stay on marked trails and limit groups to no more than 12, but these trails lead through such amazing scenery, it is well worth any restrictions.

The park is divided into two main districts: Summit and Kīpahulu. The Summit District features more than 30 miles of hiking trails, which range from short jaunts to multi-day overnight trips. Pack animals like horses, mules, and donkeys are permitted on the Keonehe'ehe'e Trail and the Halemau'u Trail. The Hosmer Grove Campground is the only drive-in campground in the park.

Visitors can take easy-to-strenuous alpine desert hikes in the Summit District that wind past ancient lava flows and pu'u (old eruption sites). Subalpine shrubland hikes offer views of native Hawai'ian trees and shrubs that provide habitat for many endemic, endangered species, such as the nēnē (Hawaiian goose). A favorite with park-goers is the Sliding Sands Loop, which combines the Keonehe'ehe'e Trail (also called the Sliding Sands Trail) with the Halemau'au Trail to form an 11-mile hike. This route can be challenging, but

◄ A rosette of a Haleakalā silversword,
or *'āhinahina* in the Hawaiian language, emerges from rocks within the park. The park service has erected fences to prevent damage from local herbivores and from visitors taking home the highly endangered flowering plants as souvenirs.

Haleakalā volcano crater. The dormant Haleakalā ("house of the sun") volcano last erupted sometime between 1480 and 1600 CE. In Hawaiian folklore, the crater was home to the demigod Māui's grandmother, who helped him capture the sun and force it to slow its journey across the sky in order to lengthen the day.

▶ **A mauve and purple sunrise** lights the complex of buildings that form the Haleakalā Observatory. The 18 acres near the summit, known as "Science City," is unfortunately closed to the general public.

▼ **Pīpiwaī Trail,** in the Kīpahulu District of the park, leads visitors through a lush bamboo rainforest to end at the graceful Waimoku Falls.

DID YOU KNOW?

On a gated road just past the summit near the park's visitor center, stand the buildings of the Haleakalā Observatory, which is not actually part of the park. The University of Hawaii Institute for Astronomy has managed this site for 40 years, conducting astrophysical experiments.

the myriad, ever-changing views of the Haleakalā crater are sublime. Be forewarned that this option is for those healthy and in shape. As well as demanding, trails in the Summit Area wind through high elevations, and altitude sickness is a concern. A popular destination on Halemau'u Trail is the "Rainbow Bridge," a natural land bridge about a quarter mile from the first crater viewpoint.

The remote Kīpahulu District, only accessible via the Hana Highway, is a coastal area in which native people have lived for hundreds of years, and it remains a thriving element of the culture. This district offers cultural demonstrations and exhibits, car camping, and archaeological sites, as well as engaging hiking trails. The Pīpiwaī Trail winds along a freshwater stream and leads through a bamboo forest with boardwalks and footbridges. About a half mile in, the Makahiku Overlook provides a view of Makahiku Falls, and at the end of the trail is the Waimoku Falls viewing area. The Kūloa Point Trail, which starts at the visitor center, leads to Kūloa Point at the mouth of 'Ohe'o Gulch and to the Pools of 'Ohe'o, also known as the "Seven Sacred Pools." At the

junction of the Pīpīwai and Kūloa Point trails stands Hale Hālāwai, a reconstruction of a traditional meeting house.

WILDLIFE AND PLANT LIFE

The Hawai'ian Islands are home to a unique assortment of flora and fauna found only here. Evolving over 70 million years ago in near-complete isolation in the middle of the Pacific, more than 90 percent of the state's endemic species are descendants of birds, bats, and insects that could fly here or were light enough to be carried by them, as well as those blown here by the wind or washed ashore on the ocean currents. Evolutionary curiosities, such as mintless mints and nettleless nettles, adapted to an environment free of plant-eating mammals. On a trip here, one might see the low-growing rosette of a Haleakalā silversword at the aeolian desert cinder slopes of the crater or the Haleakalā greensword in the high mountain bogs.

Some charismatic birds find home in the park, such as the 'Ua'u kani (wedge-tailed shearwater) and the endangered 'Ua'u, or Hawai'ian petrel, which has its largest known nesting colony at the top of Mount Haleakalā. In the forest are several species of colorful honeycreepers, such as the 'apapane 'i'iwi, 'amakihi, 'alauahio, and kohekohe, as well as the kiwikiu (Maui parrotbill).

SAVING THE NĒNĒ

Hawai'i's state bird is the nēnē, or Hawai'ian goose. At the time of European first contact, these birds were only known with certainty on the island of Hawai'i. Their population decline was sparked by the American and European establishment of such endeavors as sugarcane cultivation and cattle ranching, which resulted in habitat loss, and was exacerbated by the impact of the introduction of non-native mammals. Between the 1850s and 1940s, the decline accelerated, and by 1952, an estimated 30 nēnēs remained in Hawai'i. Efforts to reintroduce this bird commenced in 1962, with Haleakalā on Maui the chosen site. From 1962 until 1978, approximately 500 birds were released through a captive propagation program. The efforts to protect these birds continue today, with strategies such as population monitoring, predator control in known nesting areas, and fence maintenance to prevent damage by goats, pigs, and dogs. Public education and outreach is an important factor in saving these birds, and programs like the Adopt-A-Nēnē is run cooperatively with the Friends of Haleakalā National Park.

▶ **A nēnē** stands on a slope of Haleakalā Crater.

▼ **With its long and slender** pale orange bill and striking red color with jet black wings, the adult 'i'iwi stands out amid the forest greenery. Hawai'ian royalty once prized the brilliant scarlet feathers of these birds for their capes.

A panoramic view of the park gives a sense of the vastness of the cinder-cone-dotted crater valley, which sits more than 10,000 feet above sea level.

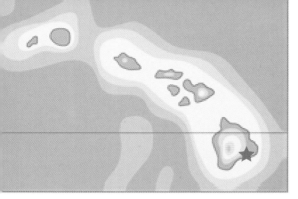

BIG ISLAND, HAWAI'I
HAWAI'I VOLCANOES

Sea and fire explosively contend with each other in this breathtaking landscape of awe-inspiring active volcanoes.

LOCATION Hawai'i County, HI

CLOSEST CITY Hilo, HI

AREA 323,431 acres (1,308.88 km²)

ESTABLISHED August 1, 1916, as Hawai'i National Park (with Haleakalā); July 1, 1961, as Hawai'i Volcanoes National Park

VISITORS 1,116,890+

ELEVATION 13,679 feet (4,169 m) at Mauna Loa

GEOLOGY Volcanic rock

WHAT TO LOOK FOR

Home to two volcanoes, the park offers the chance to get close to them, while also offering wilderness adventures.

> Volcano House Hotel

> Volcano Art Center

> Turston Lava Tube

> Mauna Loa

> Kīlauea Crater

> Hawai'i Volcanoes Wilderness

Protecting a cherished geological, biological, and cultural landscape, Hawai'i Volcanoes National Park encompasses the summits of two of the world's most active volcanoes—Kīlauea and Mauna Loa. Established in 1916, it was at originally combined with Haleakalā as Hawai'i National Park, but the two were later split into distinct parks. This magical destination has also been designated an International Biosphere Reserve and UNESCO World Heritage Site.

THE VOLCANOES

Two active volcanoes reside within the park: Kīlauea, one of the world's most active, and Mauna Loa, the world's most massive shield volcano. Recently eruptive sites include the main caldera of Kīlauea and a more active but remote vent called Pu'u Ō'ō. Kīlauea and its Halema'uma'u caldera were traditionally considered the sacred home of the volcano goddess Pele, and Hawai'ians visited the crater to offer gifts to the goddess.

Visitors have many options for exploring the volcanoes, such as day hiking the volcanic terrain or taking a walk in the dark through Nahuku, known as the Thurston Lava Tube, a lava cave on Kīlauea Crater. Located on the shoulders of Mauna Loa, the park's Kahuku unit also has a variety of options for day hikes.

VOLCANO HOUSE

Since 1846, the lure of witnessing active volcanoes has drawn visitors to the many incarnations of the iconic Volcano House, which stands at the summit of Kīlauea. The first was a four-walled thatched shelter "in the native style" built by Benjamin Pitman. The Volcano House register book that originated here provides some of the oldest records of volcanic activity within the caldera. That structure proved less than guest-worthy, however, so in 1866, a joint investment by local businessmen resulted in a comfortable thatched inn. A more permanent western-style Volcano House hotel was erected near the site of the present hula platform in 1877. Princess Lili'uokalani (the final monarch of the Hawaiian kingdom), witnessed the start of the 1880 rift zone eruption of Mauna Loa from this building. Eventually, the hotel's popularity called for expansion, so a two-story Victorian-

style addition went up in 1891. In 1921, with space tight as business boomed, the 1877 section of the building was removed from the 1891 addition, and a massive two-story wing was added. After a disastrous fire in 1940 burned that grand version of Volcano House to the ground, an entirely new building was constructed in 1941. It is still in use today, and many volcanic events have taken place since then, allowing guests to witness up close the lava glows and occasional eruptive activity.

ACTIVITIES

From sea level to the 13,679-foot summit of Mauna Loa, the park features diverse landscapes. Visitors can experience a vibrant tropical rainforest or the barren Ka'ū Desert. For hikers and campers, the Hawai'i Volcanoes Wilderness area provides thousands of acres of backcountry in which to enjoy serene solitude and lush scenery. The Crater Rim Drive Tour takes a scenic route around the summit of Kīlauea, and the Chain of Craters Road Tour affords spectacular views on a drive down its slopes to the sea. The main visitor center, located just within the park entrance, includes info about the park's features. The nearby Volcano Art Center houses historical displays and an art gallery.

DID YOU KNOW?

Beginning on January 3, 1983, the longest-lasting rift-zone eruption of the last two centuries created Pu'u Ō'ō, a volcanic cone on the eastern rift zone of Kīlauea, and continued nearly continuously until April 30, 2018.

▲ Gifts of beads, leis, and flowers for the goddess Pele are left on the hardened lava.

"HAWAI'I IS A PARADISE BORN OF FIRE."

— Rand McNally

For U.S. military personnel, Kīlauea Military Camp provides accommodations.

WILDLIFE AND PLANT LIFE

As on all of the Hawai'ian Islands, the fauna is limited to what could fly or be carried by birds, be blown by winds, or wash ashore. There are no native terrestrial mammals, other than one bat, but visitors might spot a host of gorgeous birds, fascinating insects like a carnivorous caterpillar, or an endangered sea turtle. The park's landscape offers up unique plants, such as the 'ae fern peeking from a crack in hardened lava or the giant hāpu'u, a towering tree fern in the rainforest. The park is currently in a race against time to protect endemic plants, which have survived here for millennia, from the threats posed by alien invasive plants and wildlife species. Within the park are 23 species of endangered vascular plants, including 15 species of endangered trees.

▶ **Inside Nahuku,** or the Turston Lava Tube. This fun, short hike takes visitors through a 500-year-old lava cave located on Kīlauea Crater.

▶ **Old Volcano House No. 42** was used as the Volcano House Hotel from 1877 to 1921. It now houses a gallery for the Volcano Art Center.

The Kamokuʻna ocean entry at Kīlauea allows visitors to catch the awe-inspiring sight of fresh lava streams cascading into the ocean at the former lava delta site.

MORE TO EXPLORE

NATIONAL SEASHORES AND LAKESHORES

The National Park Service also oversees 13 protected coastal areas composed of 10 National Seashores and three National Lakeshores—regions federally designated by Congress as possessing "natural and recreational significance."

The shorelines of major bodies of water are highly attractive to developers and particularly vulnerable to destruction. The latter is especially true as the effects of climate change steadily accumulate: higher temperatures cause lake water to recede, rising sea levels imperil low-lying islands and coastal habitats, and storm surges and hurricanes erode beaches.

FEDERAL INTERVENTION

The first time the government interceded to protect a recreational coastal region was in Minnesota in 1930, when it first advocated "the principle of conserving the nature beauty of a shoreline for recreational use." During the Great Depression, the government created much-needed jobs by expanding the National Park Service's role beyond managing national parks and national monuments to protecting historical sites and recreation areas, including shorelines.

Erosion of the Outer Banks in North Carolina was an early concern, and Cape Hatteras was considered for possible designation as a national recreation area. But some of the proposed park was private land, making it unsuitable for national park usage. Eventually, the government came up with a framework that allowed the protection of a wide variety of resources, including recreational areas. Cape Hatteras National Seashore was authorized by Congress in August 1937, but the park did not open to visitors until 1953, after the government had acquired sufficient land.

In 1955 a park service survey of the Atlantic and Gulf coasts determined 16 areas that possibly required protection; five of these were ultimately made national seashores. Studies of the Pacific coast and the Great Lakes resulted in even more designations, included Pictured Rocks in upper Michigan, the first lakeshore chosen.

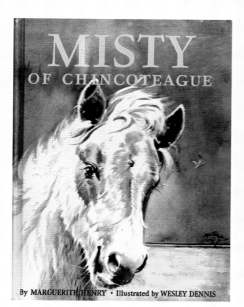

▶ **Assateague Island National Seashore**

Location Atlantic coast of Maryland and Virginia
Established 1965
Area 39,726 acres (160.8 km²)

Famous for its diminutive wild horses, this barrier island lies within two states. The beach, which is sculpted by wind and water, is open for swimming—and occasional equine encounters—during warm weather. Wildlife watchers might spot fox, deer, crab, wading birds, waterfowl, gulls, and migrating snow geese. Vegetation includes American beach grass, saltmarsh cordgrass, and sea rocket.

◀ *The barrier islands Chincoteague and Assateague became familiar to many children after the publication of Marguerite Henry's 1947 book, Misty of Chincoteague.*

▶ *A herd of the famous Chincoteague ponies, also known as the Assateague horse, gather on the shoreline of Assateague Island.*

▼ **Canaveral National Seashore**

Location Atlantic coast of Florida
Established 1975
Area 57,661 acres (233.3 km²)

Adjacent to the Kennedy Space Center, this barrier island offers Florida's longest undeveloped Atlantic beach. It surrounds Mosquito Lagoon, a haven for manatees, dolphins, and sea turtles, along with migrating birds. Activities include boating, fishing, and hiking. The Seminole Rest historic site features ancient Native American shell mounds, while Eldora Statehouse showcases historic life on the lagoon.

▲ *A trail at Canaveral National Seashore leads to Turtle Mound, a large Native American Indian shell midden named for its similarity to a turtle.*

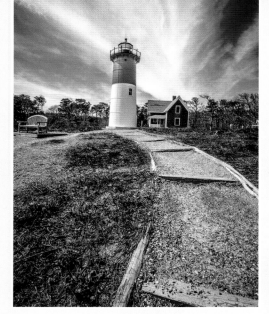

▲ *Nauset Light, officially the Nauset Beach Light, is a restored lighthouse on the Cape Cod National Seashore near Eastham, Massachusetts.*

▲ Cape Cod National Seashore

Location Atlantic coast of Massachusetts
Established 1966
Area 43,608.48 acres (176.5 km²)

Along with almost 40 miles of beaches, this peninsula features a Marconi Station, the Three Sisters Lighthouses, and a former Air Force station. Hiking cranberry bogs, marshes, and woodland trails offers a close-up view of the Cape's animal and plant life.

► Cape Hatteras National Seashore

Location Atlantic Coast of North Carolina
Established 1953
Area 30,350.65 acres (122.8 km²)

North Carolina's Outer Banks are home to this national seashore, which is known for the Bodie Island and Cape Hatteras Lighthouses. Activities include birding, fishing, beachcombing, windsurfing, and kayaking. Endangered piping plovers, sea turtles, and seabeach amaranth find refuge here.

► *Standing at the northern end of Cape Hatteras National Seashore, Bodie Island Lighthouse was first lit on October 1, 1872.*

▲ *Morning dawns over the Atlantic Ocean at Cape Hatteras National Seashore.*

▼ Cape Lookout National Seashore

Location Atlantic coast of North Carolina
Established 1966
Area 28,243.36 acres (114.3 km²)

Made up of three islands of the Outer Banks, this park is accessible only by boat. It boasts a herd of wild horses, two historic villages, and the distinctive Cape Lookout Lighthouse. Activities include fishing, birding, hiking, and camping.

▲ *The distinctive Cape Lookout Lighthouse, visible at least 12 miles out to sea, flashes every 15 seconds, even during the day.*

▲ Cumberland Island National Seashore

Location Atlantic coast of Georgia
Established 1972
Area 36,415.13 acres (147.4 km²)

Georgia's largest and southernmost barrier island is accessible only by ferry. It is home to the lavish Plum Orchard estate, Thomas Carnegie's restored mansion, as well as an African Baptist church. The mainland museum covers Timucua Indian and African American history and the War of 1812.

▲ A wild horse grazes on the grounds of the Dungeness Ruins Historical Site in the Cumberland Island National Seashore.

▼ Padre Island National Seashore

Location Gulf coast of Texas
Established 1968
Area 130,434.27 acres (527.8 km²)

The world's longest undeveloped barrier island is a nesting ground for the highly endangered Kemp's ridley sea turtle and a migratory refuge for least terns, brown pelicans, and piping plovers. Malaquite Beach offers swimming and camping, while Novillo Line Camp features the remains of a cattle ranch. Part of the island was used as a bombing range during WWII.

▲ The ruins of historic Fort Pickens lies within the Gulf Islands National Seashore.

▲ Gulf Islands National Seashore

Location Gulf Coast of Florida and Mississippi
Established 1971
Area 137,990.97 acres (558.4 km²)

The Florida portion, near Pensacola, features white-quartz sand beaches, wildlife trails, and military forts, all accessible by automobile. The Mississippi portion's beaches, bayous, wildlife trails, historic sites, and barrier islands are accessible only by boat. Gulf Islands suffered massive damage in 2020 due to Hurricane Sally, but restoration efforts are underway.

▼ Fire Island National Seashore

Location Atlantic coast of New York
Established 1964
Area 19,579.47 acres (79.2 km²)

This barrier island along the southern coast of Long Island is a popular summer destination for New York City residents. It features dunes, a sunken forest, wetlands, the William Floyd House, the Fire Island Lighthouse, and 32 miles of pristine beaches.

▲ The Fire Island Lighthouse is a visible landmark on the Great South Bay, in southern Suffolk County, New York

▲ Brown pelicans gaze out to the Gulf of Mexico.

▶ A Kemp's ridley sea turtle nests in the sand.

▲ In many spots, vegetation stabilizes the windswept sand dunes on the Padre Island shore.

▼ Apostle Islands National Lakeshore

Location Wisconsin shoreline of Lake Superior
Established 1970
Area 69,371.89 acres (280.7 km²)

These 21 islands at the northern tip of Wisconsin feature boating, kayaking, fishing, hiking, and camping, plus scuba diving at four shipwrecks. The landscape features sandstone sea caves, old-growth forest remnants, animal habitats, and eight lighthouses, the most found in any national park.

▼ Pictured Rocks National Lakeshore

Location Michigan shoreline of Lake Superior
Established 1966
Area 73,235.83 acres (296.4 km²)

Here, colorful sandstone cliffs jut into Lake Superior. In winter the sea caves become enchanted ice caves, while waterfalls turn into crystal curtains. Great Sable Dunes, located near the 1874 Au Sable Light, are more than 300 feet high and 5 miles in length. Beaver Basin Wilderness is a protected area of the park.

▲ *A stunning sea stack stands along the rocky shoreline of Lake Superior.*

◄ *A frozen waterfall shelters the ice caves of the Apostle Islands.*

▲ *Pictured Rocks National Lakeshore features colorful formations along the Lake Superior shoreline of Michigan's Upper Peninsula.*

▼ Sleeping Bear Dunes National Lakeshore

Location Michigan shoreline of Lake Michigan
Established 1970
Area 71,198.48 acres (288.1 km²)

Explore the towering 450-foot sand dunes situated on 4 square miles of glacial moraine, as well as the two wilderness islands, wetland marshes, maple forests, and historic farmsteads that feature 1,500 species of wildlife and plant life. Activities include camping, hiking, and canoeing.

◄◄ *A northern elephant seal bull comes ashore at Point Reyes.*

◄ *Tule elk wander the hilly grasslands.*

▼ *Rocky cliffs mark the dramatic landscape of Point Reyes National Shoreline.*

▲ *A spot at the top of Sleeping Bear Dunes National Lakeshore looks out over Lake Michigan.*

► Point Reyes National Seashore

Location Pacific coast of California
Established 1972
Area 71,067.78 acres (287.6 km²)

A UNESCO Biosphere Reserve, Point Reyes Peninsula ranges from sandy beaches to open grasslands and features a lighthouse, a lifeboat station, and a recreated Coast Miwok village. Migrating gray whales pass along the shore, while elephant seals and tule elk are found on the rugged cliffs.

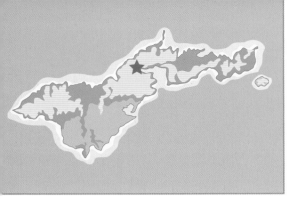

AMERICAN SAMOA

AMERICAN SAMOA

The cobalt blue Pacific, verdant rainforests, and colorful marine life attract visitors to the only U.S. park south of the equator.

LOCATION American Samoa, US
CLOSEST CITY Pago Pago
AREA 8,256.67 acres (33.4136 km²)
ESTABLISHED October 31, 1988
VISITORS 28,600+
ELEVATION 3,170 feet (970 m) at Lata Mountain on Tutuila
GEOLOGY Breccia, volcanic tuff, basalts, andesites, and trachytes

WHAT TO LOOK FOR

This tropical park offers lovers of water sports and of history a place to explore and relax.

> Diving from shore on Tutuila Island

> Snorkeling on Ta'ū and Ofu

> Visitor center for cultural and ecological exhibits

> World War II Heritage Trail

With a mission to preserve and protect tropical rainforests, fragile coral reefs, endangered fruit bats, and the Samoan culture, the National Park of American Samoa lies in the U.S. territory of American Samoa. Its acreage, distributed across the South Pacific islands of Tutuila, Ofu, and Ta'ū, also encompasses 2,500 acres of coral reefs and ocean waters.

HISTORY OF THE ISLANDS

Southeast of the independent state of Samoa, American Samoa consists of five main islands and two coral atolls. The islands show no evidence of current volcanism, but volcanic islands dominate the park's acreage. Developed from a hot spot on the Pacific Plate, they emerging sequentially from west to east. Tutuila, the largest and oldest island, dates from the Pliocene Epoch, approximately 1.24 to 1.4 million years ago, while the smaller islands probably date to the Holocence (the current geological epoch, which began about 11,650 years ago). Ta'ū island, the youngest of the park's islands, is all that remains from the collapse of a shield volcano during the Holocene. Rather than individual volcanoes, the islands are formed from overlapping and superimposed shield volcanoes built by basalt lava flows.

Estimates of the first human settlements in the Samoan archipelago range between 2,900 and 3,500 years ago. Very little is known about the history of human activity here before 1000 CE. It was not until the early 18th century that Samoans came in contact with Europeans, when Dutch explorer Jacob Roggeveen arrived in 1722.

By the mid 19th century, the Samoan Islands had become prime targets for European missionaries and traders. During the second half of the 19th century German-owned plantations began cultivating coconut, cacao, and hevea rubber, while the British set up their own businesses and consulate office and claimed harbor rights. The United States, with operations at the harbor of Pago Pago, formed alliances with local native chieftains. By the 1880s indigenous in-fighting resulted in the First Samoan Civil War. It was soon followed the Second Samoan Civil War, during which Germany, Great Britain, and the United States disputed one another's claims for control of

the islands. The resulting Tripartite Convention of 1899 split the islands between the three nations, with the United States gaining control of Tutuila and Manu'a. The following year, a smaller group of eastern islands, one of which contains the noted harbor of Pago Pago, fell under U.S. jurisdiction. When the navy took possession of eastern Samoa, it expanded the existing coaling station at Pago Pago Bay into a full naval station. In 1911, the U.S. Naval Station Tutuila, composed of Tutuila, Aunu'u and Manu'a, was officially renamed American Samoa. U.S. Marines stationed in Samoa during World War II outnumbered the local population, exerting a strong cultural influence on them.

The history of the park began when delegate to the U.S. House of Representatives Fofó Iosefa Fiti Sunia introduced a bill in 1984 to include American Samoa in the Federal Fish and Wildlife Restoration Act, with the goal of protecting the habitat for the flying fox, as well as old-growth rainforest. The park was officially established on October 31, 1988.

ACTIVITIES AND ATTRACTIONS

The park is a haven for divers and snorkelers, and hikers will have much to appreciate in the park's rainforest habitat. Subsistence fishing is allowed with permits. A visitor center gives park-goers a glimpse into the heart of Samoan life.

On the north end of the island, near Pago Pago, is the Tutuila island unit of the park, which is the only area of the park accessible by car. Points of interest here include the Amalau Valley, Craggy Point, Tāfeu Cove, and the islands of Pola and Manofā. The World War II Heritage Trail through dense forest leads to the top of Mount Alava, and along the way visitors can view the remains of historic World War II gun emplacement sites at Breakers Point and Blunt's Point.

▲ **A World War II** gun emplacement lies moldering in the rainforest.

The Manu'a Island group includes the Ofu unit and the Ta'ū unit. Accommodations are available on Ofu, but the island is only accessible via small fisher boats from Ta'ū. Flights from Tutuila to Fiti'uta village brings park-goers to Ta'ū. There hikers can follow a trail that runs from Saua around Si'u Point to the southern coastline, with stairs leading to the summit of Lata Mountain.

WILDLIFE AND PLANT LIFE

One of the park's roles is to ensure the species endemic to the islands thrive and to control and eradicate invasive plant and animal species. Only about a third of the plant life is endemic. Still, the tropical rainforest that covers most of the islands, including a cloud forest on Ta'ū and lowland ridge forest on Tutuila, are places of beauty. There are 343 flowering plants and 135 ferns.

Three species of bat account for the park's only native mammals: one small insectivore, the Pacific sheath-tailed bat, and two large fruit bats, the Samoa flying fox and the white-naped flying fox. Reptiles include the pelagic gecko, Polynesian gecko, mourning gecko, stump-toed gecko, Pacific tree boa, and seven skink species. Birders can look for the wattled honeyeater, Samoan starling, and Pacific pigeon.

Marine life is abundant, with more that 950 fishes, and other treats like sea turtles and humpback whales also swim in the Pacific waters. Ta'ū island can boast of some of the largest living coral colonies in the world, in which over 250 coral species live.

▲ **A Samoan flying fox,** also known as a fruit bat. This native bat was featured on the 2020 American Samoa quarter

Cockscomb Point at the end of Pola Island juts out into the ocean. This often-photographed site is in the Tutuila unit of the park, on the north end of the island near Pago Pago.

DID YOU KNOW?

The new visitor center, which gives park-goers the opportunity to understand and enjoy the cultural and natural wonders the park seeks to protect, was built to replace the previous one that was destroyed by the horrific 2009 tsunami.

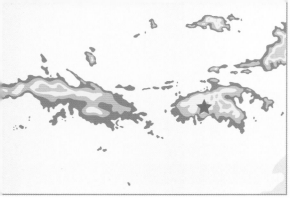

ST. JOHN
VIRGIN ISLANDS

Stunning natural beauty meets complex colonial and indigenous history in "America's paradise."

LOCATION St. John, VI

CLOSEST CITY Charlotte Amalie, St. Thomas, VI

AREA 14,737 acres (59.64 km²)

ESTABLISHED August 2, 1956

VISITORS 112,280+

ELEVATION 1,286 feet (392 m) at Bordeaux Mountain

GEOLOGY Volcaniclastic turbidites, basalt, and andesite

WHAT TO LOOK FOR

Virgin Islands offers a rare national park experience akin to indulging in a tropical island getaway.

> Snorkeling trail off Trunk Cay

> Kayaking off Honeymoon Beach

> Camping at Cinnamon Bay

> Hiking the Lind Point Trail

> Reef Bay Sugar Factory Historic District

> Annaberg Historic District

> Caneel Bay Resort

St. John is just one of the Virgin Islands' approximately 90 islands, islets, and cays that lie in the aquamarine waters of the Caribbean. Here, on the smallest of the three main U.S. Virgin Islands, lush tropical forest might open up to reveal the ruins of a colonial sugar plantation or lead visitors to pristine white beaches.

EARLY ISLAND HISTORY

Humans migrating from South America first arrived in what is now the Virgin Islands approximately 2,500 to 3,000 years ago, eventually settling in the islands around 480 BCE to 722 CE. Little is known about these earliest inhabitants, except that they were most likely nomadic hunter-gatherers living in caves or out in the open. A wave of immigration about 1,000 to 1,300 years ago brought the Taino people, who established villages at Cinnamon Bay, Coral Bay, Caneel Bay, and Lameshur Bay. Archaeological sites on St. John suggest that the Taino built communal villages, used stone tools, and cultivated cotton to make items like clothing and hammocks. Evidence also suggests that, as well as agriculture, they developed complex religious ceremonies and games of skill. Today, park visitors can explore some of these sites at Cinnamon Bay and view the petroglyphs they left behind along Reef Bay Trail, located at the base of the valley's highest waterfall.

A darker side of the islands' history commenced in the early 1600s, when European slave ships began to transport millions of African people from their homes in Africa to a life of bondage in the Caribbean. By the early 1670s, the Danish West India company had established a slave market in the St. Thomas port of Charlotte Amalie. Slavery was abolished in the Danish West Indies in 1848, but echoes of this brutal era still resound throughout the islands. Today, ruins and artifacts left behind from the Danish colonial era are scattered across the island.

MODERN HISTORY

In 1917, during World War I, the United States purchased what became the U.S. Virgin Islands from Denmark with the intention of establishing a naval base. Later in the 20th century, private investors began acquiring land on St. John, redeveloping some of the plantation houses into holiday resorts, the most famous being Laurance Rockefeller's Caneel Bay Resort. This launched a wave of tourism to the island, with service jobs becoming a vital part of its economy. In 1956, the Jackson Hole Preserve, an organization founded in 1940 by Laurance Rockefeller with the mission to conserve natural areas, donated its extensive lands on St. John to the National Park Service, with the stipulation that the lands would be protected from future development. These lands

◀ **A green sea turtle** feeds on the seagrass in shallow waters off St. John.

included Rockefeller's Caneel Bay Resort, which still operates on a lease arrangement with the NPS. The park land now makes up nearly three-quarters of the island.

ATTRACTIONS AND HISTORIC SITES

With an array of white-sand beaches, stunning coral reefs, engaging hiking trails, and captivating natural and historic sites, this park offers visitors a truly memorable experience. Along with the Caneel Bay Resort on the island's north shore, there are numerous other resorts, hotels, and vacation villas near the park. For overnight boaters, there are mooring balls available, and for campers, the Cinnamon Bay Campground is located within the parklands.

Behind the Virgin Islands National Park Visitor Center in Cruz Bay is the mile-long Lind Point Trail that leads up to Lind Point, overlooking the harbor of Cruz Bay, before continuing on to Honeymoon Beach on the north shore of St. John. Here visitors find soft white sand under the shade of coconut palm trees, and they can also rent kayaks and snorkel equipment to explore the turquoise waters.

Also starting in Cruz Bay, the Caneel Hill Trail leads visitors up a steep incline to the summit of Caneel Hill, where an observation

The turquoise waters of Trunk Bay are surrounded by St. John's lush green forest. The bay is a favorite with snorkelers, who can follow the underwater trail around the coral reefs of Trunk Cay, which lies in the middle of the bay.

DID YOU KNOW?

The leatherback turtle, endemic to the Virgin Islands and locally known as a "trunk," gives its name to Trunk Bay.

▲ **An aerial view of Caneel Bay** gives a view of verdant St. John, with St. Thomas in the distance.

► **On an island known** for attracting newlyweds, Honeymoon Beach is aptly named.

platform offers views of St. Thomas, Jost Van Dyke, and many smaller islands. On a clear day, a hiker might spot St. Croix and even Puerto Rico in the distance.

Regularly cited as having some of the best beaches in the world, the park offers visitors a wealth of choices for enjoying the sun and surf. Trunk Bay is divided into the main beach and swim area and Burgesman Cove at its west end near Jumbie Bay. Trunk Cay, a small grass-covered islet, sits in the bay, and the park service offers underwater snorkeling trails around the cay's coral reefs.

On the north shore of the island is Cinnamon Bay, a long, wide sandy stretch perfect for sunbathing, snorkeling, and water sports. As well as its campground, Cinnamon Bay also offers water sports rentals. Hikers in the park can also follow the Cinnamon Bay Nature Trail, with its mix of boardwalks and paved paths that leads them past the remnants of one of St. John's sugar factories.

The soft sand lining Maho Bay slide into calm, shallow waters with a seagrass floor in which sea turtles and stingrays might be spotted. On the island's south shore, Salt Pond Bay is a popular snorkeling spot with seagrass in the center, a deep coral reef set far out in the middle, and reefs fringing both sides. Boaters can stay overnight, and hikers can access Drunk Bay and the Ram Head Trail that travels down a rocky peninsula to the island's southernmost point. For those up for a challenge, the steep, rocky Bordeaux Mountain Trail guides them from Little Lameshur Bay to the island's highest point.

The Reef Bay Trail is a lure to both nature lovers and history buffs, guiding them through the lush island forests to a spring-fed waterfall and reflection pool and to the Reef Bay Sugar Factory Historic District and Taíno petroglyph rock carvings. A ranger-guided hike is offered for this strenuous hike, which includes a boat ride back to Cruz Bay from Reef Bay.

The park protects dozens of historic ruins, which range in date from the colonial and plantation eras through the 1950s. Most notably is the Annaberg Historic District that protects a partially restored sugar factory and windmill located just east of Mary's Point. Visitors can follow signs through the site that explain the process of turning sugar cane into molasses. The bake house hosts cooking demonstrations and offers samples of dumb bread, a rich, round loaf that is an island specialty. The windmill provides views of Tortola, Great Thatch Island, and the Narrows.

The well-preserved Catherineberg Sugar Mill Ruins also features a windmill tower, as well as a horse mill. Also part of the park is Fort Willoughby on Hassel Island.

WILDLIFE AND PLANT LIFE

With 140 species of birds, 302 species of fish, 7 species of amphibians, inhabiting the island, St. John is rich in wildlife. The approximately 50 corals species and numerous gorgonians and sponges also ensure that visitors will experience some of the best snorkeling and diving in the world. Although there are 22 species of mammals on St. John, the bat is the only native. Some species are key pollinators for many of the island's flowers and important seed dispersal agents for fruit-bearing trees and shrubs. Other species help keep insect populations manageable, consuming vast quantities of insects, including mosquitoes.

The island's diverse plant life—with about 740 species—is set in mangrove shorelines, offshore seagrass beds, dry cactus scrubland, and algal plains.

▲ **The Annaberg Plantation windmill.** Once one of 25 active sugar-producing factories on St. John, the Annaberg Plantation, built between 1810 and 1830, now lies in ruin.

▶ **Caneel Bay,** a luxury resort hotel located on St. John, was first opened in 1956. Devastated by back-to-back Category 5 Hurricanes Irma and Maria in 2017, work to reopen it continues.

▼ **A coconut palm tree** stands ready to shade beach-goers during a visit to Cinnamon Bay.

▲ **An iguana** basks in the island's sunshine.

INDEX

A

Acadia National Park, Maine, 12–17

Alagnak Wild River, Alaska, 57

Allagash Wilderness Waterway, Maine, 55

Apostle Islands National Lakeshore, Wisconsin, 263

Arches National Park, 80–83

Arctic National Wildlife Refuge, Alaska, 25

Ash Meadows National Wildlife Refuge, Nevada, 24

Assateague Island National Seashore, Maryland and Virginia, 260

B

Badlands National Park, South Dakota, 156–159

Big Bend National Park, 84–85

Biscayne National Park, Florida, 40–43

Black Canyon of the Gunnison National Park, 86–89

Bridger-Teton National Forest, 104

Bryce Canyon National Park, 90–95

Buffalo National River, Arkansas, 55

C

Canaveral National Seashore, Florida, 260

Canyonlands National Park, 96–101

Cape Cod National Seashore, Massachusetts, 261

Cape Hatteras National Seashore, North Carolina, 261

Cape Lookout National Seashore, North Carolina, 261

Capitol Reef National Park, 106–111

Carlsbad Caverns National Park, 112–115

Channel Islands National Park, California, 160–163

Chattooga Wild and Scenic River, South Carolina and Georgia, 55

Chincoteague National Wildlife Refuge, Virginia and Maryland, 23

Coconino National Forest, 103

Congaree National Park, South Carolina, 44–45

Crater Lake National Park, Oregon, 164–167

Cumberland Island National Seashore, Georgia, 262

Cuyahoga Valley National Park, Ohio, 18–19

D

Death Valley National Park, California and Nevada, 168–169

Delaware River, Pennsylvania, New Jersey, New York, and Delaware, 56

Denali National Park and Preserve, Alaska, 170–175

Dry Tortugas National Park, Florida, 46–47

E

Edwin B. Forsythe National Wildlife Refuge, New Jersey, 22

Eel Wild and Scenic River, California 56

El Yunque National Forest, 104

Everglades National Park, Florida 48–53

F

Fire Island National Seashore, New York 262

G

Gates of the Arctic National Park and Preserve, Alaska 176

Gateway Arch National Park, Missouri, 20–21

Gifford Pinchot National Forest, 102

Glacier Bay National Park and Preserve, Alaska, 186–187

Glacier National Park, Montana, 178–179

Grand Canyon National Park, 116–121

Grand Teton National Park, Wyoming, 188–191

Great Basin National Park, 122–123

Great Sand Dunes National Park and Preserve, 124–125

Great Smoky Mountains National Park, North Carolina and Tennessee, 58–63

Green Mountain National Forest, 105

Guadalupe Mountains National Park, 126–127

Gulf Islands National Seashore, Florida and Mississippi, 262

H

Haleakalā National Park, Maui, 254–257

Hart Mountain National Antelope Refuge, Oregon, 25

Hawai'i Volcanoes National Park, Big Island, Hawai'i, 258–259

Horicon National Wildlife Refuge, Wisconsin, 23

Hot Springs National Park, Arkansas, 26–29

I

Indiana Dunes National Park, Indiana, 30–31

Inyo National Forest, 105

Isle Royale National Park, Michigan, 32–35

J

J. N. "Ding" Darling National Wildlife, Florida, 24

Joshua Tree National Park, 192

K

Katmai National Park and Preserve, Alaska, 198–201

Kenai Fjords National Park, Alaska, 202–203

Kings Canyon National Park, California, 204–205

Kobuk Valley National Park, Alaska, 206–207

L

Lake Clark National Park and Preserve, Alaska, 208–209

Lassen Volcanic National Park, California, 210–211

M

Mammoth Cave National Park, Kentucky, 64–67

Mesa Verde National Park, 128–131

Mount Rainier National Park, Washington, 212–215

N

Nashua River, New Hampshire and Massachusetts, 57

National Forests, 102–105

National Park of American Samoa, 264–265

National Preserves, 182–185

National Seashores and Lakeshores, 260–263

National Wild and Scenic Rivers, 54–57

National Wildlife Refuges, 22–25

New River Gorge National Park and Preserve, West Virginia, 68–71

Niobrara National Scenic River, Nebraska, 57

North Cascades National Park, Washington, 216–217

O

Olympic National Park, Washington, 218–219

P

Padre Island National Seashore, Texas, 262

Parks of Hawai'i and Other U.S. Islands, 253–269

Parks of the Northeast and Midwest, 11–37

Parks of the South, 39–77

Parks of the Southwest, 79–153

Parks of the West , 155–197

Petrified Forest National Park, 132–137

Pictured Rocks National Lakeshore, Michigan, 263

Pinnacles National Park, California, 222–223

Pisgah National Forest, 102

Point Reyes National Seashore, California, 263

R

Rachel Carson Wildlife Refuge, Maine, 22

Red Rock Lakes National Wildlife Refuge, Montana, 23

Redwood National Park, California, 224–227

Rio Grande Wild and Scenic River, New Mexico, 54

Rocky Mountain National Park, 138

Rogue National Wild and Scenic River, Oregon, 56

S

Sachuest Point National Wildlife Refuge, Rhode Island, 25

Saguaro National Park, 142–145

Sequoia National Park, California, 228–233

Shawnee National Forest, 104

Shenandoah National Park, Virginia, 72–77

Sleeping Bear Dunes National Lakeshore, Michigan, 263

Superior National Forest, 105

T

Theodore Roosevelt National Park, North Dakota, 234–235

Tongass National Forest, 103

V

Vieques National Wildlife Refuge, Puerto Rico, 24

Virgin Islands National Park, St. John, 266–269

Voyageurs National Park, Minnesota, 36–37

W

White Mountain National Forest, 103

White River National Forest, 105

White Sands National Park, 146–147

Wichita Mountains Wildlife Refuge, Oklahoma, 24

Wind Cave National Park, South Dakota, 236–237

Wrangell-St. Elias National Park and Preserve, Alaska, 238–239

Y

Yellowstone National Park, Wyoming, Montana, and Idaho, 240–245

Yosemite National Park, California 246–251

Z

Zion National Park, 148–153

CREDITS

KEY

DT = Dreamstime.com

SS = Shutterstock.com

NPS = National Park Service

USGS = U.S. Geological Survey

USFWS = U.S. Fish and Wildlife Service

CC = Creative Commons* PD = Public Domain**

t = top m = middle b = bottom l - left r = right

Cover: © evenfh | Shutterstock.com

Back cover: From top to bottom: F11photo/DT; Vladimir Grablev/SS; Maciej Bledowski/DT; anthony heflin/SS; topseller/SS

Title Page: Yunpeng Li/SS

Contents: Chapter 1 YP_Studio/SS; Chapter 2 Dave Allen Photography/SS; Chapter 3 Paul Brady/DT; Chapter 4 kojihirano /SS; Chapter 5 Alexander Demyanenko/DT

Introduction: 7tl Everett Collection Historical/Alamy Stock Photo; 7tr Everett Collection Historical/Alamy Stock Photo; 7b Library of Congress; 8–9 Kelsey Mcquisten; 9tl NPS

Locator maps: Stan Parkh/DT

CHAPTER ONE
PARKS OF THE EAST AND THE MIDWEST

10–11 YP_Studio/SS; 12 Harry Collins/DT; 13 F11photo/DT; 14–15 Jarvin Hernandez/SS; 16tr Jon Bilous/SS; 16–17 pisaphotography/SS; 17t Mihai Andritoiu/DT; 17m Harry Collins Photography/SS; 17b Jim Ekstrand/DT; 18bl Pat Dooley/SS; 18–19 Keri Delaney/SS; 19tr Zack Frank/SS; 20bl Sean Pavone/SS; 20–21 Zac Carter/SS; 22br Joseph Sohm/SS; 22tl David Des Rochers/DT; 22–23 Elizabeth Paige Brown/DT; 23tl USFWS Wilderness Fellow, Erin Clark; 23tr melissamn/SS; 23m Stacey Steinberg/DT; 23br Tony Savino/SS; 24tl VIKVAD/SS; 24m William Cushman/SS; 24bl Richard G Smith/SS; 24tr Dominic Gentilcore PhD/SS; 24mr Olin Feuerbacher/SS; 24br Stefania Moehring_CC BY-2.0; 25tl Joshua Mcdonough/DT; 25ml chris_dagorne/SS; 25bl Danita Delimont/SS; 25tr Bob Weaver/USFWS; 25br William T Smith/SS; 26bl Zack Frank/SS; 26–27 jprom/SS; 27tr picturin/SS; 28l Zack Frank/SS; 28 inset Steve Shook/CC BY-2.0; 28–29 Sandra Foyt/SS; 29tr Zack Frank/SS; 30b Tom_Gill_CC BY-NC-ND-2.0; 30–31 Jon Lauriat/SS; 31tr GARRETTGCRAIG/SS; 32br rizz5447/SS; 32 inset DOM STOCK/SS; 32–33 Steven Schremp/SS; 34–35 Steven Schremp/SS; 35tr dbabbitt12/SS; 35br Jacob Boomsma/SS; 35m Matipon/SS; 36br swarn'o/SS; 36–37t BlueBarronPhoto/SS; 36–37b Kelly Vandellen/DT; 37bl Noah Lang /SS

CHAPTER TWO
PARKS OF THE SOUTH

38–39 Dave Allen Photography/SS; 40 NPS; 40–41 Francisco Blanco/DT; 41 inset Michael Thompson/DT; 42tl Francisco Blanco/DT; 42m Francisco Blanco/DT; 42mr Lawoel/DT; 42br William C. Bunce/DT; 43ml Rudy Umans/DT; 43tr Francisco Blanco/DT; 43b Fotoluminate/DT; 44tr Andy Morgan/DT; 44–45 Alex Grichenko/DT; 45t Pierre Leclerc/DT; 45m Jonathan Mauer/DT; 45b Steven Prorak/DT; 46l Mmorell/DT; 46–47 Mia2you/SS; 46tr AG Technology Solutions/SS; 47t BlueBarronPhoto/SS; 48–49 pisaphotography/SS; 49 jo Crebbin/SS; 50–51 allouphoto/SS; 51tr Mia2you/SS; 51tl Brian Lasenby/SS; 52t Mia2you/SS; 52m Nick Fox/SS; 52b DmHall/SS; 53t migueldotv/CC BY-SA 3.0; 53b Bildagentur Zoonar GmbHv/SS; 54tr Dennis W Donohue/SS; 54–55 gmeland/SS; 55tl Glenn W. Wheeler/SS; 55tr Allagash_Jack_Heddon/CC BY-NC-ND 2.0; 55br JayL/SS; 56tl James Kirkikis/SS; 56tr Zadranka/SS; 56mr JKendall/SS; 56bl Anna Westman/SS; 57tl Jon Bilous/SS; 57 tr Jon Bilous/SS; 57m marekuliasz/SS; 57br Chris Oggerino/SS; 58bl Abbey_Hambright/CC BY-NC-SA 2.0; 58–59 jadimages/SS; 59tr Bittersalt Studio/SS; 60t Jason Sponseller/SS; 60b ehrlif/SS; 61 Kelly vanDellen/SS; 62–63 Keneva Photography/SS; 63 jadimages/SS; 64 Khairil Junos/DT; 64–65 Sequential5/DT; 65 inset Steve Shook/CC BY-2.0; 66t Kostya Zatulin/SS; 66bl Kelly Vandellen/DT; 66t Kostya Zatulin/SS; 67b ZakZeinert/SS; 67tr Kostya Zatulin/SS; 67tl Zack Frank/SS; 68bl patrimonio designs ltd/SS; 68–69 Zack Frank/SS; 69tr Malachi Jacobs/SS; 70–71 Malachi Jacobs/SS; 71tr Zack Frank/SS 71br Gestalt Imagery/SS; 72bl Ivan Kokoulin/DT; 72–73 Danita Delimont Shenandoah/SS; 73t NPS; 74–75 Vladimir Grablev/SS; 76bl Jon Bilous/DT; 77br Joe Sohm/DT; 76–77; Ralf Broskvar/SS; 77t Boston Public Library

CHAPTER THREE
PARKS OF THE SOUTHWEST

78–79 Paul Brady/DT; 80bl Darren J. Bradley/SS; 81tl Kevynbj/DT; 80–81 dibrova/SS; 82b anthony heflin/SS; 83m My Good Images/SS; 83 Chris Hill/SS; 82–83 KENNY TONG/SS; 84tr BlueBarronPhoto/SS; 84–85 Zack Frank/SS; 85t jordaneil/SS; 85m Mark Taylor Cunningham/SS; 86 Keith J Finks/SS; 87 Kelly vanDellen/SS; 88tl Zack Frank/SS; 88–89 Danielsen_Photography/SS; 89tr Zack Frank/SS; 89m corlaffra/SS; 89br drewthehobbit/SS; 90 Gleb Tarro/SS; 91 Ami Parikh/SS; 92 Rex Wholster/SS; 93 jrtwynam/SS; 94tl Peter Wey/SS; 94–95 Alexander Lozitsky/SS; 95tr James Marvin PhelpsSS; 96–97 Colin D. Young/SS; 97tr Rudy Balasko/SS; 98–99 TomKli/SS; 100t Kyle T Perry/SS; 100bl USDA-FSA-APFO; 100–101 LHBLLC /SS; 101tl Arlene Waller/SS; 101tr Doug Meek /SS; 102bl Sean Pavone/SS; 102tr Petrarch1603_CC BY-SA-1.0; 102m Gary Gilardi/SS; 102mr Heidi Ihnen Photography/SS; 103t Harry Beugelink/SS; 103tl Maundy/SS; 103mr Jon Bilous/SS; 103bl Ken Marsh/SS; 103br YegoroV/SS; 104tl Sierralara/SS; 104bl Dennis van de Water /SS; 104tr Tonya Kay/SS; 104mr Eddie J. Rodriquez/SS; 104br Dennis van de Water/SS; 105tl Jacob Boomsma /SS; 105ml Joseph Rossbach/SS; 105tr Kristi Blokhin/SS; 105mr Noah Lang/SS; 105br Don Paulson | Jaynes

CHAPTER FOUR
PARKS OF THE WEST

CHAPTER FIVE
PARKS OF HAWAI'I AND OTHER U.S. ISLANDS